ADDITIONAL PRAISE FOR *THE LEADING INDICATORS*

"Zachary Karabell's lively account, *The Leading Indicators*, is a terrific introduction to the range of statistics economists and governments use to address these questions."

—*The New York Times Book Review*

"Karabell offers an engaging account of the history of these indicators, and his explanation of their flaws is both readable and useful for non-economists trying to make sense of the barrage of numbers with which they're pelted on a regular basis."

—*The Wall Street Journal*

"[*The Leading Indicators*] demystifies a lot of current debates, explains its subject matter clearly and shows that the major published macroeconomic statistics are neither nonsense nor conspiracy. Most people could read this book with enjoyment and profit."

—Tyler Cowen, for *The Washington Post*

"How did we get to the era of Big Data? Karabell . . . mines little-known tidbits in the history of economics to explain how individuals, companies, and countries came to rely on statistics like unemployment, inflation, and gross domestic product to describe the wealth of nations. . . . In Karabell's hands economics is no longer 'the dismal science.' More storyteller than analyst here, he succeeds in livening up how 'the economy' came to be."

—*Publishers Weekly*

"*The Leading Indicators* presents a potentially dry but important topic in an engaging manner, with wit and intelligence."

—*The Cleveland Plain Dealer*

"[A] lucid measurement of how the United States is faring. . . . Readers of this intelligent introduction to iconic economic indices will agree that Karabell makes an excellent case."

—*Kirkus Reviews*

"An amusing and eye-opening romp through the history of the powerful numbers, such as the unemployment and inflation rates, that influence the course of national policy. They're not only out of date, they often point us in the wrong direction. Karabell's surprising book shows that we don't know what we think we know, and trillions of dollars hang in the balance."

—Jane Bryant Quinn, author of *Making the Most of Your Money Now*

"Karabell tells the story of statistics vividly, illuminating the forgotten characters who shaped our numbers."

—*The Week*

ALSO BY ZACHARY KARABELL

Sustainable Excellence: The Future of Business
in a Fast-Changing World (with Aron Cramer)

Superfusion: How China and America Became One Economy
and Why the World's Prosperity Depends on It

Peace Be upon You: The Story of Muslim,
Christian, and Jewish Coexistence

Parting the Desert:
The Creation of the Suez Canal

Chester Alan Arthur

Kennedy, Johnson, and the Quest for Justice: The Civil Rights Tapes
(with Jonathan Rosenberg)

The Generation of Trust: Public Confidence in
the U.S. Military Since Vietnam (with David C. King)

A Visionary Nation: Four Centuries of American Dreams
and What Lies Ahead

The Last Campaign: How Harry Truman Won the 1948 Election

Architects of Intervention: The United States, the Third World,
and the Cold War, 1946–1962

What's College For? The Struggle to Define
American Higher Education

A SHORT HISTORY

of the

NUMBERS

That

RULE OUR WORLD

The
LEADING
INDICATORS

ZACHARY KARABELL

SIMON & SCHUSTER PAPERBACKS

NEW YORK   LONDON   TORONTO   SYDNEY   NEW DELHI

Simon & Schuster Paperbacks
A Division of Simon & Schuster, Inc.
1230 Avenue of the Americas
New York, NY 10020

First Simon & Schuster trade paperback edition January 2015

SIMON & SCHUSTER PAPERBACKS and colophon are
registered trademarks of Simon & Schuster, Inc.

For information about special discounts for bulk purchases,
please contact Simon & Schuster Special Sales at
1-866-506-1949 or business@simonandschuster.com.

The Simon & Schuster Speakers Bureau can bring authors to your live event.
For more information or to book an event, contact the
Simon & Schuster Speakers Bureau at 1-866-248-3049
or visit our website at www.simonspeakers.com.

Interior design by Ruth Lee-Mui
Jacket art: Arrows © SkillUp/Shutterstock; grid © Ivancollad/Shutterstock

Manufactured in the United States of America

1   3   5   7   9   10   8   6   4   2

The Library of Congress has cataloged the hardcover edition as follows:

Karabell, Zachary.
The leading indicators : a short history of the numbers that rule our world / Zachary
Karabell. — First Simon & Schuster hardcover edition.
pages cm
Includes bibliographical references and index.
1. Economic indicators—History. 2. Economics—Statistical methods—History. 3.
Economic indicators—United States—History. 4. Economics—United States—History.
5. United States—Economic conditions. I. Title.
HB137.K36 2014
330.01'5195—dc23
2013039641

ISBN 978-1-4516-5120-1
ISBN 978-1-4516-5122-5 (pbk)
ISBN 978-1-4516-5125-6 (ebook)

Contents

Contents

THE LEADING INDICATORS

INTRODUCTION

What if I told you that many of the assumptions we make about our economic life are wrong? What if those assumptions shaped our domestic economic policies? What if they determined core aspects of our international strategy? What if they bolstered the deep and intractable funk that seized the developed world after the financial crisis of 2008–09? What if indeed.

We live in a world defined by economic numbers. We assess how we are doing personally and collectively based on what these numbers say. How fast our country is growing economically or how slow, how much prices are increasing, how much income we have, whether we are employed—these numbers rule our world. We treat our economic statistics as absolute markers of our success or failure. None of these numbers, however, existed a century ago. Most of them didn't exist in 1950. Yet we enshrine them almost as laws of nature.

Take two recent examples: in 2012, the unemployment rate was a central factor in the US presidential election. It was widely reported that no president had ever been reelected with an unemployment rate more than 7.2%. The monthly release of the unemployment report became one of the most watched events that summer and fall, and each new number ushered in assertions that the economy was recovering and accusations that it was not. Through election day, the rate never dropped to that supposedly portentous 7.2% level, and was hovering close to 8% when Barack Obama was reelected. Obama's victory had seemingly broken with a strong historical pattern. But did it? The answer is no, for reasons that will become clear in these pages. Our sense of probability and likely outcomes was wrong. How we came to place such stock in these numbers—and what to do now—is the subject of this book.

The other example is a widely accepted "fact" that has dramatic social and political consequences: the trade deficit between the United States and China. Few issues have weighed more heavily than this gap, and it has created substantial tension between the United States and China at least since 2001. Regardless of political party, Americans have decried unfair Chinese trade practices, the undercutting of American wages and manufacturing jobs, and the negative effects of the relationship on the global financial system. But what if the actual size of the trade deficit is significantly less, or perhaps even nonexistent? That may seem an outlandish question, but it is not. We rely on trade numbers compiled every month by the government, and those numbers tell us that there is a deficit. As we shall see, however, the world these statistics say we are living in and the one we are actually living in often diverge; the world we are living in is not the one that these statistics depict.

Every day we are showered with economic statistics such as GDP, unemployment, inflation, trade, consumer sentiment and spending, the stock market, and housing. This suite of statistics intimately shapes our perceptions of reality. We now refer to them as our "leading indicators," and they are thought to provide key insights into the health of the economy. But they measure only what they were designed to measure at the time they were invented. The world, however, has not stayed the same.

Just how much it has changed was brought home in the middle of 2013. You may not have noticed, but one day in 2013, the US economy grew by $400 billion overnight.

That wasn't because of normal economic growth. After all, given that the gross domestic product (GDP) of the United States is in excess of $16 trillion, even at a modest clip it will get hundreds of billions of dollars larger each year.

No, the reason for that boost was not a sudden surge of activity. One day, those billions just appeared. And not only just appeared, but apparently had been there all along. On July 31, 2013, the US Bureau of Economic Analysis (BEA), which is the government agency responsible for calculating the size of the US economy, announced that it had shifted the way it measured national output. The result was a $400 billion adjustment.

Given the language used by the agency in describing the revision, you could be forgiven for missing the import. Months before the official new number, the BEA had announced the change. But few of us sit up and take notice when greeted with this headline: "Preview of the 2013 Comprehensive Revision of the National Income and Product Accounts: Changes in Definitions and Presentations." The subsequent official announcement in July was hardly catchier. In its bulletin describing the new methodology, the BEA stated that it would now include "creative work undertaken on a systematic basis to increase the stock of knowledge, and use of this stock of knowledge for the purpose of discovering or developing new products, including improved versions or qualities of existing products, or discovering or developing new or more efficient processes of production."[1]

This inelegant prose masked a profound shift in the way that we understand the economy. Until the Great Depression, no country measured its national output. The global economic crisis of the 1930s led to efforts in both the United States and Great Britain to develop statistics that would provide some clarity about what was going on. National income and GDP were two of the most important statistics to emerge from that era. By the middle of the twentieth century, countries everywhere were using these numbers.

The world those numbers measured, however, was very much a world of nation-states making stuff. Economies were based on the output of goods, on manufacturing, farming, and production. In the decades since, however, the nature of the United States and many other economies has changed dramatically, away from manufacturing and toward services; away from making stuff in factories to inventing ideas.

For many years, the keepers of these statistics recognized that ideas and intellectual property are central to today's economies. When the numbers were created, however, the decision was not to include activities such as research and development (R&D) as part of national output. That meant that until the BEA announced its shift in 2013, the billions spent by a pharmaceutical company to develop new drugs to save and improve lives were treated simply as an expense rather than as an investment that could yield massive future returns. When a company bought a robot for a factory, it counted as part of GDP. When Apple spent a fortune to develop the iPhone, it didn't.

Also uncounted had been many of the creative endeavors that go into television shows, movies, and music. By adding up all of these investments—the money Lady Gaga spends writing songs, the amount Apple spends on the next iPad, the amount Pfizer invests in a new medicine—the BEA found that it had been underestimating the size of the US economy by $400 billion, an amount larger than the GDP of more than one hundred countries.

Our indicators have become so intimately woven into our lives and our sense of what is going on around us that we forget that for most of human history, there were no economic indicators, and without those numbers, there was no "economy." Now, the "economy" is a central factor in our lives. The financial crisis of 2008–09 cemented that fact. The primary way that we relate to the economy is through numbers, through statistics that are released regularly by the government, by industry groups, and by companies. The leading indicators are a data map that we use to navigate our lives.

So when the agency responsible for maintaining key elements of that map decides to redefine one of those numbers, it alters our perception of reality. Lost in the verbiage of the Bureau of Economic Analysis bulletin announcing that $400 billion "adjustment" was the fact that these changes shape how we assess our lives, collectively and individually. While most of us pay little attention to the waves of economic numbers that come at us day after day, few of us are immune to the effects of this wave of data. We are inundated by economic statistics, and there is hardly a country in the world that does not mark its success or define its failings by what these statistics tell us.

Not only do US presidential elections now hinge on what those economic statistics say, but all of Europe has been locked in a downward spiral because of economic policies that are based on the relationship between debt and GDP. And, of course, there is China, whose ruling Communist Party sets targets of economic growth that become the party's claim to legitimacy. Leaders everywhere trumpet strong economic statistics, and challengers use weak numbers to criticize incumbents.

The leading indicators occupy a place in our world that no one who invented them could have imagined. They were all designed with limited goals, and yet now they are used as absolute gauges of how we are doing. That is why, perhaps, the news that our economy is bigger than we thought was greeted by many with derision. Said one headline discussing the revision, "US GDP: America Is About to Look Richer—But Don't Be Fooled." Criticism ranged from the accusation that the Obama administration was juicing the numbers to burnish its record, to the belief that the new calculus only widens the gulf between those doing well and those struggling in today's economy.

And indeed, just saying that we are statistically richer than we thought doesn't actually make anyone richer. If I told you that you had $1,000 more than you thought you did five years ago, you would not suddenly have more money in your bank account, nor would you reevaluate your past experiences. In order to maintain the integrity of GDP, the BEA did not simply change its current methods of calculating; it revised all the numbers going back to 1929, so that now the money spent by Warner Bros. on blockbusters in 1955 and the R&D budgets of Hewlett-Packard and the Ford Motor Company in their mid–twentieth century heydays will be included in the GDP for those years. None of that, however, will have altered the ability of your parents or grandparents to afford a house or a new car retroactively.

The fact that knowledge work will now be integrated into our indicators does indeed make more acute the already sharp distinction between winners and losers in the contemporary economy. While GDP is a national number, it is not nationally experienced the same way. That is an often overlooked limitation of our statistics: they measure us in toto, but we then act as if they measure us individually. They do not, and they were not designed to. They were invented as tools to gauge an economy as a national system, not our own individual economic lives. The recent revisions show that those who are inventing new ideas have been benefiting even more than the numbers have shown. The fact that those efforts make us richer collectively and thereby statistically increase our "per capita income" does not mean that we each have become that much wealthier.

All of this is simply a case in point for how our numbers shape our sense of reality. For almost a century, people have been inventing statistics to measure our lives, and since the middle of the twentieth century, our understanding of the world has been integrally shaped by those numbers. Our statistical map, however, is showing signs of age. In our desire to have simple numbers to make sense of a complicated world, we forget that our indicators have a history—a reason that they were invented in the first place—and that history reveals their strengths and limitations just as our own personal histories do. Knowing how we came to live in a world defined by a few leading indicators is the first step to assessing whether we are still well served by them.

The history of these numbers is not well known, save by those academics and professional statisticians who look back for guidance on how to move forward. The impetus to invent statistics to measure what we now call "the economy" was a combination of the passion to conquer the unknown and the desire to create more social justice and equity. Our leading indicators are the offspring of progressive reform movements and the scientific drive to quantify in order to control.

The indicators were inventions meant to measure industrial nation-states of the mid-twentieth century. In their time, they did so brilliantly. The twenty-first century, however, is different. Industrial nation-states have given way to developed economies rich in services, and to emerging world industrial economies exporting goods made by multinational companies. The statistics of the twentieth century were not designed to capture that, and the assiduous efforts of statisticians notwithstanding, they cannot keep up.

The following pages tell the story of these numbers and the men (and yes, they were mostly men) who invented them. They tell as well how these statistics morphed from limited tools used by a handful of policy makers during the Great Depression and World War II into leading indicators that govern vast aspects of life in nearly every country in the world. Then, we will see how it came to pass that these statistics determine the pecking order of nations, set the parameters and shape the debate for how governments spend or refuse to spend trillions of dollars, and how all societies except for one small country measure their success.

Having traced this evolution, we will see that using these indicators to navigate today is much like using a 1950s road map to get us from point A to point B. It's possible that you will get there, but it's more likely that you'll get lost. Given that, it is no surprise that our economic policies so often fail to deliver the promised or expected results. We rely on old formulas for new realities.

The temptation, then, is to find new formulas, better indicators, new statistics. The search for better numbers, like the quest for new technologies to improve our lives, is certainly worthwhile. But the belief that a few simple numbers, a few basic averages, can capture the multifaceted nature of national and global economic systems is a myth. Rather than seeking new simple numbers to replace our old simple numbers, we need to tap into both the power of our information age and our ability to construct our own maps of the world to answer the questions we need answering.

Before we get to that, however, we need to go back, far back, to the first attempts to know the world in numbers, to the dawn not of this millennium but the last, and to one of the most famous battles in the world, the outcome of which wasn't just a shift in the political tides but one of the first attempts to measure the world.

1

THE RIPPLES OF DOMESDAY

In 1066 Duke William II of Normandy crossed the English Channel to contest the crown of the Saxon king Harold II. That October, as generations of English schoolchildren have learned, the weather turned crisp and the skies gray, and the two armies met at Hastings in East Sussex. Harold was killed; William and his army of supporters, vassals, and mercenaries emerged triumphant, thus giving way to Norman rule of England and forever earning William the sobriquet "the Conqueror."

Twenty years later, King William the Conqueror ruled a realm at peace, but that was not a recipe for ease. The world was not a peaceful place, and any contest with adversaries foreign or domestic would require resources. But what resources did his kingdom, in fact, possess? How much land? How much could it yield in crops and livestock? How many people were there, and how much wealth, both actual and potential? To answer those questions, William, like rulers before and like many governments since, took the first step that he could. He dispatched minions to every corner of the kingdom to ask those questions and record the answers.

As the king's chronicler explained:

[H]e sent his men all over England into every shire to ascertain, how many hundreds of "hides" of land there were in each shire, and how much land and live-stock the king himself owned in the country, and what annual dues were lawfully his from each shire. He also had it recorded how much land his archbishops had, and his diocesan bishops, his abbots and his earls—and though I may be going into too great detail—what or how much each man who was a landholder here in England had in land or in live-stock, and how much money it was worth. So very thoroughly did he have the inquiry carried out that there was not a single hide—not even one ox, nor one cow, nor one pig—which escaped notice in his survey. And all the surveys were subsequently brought to him.

And when they were done in 1086—when the manors of each of the feudal lords had been surveyed, when each village had been inspected and its inhabitants counted, when information from each county and each parish had been submitted and inspected—the findings were assembled in a vast manuscript known ever since as the *Domesday Book*, named after the Day of Judgment. "For as the sentence of that strict and terrible last account cannot be evaded by any subterfuge," explained a later courtier, "so when this book is appealed to on those matters which it contains, its sentence cannot be quashed or set aside with impunity."[1]

Hailed for its rigor and comprehensiveness, the book suffered from many flaws. Inspectors in one county did not always ask the same questions as inspectors in another. Some counties in the North, ravaged by rebellion against the Normans, were not included. Material goods were the order of first priority; people, less so. The Church, a powerful force and a major landholder, was in various parts of the country omitted altogether, either because the bishops and clerics refused to cooperate with the king's representatives or because the surveyors didn't think to include lands and goods that belonged to an institution that answered only marginally to the Crown.

Nonetheless, the *Domesday Book* is the first recorded statistical survey of economic life in Great Britain in the age after the Romans. The ancients had their own tallies: the Greeks, Romans, Persians, Babylonians, Egyptians. The Chinese and their dynasties had theirs. All rulers have understood the imperative of counting what they have: how many weapons, how much grain, and how much their subjects could be taxed, what could be levied, and what armies could be raised. Some have done better gauging those numbers, some worse, but all have tried, and few have succeeded in creating more than a temporary, fluid, and ultimately flawed snapshot. That was true millennia ago, and it is true today. The main difference is that then, the flaws lay with insufficient models and an incomplete understanding of the distinction between counting and adding versus creating statistics that allow you to measure and compare over time whether you are doing better, worse, or simply treading water.

The *Domesday Book* also revealed the central dilemma of statistics and economic indicators: how you define what is important determines what gets counted. As anyone in business or government will attest, what gets measured gets managed. What doesn't might as well not exist for all the attention it garners. By not including the Church with the same rigor as feudal manors, the *Domesday Book* undercounted the material strength and potential output of England. Because the goal was to assess the power of the king and the throne, omitting aspects of the Church made sense, but it also made the country appear weaker than it was—which subsequent monarchs came to realize and which in the end led Henry VIII to expropriate the vast wealth of the Church in order to bring all of England's resources under the sway of the Crown.

Over the following centuries, successive rulers in England and throughout Europe conducted other surveys of their realms, almost always with an eye toward figuring out just how much could be raised in taxes. That led to some of the earliest and most rudimentary efforts to measure national output, which was a precursor to the modern measurement of gross domestic product. But even as those efforts proceeded, the methods did not evolve appreciably. Innovation and imagination went into measuring the cosmos, mapping the globe, figuring out if the Earth was round or flat, devising new navigation tools and better instruments of war, and honing the skills of art, music, and architecture. Statistics did not make the list of ripe and exciting areas for innovation.

In the sixteenth century, the empires of Europe branched across the Atlantic, and then in the eighteenth century, around the globe. To survive in Western Europe, states large and small—from tiny Netherlands to the Spanish Empire—tapped into the resources of North and South America, and then Asia, and finally Africa. In order to both exploit and utilize the fruits of that trade, governments needed to know as much as possible about its extent.

Governments then and now depend on consistent sources of revenue in order to function and provide the services expected of them. Before the modern era, the primary sources of revenue were taxes on land levied from nobles and customs duties levied on trade. For centuries, it wasn't government that kept the best records; merchants did. They were the ones who refined methods of accounting, bookkeeping, costs, and incomes, and they were at the core of the development of banking and notes of credit that are the precursors to all contemporary finance.

Rulers, however, needed and coveted the revenue that merchants generated. Hence the evolution of the mercantile system, which saw various empires attempt to monopolize trade with their far-flung colonies and keep out foreign powers and foreign merchants. Mercantile or not, governments made a point of confining foreign trade to limited ports of entry and then monitored those ports very closely. Shipments were recorded and assessed, and duties were imposed. Hence the famous (or infamous, depending on your perspective) Navigation Acts passed by the British Parliament over the course of decades beginning in 1651, which confined trade with the American colonies to British ships and British merchants paying British duties to the British Crown. The French and the Spanish passed their own versions of these laws, to the point where few could trade freely without confronting imperial displeasure and onerous penalties.

With trade becoming a primary source of income and a vital one for supporting the constant wars between these powers, and with that trade tightly monitored, piracy blossomed. That sparked the daring (or devilish, if you were Spanish) acts of raiders such as Sir Francis Drake and Sir Walter Raleigh intercepting the silver ships of the Spanish king. It sparked as well the stirrings of discontent in the American colonies, which began to bristle as the eighteenth century wore on, and soon that bristling turned into outright rebellion against the efforts of the English Crown to control and tax all trade emanating from the Americas.

Trade and taxes, customs duties and ledgers—these were all fine and well for making sure that royal coffers were full and replenished. They were not, however, modern statistics or leading indicators. The evolution of those lagged behind the advances of science and math in other walks of life.

Still, as mathematics branched off from philosophy, and seventeenth-century giants such as Isaac Newton and Gottfried Leibniz explored the calculus, a few individuals began to investigate the nature of probability and the need to understand it in order to measure accurately a material world that was ever in flux, with births, deaths, wars, famines, and a bewildering kaleidoscope of political change. In the mid–seventeenth century, Blaise Pascal and Pierre de Fermat, mathematicians and philosophers both, reflected on the nature of probability. Their letters explored the nature of gambling and the most basic of all probability games: the roll of the dice. Fermat, better known for his long-unsolved mathematical theorem, was fascinated with games of chance. His correspondent, Pascal, better known for his essays that plunged with eloquence into the elemental question of why we are here, did not take life so seriously that he couldn't find time to play the seventeenth-century version of craps. With their common love of the dice, their musings ranged from how to determine the population of a dense city to how to create formulas that would account and adjust for inevitable errors in seemingly simple tabulations. They didn't speak the language of modern statistics or statisticians; they did not use terms such as *sampling error*, but they grasped a basic truth: humans make mistakes when they try to count large numbers in complicated systems. They make even greater errors when they attempt—as they always do—to reduce complicated systems to simple numbers.[2]

The word *statistics* wasn't much used before the eighteenth century, and its origins are often ascribed to a German named Gottfried Achenwall, who combined Latin and Italian words to coin the term *statistic* to refer to data about the state. The nascent field—not really a field, in fact, but rather an arcane area of interest to those rare and few men of letters who often double dipped as astronomers, alchemists, and engineers—of statistics was given some of its modern form by Pierre-Simone Laplace. Known as the French Newton (to the English-speaking world at least), Laplace was concerned mainly with mapping the solar system in the waning days of the French ancien régime, and he did his finest work just as the regime was about to crumble in blood and revolution at the end of the eighteenth century. Laplace continued his research throughout those years and found some favor with Napoléon I, who was ever on the lookout for men of science who might illuminate the meaning of the universe and help him rule it. Laplace then penned his *A Philosophical Essay on Probabilities*, which has ever since shaped the way we have constructed the indicators that govern our world.

In a concise essay of a few hundred pages, Laplace laid out the basic principles of why probability matters to everything from the selection of juries to assessing how long people live. Few of us are unfamiliar with the concept of an "average," yet Laplace showed just how complicated seemingly simple figures can be. For mortality figures, it is not enough just to take birth registers and death records, and then add them up and divide. Why? Because that will vastly overstate the chances of death at an early age. The logic is clear but easy to overlook. Far more infants and toddlers in those years failed to make it to adulthood. Their mortality rate was significantly higher, and so including them in an average significantly lowered average life expectancy. But once a child made it past those first dangerous years, life spans were considerably longer. That may seem obvious, and yet it was not.

Laplace illuminated the challenges of compiling accurate statistics. He showed that for mortality figures, you need a large sample to ensure that you assess the full range of probabilities and vagaries of life and death. One area may have been hit with disease, plague, or drought, and hence distort the results unless many other samples are included. "A table of mortality," he wrote, "is then a table of the probability of human life." For that table to be accurate, much more is required than simply counting, adding, and dividing. Laplace's essay was a paean to the mathematical and social utility of probability, and it launched the field of statistics into its modern trajectory.[3]

Over the next two hundred years, mathematical statistics became an increasingly professionalized field, as did a panoply of academic disciplines that didn't exist before the mid–nineteenth century. At the same time, another set of measurements, more political and less mathematical, evolved. As governments in the West embraced the spirit of rigor and innovation that characterized industry and science, they became ever hungrier for knowledge about the societies they governed. Nowhere was that more evident than in the United States, which had at least one statistic embedded in the heart of its founding document, the Constitution.

While seven hundred years separate the *Domesday Book* from the US Constitution, in one respect, they were cousins. The framers of the Constitution were acutely sensitive to the need for an accurate count of land, property, and citizens. Given the nature of the representative government they were forming, they particularly needed to capture changes in population and income on a regular basis. A government based on proportional representation—on the idea that each citizen should have his voice heard in national deliberations via an elected representative—demanded knowing how many voters there were in each state. Without that, it would be impossible to determine how many congressional representatives there should be from each district and how many electoral votes would go to each state. It would also be impossible to manage the national tax system, which while rudimentary compared with later years, still required an assessment of national wealth.

As a result, the framers inserted a clause into the Constitution calling for a regular census of the population to be taken every ten years. This was not an afterthought. It was front and center, and placed near the beginning of the document, in Article I, Section 2, just after the clause calling for the creation of a legislative branch and Congress:

> Representatives and direct Taxes shall be apportioned among the several States which may be included within this Union, according to their respective Numbers, which shall be determined by adding to the whole Number of free Persons, including those bound to Service for a Term of Years, and excluding Indians not taxed, three fifths of all other Persons. The actual Enumeration shall be made within

three Years after the first Meeting of the Congress of the United
States, and within every subsequent Term of ten Years, in such Manner as they shall by Law direct.

If this clause is remembered at all, it is usually for the compromise
about how to count slaves. The slaveholding southern states wanted
slaves counted in order to boost the population and hence the number
of representatives in the central government. The northern states objected on the grounds that slaves had few legal rights, could not vote,
and were therefore not truly citizens of the republic. The compromise,
necessary but not one of the bright, shining moments of American
history, was to count slaves as "three-fifths" of a person. For the next
seventy years, that enhanced the power of the South relative to its vot-
ing population but did not, in the end, preserve the peculiar institution of slavery for the perpetuity that its masters had intended.

The initial census was taken in 1790, and it was the first official government statistic of the new republic. At the time, it was the
most costly and time-consuming effort undertaken by the federal
government to collect information on the American people. As the
population grew and national economic activity became more diverse
and productive, the census also grew in complexity and cost. Today
it continues to be a decennial effort. The first census began on the
first Monday of August 1790. It employed 650 federal marshals who
fanned out across the thirteen colonies. Between gathering and assembling data, the operation lasted eighteen months and cost $45,000.
The census of 2010, by contrast, employed more than 600,000 enu-
merators and cost $12 billion, but rather than a year and a half, it took
only a few months to make its preliminary reports and less than a year
to finalize its vast report to the president and to Congress.

Of all official statistics, the census remains the most comprehensive, extensive, and time consuming to assemble. It evolved over the
nineteenth century into far more than just a count of people. Thomas

Jefferson tried assiduously to keep America out of the wars wracking Europe, and that posed a challenge to his ideal of an agrarian country. Cut off from European finished goods, Americans turned to domestic manufacturing, and that in turn sparked the need to figure out just how much, and what, the United States was producing. In 1810 a census of manufacturers was added, and for the first time, Americans had a measure of the burgeoning world of industrialization. Over the next decades, more and more data was asked for and obtained: for example, the number of people employed by the railroads, the number of shoe factories in Massachusetts, the average size of a household in Michigan, the education and literary level in Kansas City, and the number of free blacks in Baton Rouge in 1850.[4]

These initial census endeavors relied entirely on individuals dispatched across the country to ask questions door to door. There was no sampling, no use of statistical methods, and no way to check the accuracy of the numbers. The 1790 surveyors were tasked with asking every household a basic set of questions, and they were responsible for keeping meticulous records—by hand, of course—and then bringing those records back to be tabulated in Philadelphia, which was then the nation's capital. By 1850, with the country now stretching across the continent to the new state of California, the logistics had become more challenging. In addition, Congress mandated numerous new areas of study, from industry to the composition of households. There were so many questions being asked and so much information pouring into the Census Office (which was officially established only in 1840) that the agency was overwhelmed by the sheer mass of paper.

Given the sensitive political nature of the census and its role in determining congressional districts and representation, the inability of the Census Office to handle the information was taken by political opponents as proof of corruption and nefarious intent. Not for the last time would official government statistical efforts be seen as the handmaiden of dark forces, distorting the truth or propagating lies to allow one pernicious party or another to control the lives of millions.

Then as now, however, the truth was more banal and reality more prosaic. Incompetence and the sheer magnitude of the tasks could deluge even the most diligent and dedicated. In the middle of the nineteenth century, the reach of census authorities very much exceeded their grasp, and they were overwhelmed by too much information. These problems came to a head in 1850, when the census was expanded yet again to include more granular detail on the nature of slavery and the lives of both slaves and freedmen at precisely a time when conflict between North and South, slave and free, was about to rend the country in half.

Supported by Whig senator William Seward of New York, who was soon to be one of the founders of the antislavery Republican Party and a key member of Lincoln's wartime cabinet, the census of 1850 extensively surveyed the life of slaves. So combustible were these issues that Seward was accused of "ministering to that miserable fanatical spirit that would split the Union." The head of the census, Joseph Kennedy, was assailed for incompetence and corruption, hiring more surveyors than was necessary in order to line his pockets with patronage.[5] Kennedy was investigated by the Democrat-controlled Senate, charged with various infractions—including owning two of the four buildings leased to the new Census Office in Washington, DC—and forced to resign.

The miniscandal, however, was merely a sideshow to the vast expansion of government information and the particular challenges of assembling it in a timely and accurate manner. The tension over slavery, of course, far transcended arguments over who tabulated what. Slavery, in fact, was one of the first aspects of American life that was meticulously and rigorously documented. In that sense, data on slavery was the first leading indicators for economic life in the southern states. Records of births, deaths, and shipments extend back to the seventeenth century and were kept until the abolition of slavery during the Civil War. Slavery formed a crucial part of the southern economy, and those records were used to measure both wealth and prosperity in the antebellum South.

The last census to divide between slave and free was in 1860, just before the election of Abraham Lincoln and the secession of the southern states. That census provided crucial information to both the Union and the Confederacy about the strengths of both, including the ability of their respective manufacturing bases to meet the needs of war. The census of 1860 proved, if more proof was needed, that the North had an overwhelming advantage in what it could produce to fuel the war, from guns, to ammunition, to soldiers' uniforms. It proved as well that while the South may have gained representation by counting slaves as three-fifths of a person, it gained no advantage in the Civil War without arming those slaves and somehow motivating them to fight for their own continued enslavement.

The US census was the foundation for the indicators that became so ubiquitous in the twentieth century. After the Civil War, a few states, Massachusetts especially, started to assemble data on work and labor. But the census conducted every ten years remained the only national pool of information about family, living standards, education, and life expectancy. The wealth of information embedded in its reports was mined by the first wave of statisticians and others seeking to create a snapshot of the state of the nation and of the problems of industrialization. The census is still a primary source for many of our statistics today.

The census, however, is not a statistic. And it is not an indicator. It is raw data, and lots of it. The census was the foundation for future indicators, but it took decades of applied work for its data to be transformed and then augmented by sampling methods, by different questions, and by mathematics.

Other than people, the only aspects of nineteenth-century life that were subject to a similar level of measurement were trade and agricultural output. From time immemorial, agriculture along with trade defined the ability of any society to function. Though the US Department of Agriculture wasn't established until 1862, efforts to measure how much cotton, tobacco, wheat, and corn were being grown date back to the eighteenth century. With the first stirrings of mechanized agriculture after the invention of the cotton gin by Eli Whitney in the late eighteenth century, farmers slowly shifted from the age-old obsession with reaping just enough to prevent famine and starvation to growing as much as possible and focusing on the most lucrative crops. In short, agriculture shifted from being a need and a necessity to an industry, and that meant more focus on markets, grain exchanges, prices, and, above all, yields.

It's arguable that agriculture was the most important national economic activity until the late nineteenth century. Yet with the onslaught of industrialization, rapid urbanization, and the growth of indicators in the twentieth century geared toward labor and production, agriculture faded from the national debate and public consciousness. You can study American history (or English and European history, for that matter) and find remarkably little about agriculture and farming other than references here and there. You get a feel for the debates between Jefferson, who wanted a country of yeoman farmers, and Alexander Hamilton, who was more intent on industry, cities, and finance. But the centrality of crops, of fields full and fallow, of the science of soil and the taming of the land to bring forth food—most of that has been lost and seems distant, unless you grow up in a farming state such as Iowa or Nebraska.

But for much of the nineteenth century, knowledge about what was happening on farms was key to whether the country would thrive. Building on the work of English "agricultural societies," American states began to survey the output of their farms in the first decades of the nineteenth century, with Massachusetts typically leading the way. The first rudimentary census of agriculture was taken in 1840, followed by the creation of the Department of Agriculture in 1862. That was also the year of the Homestead Act, which opened up the vast enterprise of settling, and conquering, the American West. In one of history's little ironies, the first head of the department—the creation of which was hailed as an important step toward better policy and greater output based on scientific observation and calculation—was named Isaac Newton.

Though the census included some information about crops, the new department went much further. The USDA had a large statistical staff, and the first commissioners traveled to Europe regularly to meet with their counterparts in London, Paris, Berlin, and Vienna. They shared methods and approaches, and represented one of the first transnational efforts at establishing common standards of statistical measurement. The mid–twentieth-century transformation of economic indicators—from tools used by Western governments, to metrics used by every country in the world to assess national well-being—could occur only because of ongoing international collaboration. As we shall see, the United Nations played a key role in both bringing together experts from various governments and then disseminating that information globally. Nineteenth-century agricultural statistics were the precursor.

The challenges faced by the USDA and the Census were also a preview of how hard it is to measure the world as it is. The census was staffed, at great expense, by people dispatched across the country to ask questions. Even then, many mistakes were made. The Department of Agriculture and its statistics division relied on samples but had no sampling method relative to the later standards of statisticians. It relied on data collected by state agencies, but each state had its own set of priorities, and the quality and quantity of state statistics varied immensely. The department also depended on a few hundred agents in the middle of the nineteenth century and then a few thousand by the end of the century. But that was far from sufficient. There was no way a few thousand agents could go to every farm in the United States, and even if they had, they would have been limited by when they visited. If they visited in winter, fields were fallow, and surveyors would have to rely entirely on what farmers told them. In the spring, the surveyors could count seeds planted but not crops harvested. Weather patterns could alter estimates significantly, and that remains true to this day. Then there were farmers who underreported their crops, fearing higher taxes or simply distrusting the government. Later, in the twentieth century, with the advent of federal programs that paid farmers not to grow crops (in order to prevent too much supply from driving prices lower), there were incentives for overreporting. Either way, agricultural data proved to be hard to collect, of dubious quality, and consistently inaccurate.

As Jacob Dodge, the long-serving chief statistician of the Agriculture Department observed in the 1880s, "A stream cannot rise higher than its source; pure mathematics and immaculate judgment combined cannot cure the inaccuracy of erroneous original data. This is today the supreme difficulty in obtaining correct statistical results, whether in a census that requires years of time and millions of money, or in any other official or unofficial crop investigations."[6] Almost from the moment official statistics began, the goal of drawing a perfect map of the world through numbers fell far short of the actual numbers assembled. The compilers of the indicators have toiled ever since, refining, honing, learning from past mistakes, developing new math and new ways to sample, and deploying each new generation of technology to capture and analyze more data.

The statistical experts knew and know the issues and the flaws. But in the twentieth century, as those numbers moved out of the obscure bureaus that assembled them and into the political and social limelight, the public demand for simplicity trumped the endless complexity that these statistics represented. Financial markets didn't want to know about the methodological limitations of crop and livestock reports when setting prices for this year's corn or cattle. Politicians weren't interested in sampling errors or multiyear revisions when considering inflation and forward assessments of future economic growth as measured by GDP. They wanted a number, and they wanted it to be "the truth"—or at least a damn good proxy for it.

Yet while failing to match the ambitions of the people who worked so assiduously to collect the information, statistics at the end of the nineteenth century and into the twentieth were markedly better than no statistics. Even insufficient information was initially an undeniable improvement over none, just as the astrolabe and other early navigation devices, flawed compared with modern GPS systems, were vastly preferable to navigating by the eye and heavens alone. Compared with the void and the degree to which all societies had been flying blind—guesstimating their national strength and resources or, at best, counting and adding—the first stab at formalizing indicators gave governments and markets powerful tools to plan ahead and assess strengths and weaknesses.

The roiling pace of change in the final decades of the nineteenth century, however, acted as an impetus for even more information about even more aspects of economic and social life. The drive for more data and new statistics was born not of a sense of strength that prosperity was booming but from a strong suspicion that inequality was widening, social justice was weakening, and the pace of industrialization was creating as much harm as good. In order to prove that point, however, numbers—and not just ideology and good arguments—were needed. And the first order of priority was jobs.

2

UNEMPLOYMENT

Ethelbert Stewart, six feet tall and born with a stutter, got his first job in Decatur, Illinois, just after the Civil War. It was an unenviable job, but a job it was, working on the assembly line of the Decatur Coffin Company. Because of the stutter, Stewart had been homeschooled by his parents so that he would be spared the merciless taunting of other boys and the impatience of his teachers. So he read, and read, and even as he put together an endless series of coffins to house the deceased, he started working for a local newspaper and writing about conditions not just in his factory but others.

Ambitious and angry, Stewart wrangled a meeting with one of the journalistic titans of the day, Henry Demarest Lloyd of the *Chicago Tribune*. Lloyd in the 1880s was in the full bloom of his high dudgeon, railing against the new evils of the Gilded Age, too much wealth for too few, monopolies, and appalling conditions in factories that were infesting the land like locusts.

Stewart proposed writing a series of articles about labor in Illinois.

The *Tribune* rejected the idea, but Stewart wrote the articles anyway and managed to get them published in several local and labor papers. Lloyd was impressed, and Stewart's exposés came to the attention of the reformist governor, who appointed the young man to the rather obscure post of secretary to the Illinois Bureau of Labor in 1885.

So began a career that would culminate in Stewart's becoming commissioner of the federal Bureau of Labor Statistics in 1920. That in turn placed him at the pivot point when that small, underfunded agency helped define the parameters of the Great Depression. After a career spent advocating for better information about the struggles and needs of the working class, Stewart's crowning achievement was to be present at the creation of a national unemployment rate, which has ever since shaped our common picture of jobs in America.[1]

When Stewart and a coterie of others took the reins of the BLS in the early twentieth century, employment and unemployment were fuzzy concepts at best, so much so that when the Great Depression began, no one truly knew how bad things were because there was no way to measure how bad things were. Yes, by 1930, signs of economic collapse were visible everywhere, but no one could say with any certainty what was actually happening and to whom. Anecdotes were plentiful, but hard facts weren't. The dismal state of official information before the 1930s was a running joke among the few professional bureaucrats who cared. When President Warren Harding convened a conference on unemployment after a particularly severe recession in 1920–21, there were such divergent opinions about the numbers that the attendees put the question to a vote. The low end was three and a half million; the high end was five million.[2]

A vote. On a fact. Or rather on something that *should* be a fact. Yet the reality is that unemployment is an invention. It is not a simple case of counting who has a job and who doesn't, though even that isn't quite as simple as it seems. What does it mean to be employed? Full-time work, part-time, temporary, seasonal? Is a farmer employed?

How about an actor between jobs or a ranch hand in fallow months? And how do you count? Surveys? Who conducts the surveys? How many surveyors would you need to get an accurate measure of every single employed and unemployed person in a population of millions spread across thousands of miles? You couldn't possibly pay enough people to count everyone on a regular basis—except at an unfeasible cost. The census was one of the least visible pillars of American democracy, but few questioned the considerable expense. Still, it was an expense borne only once a decade. Not until 1902 was a permanent, continuously funded US Census Bureau set up by the federal government. Counting jobs, however, is more complicated than counting bodies; bodies are there or not, but jobs and employment are amorphous, so much so that until the late nineteenth century, no one even thought to bother counting.

Ask a classical economist about unemployment, and the answer might surprise you: there is no such thing. In any society, there are always jobs that need doing by someone at some price. Therefore, theoretically, there is no unemployment; there is only an individual's choice to work or not to work. Ask someone without gainful employment what he thinks of that answer, however, and the response is likely to be unprintable.

Until the nineteenth century, the concept of unemployment was alien. Most people didn't earn a wage; they did not have "jobs." They farmed, or traded, or served, or fought. Some were artisans or blacksmiths or stevedores, but most worked the land to nurse food out of stubborn soil. Factories were small, with a few dozen workers. There were mines here and there, and, of course, servants. But there was no framework of employment versus unemployment, only of want versus plenty, hard work versus idleness, good times versus bad.

That began to change in Western Europe with what we now call the industrial revolution. As steam power facilitated the growth of larger factories, and then railroads made possible the mass transportation of finished goods, jobs and wages became more central features of society. And as more people became employed and were paid a wage, more people also became unemployed. Still, it wasn't until after the Civil War in the United States that anyone thought seriously to count who had jobs and who did not.

Well until the end of the nineteenth century, people without work were indicted as lazy and degenerate. Town after town had laws against "idleness" and "vagrancy," and you could be arrested for not having a home or loitering on the streets looking for work. The idea that the government—any government—had a responsibility to help support those of able body who couldn't support themselves was alien. That was charity, and charity was the province of churches or local associations and in no way the responsibility of government.

Yet those attitudes began to shift, slowly, in the 1870s and after. In part, the shift occurred because American society in the Gilded Age was plunged into tumult with the advent of industrialization and the influx of far more immigrants. Industrialization and the growth of factory work for wages was the spur. Similar changes took place in Europe at the same time, and not because of immigration. The belief that governments should take some action to address the issue of unemployment took hold over the course of several decades in both Europe and the United States, and went hand in hand with a growing consensus that society could be structured and governed according to the same scientific principles that had made the industrialization of the nineteenth century possible.

The notion that a professionally run government could maximize a society's output and stability through the application of scientific principles had widespread appeal, but almost every country lacked one key element: information. Yes, as we saw, governments had long been keeping track of trade and agriculture—the two traditional sources of wealth and power. But scientific management of society required data, and there, most societies and most governments were largely in the dark. As of the middle of the nineteenth century, almost every metric we now take as a given—from health statistics to economic data—simply did not exist.

In the United States, the birth of economic statistics was part of an overall movement toward social and political reform. The drive to create these statistics was fueled in part by a rising national suspicion that large companies, monopolies, railroads, and banks were reaping disproportionate rewards and thereby robbing the common man of his hard-earned gains. In Europe, a similar sensibility led to an efflorescence of Socialist movements, not to mention the birth of Communism. In the United States, it led to the birth of unions. Unions, in turn, believed that labor was being deprived of its rightful share of prosperity, but they couldn't prove that. Hence the attempt to measure just what was going on in order to add weight to the widespread sense that many were suffering unnecessary hardship.

The men who were drawn to the obscure profession of measuring America were of two sorts: academics and technocrats or passionate reformers like Ethelbert Stewart. The late nineteenth century was rife with the creation of countless associations, from academic guilds such as the American Political Science Association (1903) and the American Economic Association (1885), to professional interest groups such as the National Association of Manufacturers, founded in Cincinnati, Ohio, in 1895 by a group of businessmen concerned about the deep economic panics that regularly dented American progress at least once a decade. The American Statistical Association was founded before them all, in Boston in 1839. But without the tools provided by these other, later groups, its work had minimal impact on defining the contours of the modern economy.

Without the passionate reformers, however, statistics and economics may have stayed on the fringes of society, or in the background along with ornithology and mountaineering. What animated Stewart was anger at how hard most Americans worked, how little they earned, and how appalling labor conditions were. By developing tools to measure precisely how bad and precisely how unsafe and exactly how tenuous the plight of the workingman was, Stewart believed that conditions could be changed, laws enacted, protections created. As long as the world remained unmeasured, however, anecdotes could always be trumped by anecdotes, and those with power and money could always argue that things were better than what a few malcontents claimed.

Stewart worked for the state of Illinois until the sleepy Federal Bureau of Labor recruited him in 1897. That agency, founded in 1884 and underfunded, had sprang out of the wave of disruptive and violent strikes that pockmarked industrial America. Its mandate was to address the perilous state of labor relations and act both as an advocate for workers and a mediator with owners. Along with so many institutions, its birth was part of what we now call the Progressive movement, which seized much of American society toward the end of the nineteenth century, and Stewart was in that respect very much a man of his time. Today we pay little attention to the countless public servants who staff numerous agencies; the government has become a bureaucracy with a history. But at the turn of the twentieth century, these agencies were all new, and many were yet to be created. With the passage of the Pendleton Civil Service Act in 1883, civil service became a profession rather than a reward for political support, and with the spirit of reform on the rise, more people were drawn to government as an agent of positive change. Stewart embodied that spirit, and he went about his work with pride and urgency. He spent years in assorted roles ranging from manager to mediator until he was recruited to be the second in command to the head of the Bureau of Labor Statistics, Royal Meeker, in 1913.

The creation of the Bureau of Labor Statistics had followed the initiatives of several states. The ever-progressive Massachusetts had led the way in 1869 and was the first state to create a labor department focused on collecting and assembling information about employment and working conditions. A dozen other states followed suit over the next twenty years. In all cases, the impetus was the same: labor unions pushed for official collection of information that would support their contention that conditions were poor, wages insufficient, safety nonexistent, and companies indifferent. The federal government was then spurred, somewhat reluctantly, to action when President Chester Alan Arthur, an accidental president if there ever was one, signed into law the creation of the Federal Bureau of Labor, along with its statistics office, in 1884.[3] In 1913, it became part of the cabinet as the Department of Labor.

By the time Stewart arrived, the Bureau of Labor Statistics (BLS) had been in existence for nearly thirty years, but in terms of measuring employment, it could just as well not have existed. Yes, its staff was imbued with a sense of noble purpose. Stewart was not alone in his zeal. As part of a general trend to celebrate efforts to define and measure reality, many of the men who worked for the agency viewed their profession as an enlightened pursuit and as central to making the world a better place. They believed that better numbers would ameliorate diseases, increase the food supply, enrich the world, and empower the nation. Said Carroll Wright, the first BLS commissioner, "Statistics are the fitting and never-changing symbols . . . to tell the story of our present state." Wright himself was a former head of the American Statistical Association and a forceful advocate for the role that better statistics could play in crafting a stronger country. He spent his life preaching the gospel of statistics as key to good government and better labor relations, and as tools that would allow governments and businesses to design the right policies and make it possible for people to learn over time by giving them the means to compare their own present to the past.[4]

Stewart, however, was less of an intellectual and more of a pugilist. He was idealistic about the capacity for change, but he was also an ornery pragmatist. Hence he saw numbers and data as weapons in the fight against ignorance and foolishness. He saw facts as a potent force, impossible to refute provided they were supported. "So long as the Bureau of Labor Statistics sticks strictly to the question of facts, then all I have to say . . . is that anybody who dislikes the facts is in hard luck!" Stewart also zealously defended his agency's turf, what little there was. When a congressional committee demanded that he hand over data on individual automobile manufacturers' labor patterns, he refused on the grounds of confidentiality. When the committee chair threatened him with a subpoena, he flatly refused. "You do," he said, "and I'll burn them first." The matter was quickly dropped.[5]

Sardonic and pithy, Stewart was very much what Mark Twain would have been had Twain been a statistician. He had little truck with homilies and ignorance, and saw in statistics a way to force society to deal with pressing issues of justice, fairness, and decency. "The working people of the United States," he declared, "are entitled to know what the changing industrial conditions are . . . and the nature of and extent of the occupational readjustment which is necessary to meet them without loss of earning power." As an advocate for a minimum wage law long before that was fashionable, Stewart saw the issue as one of simple social utility: unless people had sufficient means to meet their needs, their lives would be diminished, as would the strength of the country.

Even so, he was skeptical of too much reliance on science and math. Statistics were a guide and could provide a map, but he was wary of the "mania for statistics" that accompanied the early–twentieth century mantra of rigorous measurement. The belief that society could be treated as a machine and that by understanding the inputs you could determine outcomes had limits. "The things that make human life human do not lend themselves readily to the statistical method," he wrote. Decades later, as we shall see, similar sentiments would be expressed more poetically by Robert Kennedy.

Stewart was hardly alone in his progressive beliefs. In fact, many of the individuals who worked for the bureau strove for social justice. Royal Meeker, the BLS commissioner before Stewart, and an advocate for workmen's compensation for accidents, remarked, "I do not happen to be a Socialist, but if it is socialism to provide adequate protection to the lives, health, and well-being of our working population, then let us have more of the same." These sentiments were inseparable from the impulse to define and delineate what had until then been an amorphous issue: just who was and was not employed and why.[6]

Census takers had included questions about "gainful employment" in 1890 and 1900. In 1910 those questions were broadened so that the census could determine who was employed in what industries and whether they had been out of work at any point during the previous year. Yet those questions were then dropped in the census of 1920, just before the United States was about to enter a very sharp and unexpected recession after the demobilization of millions of soldiers from World War I. That recession blindsided policy makers and startled the rather placid administration of Warren Harding, whose most energetic cabinet secretary, Herbert Hoover at the Commerce Department, used the opportunity to organize the "Conference on Unemployment" in 1921.

Hoover had achieved fame and fortune as a mining executive and then as head of the American Food Administration during World War I before accepting Harding's invitation to join his cabinet. The Commerce Department was among the smallest federal agencies and seen less as a stepping stone to greater things than as a political reward for party loyalists. Yet Hoover was uninterested in patronage. He was instead devoted to the marriage of science and industry and then science and government—more devoted, in fact, than he was to almost any flesh-and-blood person. Hoover was many things: whip smart, focused, intense, methodical, and even visionary, but warm, friendly and compassionate he was not.[7]

Hoover was an apostle of "the efficiency movement," which was the animating force behind many of the Progressive reforms of the early twentieth century as well as the driving factor in the evolution of business and industry in these years. At heart, the movement sought to apply scientific principles to the management of all major aspects of society. If that were done, its proponents believed, the result would be lasting prosperity, high productivity, general enrichment, and permanent peace among nations. In industry, Frederick Winslow Taylor had spent decades studying the nature of factory work and creating methods to boost production and eke the most out of each process and each worker. Hoover was dedicated to the tools of measurement and organization as means to eliminate waste and enhance output, and with every plaudit he received and riches he earned, he became that much more convinced that those methods could transform America and the world.

Yet as he became commerce secretary, the country was wracked by an economic downturn. Production and prices plummeted, banks shuddered, and millions found themselves struggling for work. Lacking hard data, however, it wasn't clear how many were out of work or what that really meant. Was a demobilized soldier who hadn't found gainful employment for several months "unemployed"? And if so, was that a problem with the system or simply a natural, albeit uncomfortable, adjustment as the country shifted from wartime to peace? Though no one really knew it at the time, the 1920–21 recession was and remains one of the sharpest declines in American history, ameliorated in retrospect only by how quickly the situation improved after 1921. But the Harding administration had to be seen as addressing the crisis and hastily convened the Conference on Unemployment spearheaded by Hoover.

True to the spirit of the era, few people in positions of power believed that government should take aggressive, direct action. Hoover's view of a "new economic system" entailed not government spending or relief aid but rather government as a coordinator of private endeavors for the greater public good. Volunteerism, not government action, was the mantra, and while all participants saw the widespread lack or loss of jobs as a serious problem, they believed that the role of government was to motivate businesses and various groups to tackle that problem. Recessions and downturns were seen as a symptom of market failures that society hadn't yet resolved, but unemployment per se was not seen as an issue. It was perceived purely as a by-product of market failures.

The fact that there was no reliable information about employment made it that much easier to treat lack of work as a secondary issue that required systemic changes but not government policies targeted at employment itself. For Hoover, unemployment simply exposed a mismatch between what the system was capable of and what it was currently generating. The issue wasn't lack of jobs, it was economic inefficiency. "There is no economic failure so terrible," Hoover declared, "as that of a country possessing a surplus of every necessity of life in which people, willing and anxious to work, are deprived of the necessities." The country was rich, with ample food and industry. Hence, there should be no reason for unemployment save for some temporary breakdown in the economic machine that could be fixed by the same human ingenuity that had created it in the first place.[8]

While there was no evidence that the 1921 conference actually improved conditions, the country did soon return to prosperity, for which Hoover was not unwilling to take credit. He continued his foray into labor issues, which the actual labor secretary at the time seemed disinclined to address, and in the belief that too much work led to decreased productivity, he expended considerable energy pressuring the steel industry to end the practice of twelve-hour shifts, seven days a week.

One solid and uncontroversial conclusion of the unemployment conference, however, was that there weren't adequate statistics about unemployment. This wasn't just an American problem. European nations were also grappling with the mismatch between the information they wanted and the information they had. On both sides of the Atlantic, governments had become ever more adept at compiling data, but few had made the next step to creating actual statistics. In essence, the challenge was how to mold information into numbers that could consistently and over time create a picture of what was taking place.

What government and society confronted in these years was the recognition that all the counting in the world would get you no closer to clarity and no more able to manage society efficiently. Statistics use counting and data as raw materials, but they aren't the same as counting and data. The rise of statistics in the nineteenth century was tied to the same scientific movements that propelled the industrial revolution: the belief that quantifying the world could allow society to craft systems and institutions that would lead to more prosperity and power and eliminate the chaos and insecurity so endemic in human history. Statistics, the transformation of raw data into consistent numbers, are "an authoritative way to describe social problems," and that, in turn, is a necessary first step in solving those problems.[9]

Until the 1930s, employment was a perfect illustration of a mountain of data without coherence. Unemployment was a problem that many people recognized but which few felt the urgency to remedy. That left technocrats such as Ethelbert Stewart to exert what pressure they could and continually remind congressional committees in testimony and the general public in articles that America was flying blind when it came to employment. These arguments did have some sway. In 1927, Senator Robert Wagner of New York, then newly elected and not yet the force he was to become later, introduced bills in Congress to rectify matters and improve the way in which the government collected information about unemployment so that it could take action to help the unemployed. The bills went nowhere.

In the meantime, the country was prospering, and there was little public interest or pressure to spend more money on government counting. Stewart and his colleagues soldiered away, working diligently on improving the methods and surveys and striving ahead of the 1930 census to define more accurately what was meant by "unemployment." Then the storm arrived.

Hoover glided into the presidency in 1929 buoyed by his sterling reputation as a brilliant manager of society's needs and unhindered by a personal aloofness that would have made him all but unelectable in our contemporary politics. His serene and supreme confidence in his own capacity, combined with a zealous faith in the scientific methods that he had injected into the federal bureaucracy, were well suited for a prosperous world; they were nearly disastrous when crisis engulfed the country.

To be fair, the speed at which the economic system unraveled in late 1929 and into 1930 was breathtaking. What made it even more difficult to grasp was that no one truly knew what was going on. In the absence of coherent government data about prices, output, and employment, gauging what we now call the Great Depression was impossible. Government and society were like an airplane steering into a storm with minimal instruments other than what the naked eye could perceive. Everyone knew the weather was really, really bad, but no one could say just how bad, how extensive, and how long it might last.

In the absence of clear information—in the absence of reliable statistics—people did what they had always done: filtered available information through the lens of their worldview. Hoover and the Republicans treated the downturn that followed the stock market crash of October 1929 as akin to earlier panics and recessions, like the severe one that had rolled across the country in 1920–21. In that view, the only thing to be done was batten down the proverbial hatches and wait out the storm until the system righted itself.

As evidence of severe cracks in the system mounted in late 1929 and intensified into 1930, Hoover remained convinced that a steady hand, a lack of panic, and no radical change in current policies were the right approach for the executive branch and for the federal government. Stories of breadlines and massive layoffs in industrial America were not sufficient to change course. To be fair, Hoover's complacency about industrial unemployment was a reflection of the fact that only part of the workforce worked in industry. In 1930 there were still considerable numbers of farmers. Of the approximately 38 million men and 10 million women employed out of a population of 120 million, more than half were in services or in industry, but more than 10 million were on farms, and almost all farmers were men. Still, Hoover almost certainly underestimated the struggles faced by farmers. If you owned one of the nation's six million farms, you couldn't be "unemployed," but you certainly could be poor, hungry, and economically insecure. If you lost that farm, given that you had not previously had a job as defined by a wage paid by an employer, you were not, statistically speaking, unemployed. You were, however, in serious trouble.

The crisis of the Great Depression is usually understood as a crisis of the financial system leading then to an employment crisis along with a severe contraction of prices and production. But there was also a profound and essentially permanent rupture with agricultural America that was precipitated by the rise of industry, the mechanization of farming, and several years of crop failures. What is striking about all of these various currents, however, is that at the time, no one really recognized that the system was undergoing such radical transformation.

And this is where the forces that Hoover had been so central in unleashing came to overwhelm his presidency. A man who had stood for applying scientific principles to government would soon find his presidency and reputation in tatters because so many demanded that the problem of employment be confronted with hard evidence. That meant not relying on an ideology of how employment was supposed to ebb and flow during crises but instead actually trying to determine who was employed, who was not, and how to define "unemployment."

Hoover had been an avatar of hard data and unsentimental analysis. The quest for those as they applied to employment fatally undermined his presidency as the economic landscape eroded.

Until 1929, Ethelbert Stewart and his cohort had been staunch advocates for better statistics. Their voices had been largely ignored or taken less than seriously outside of the American Statistical Association and the burgeoning field of economics. As the crisis erupted, however, Hoover wanted to rebut his critics with data, certain that the numbers would justify his conviction that the events of 1929 were but a brief disruption rather than a systemic crisis. So in early 1930 he authorized the Bureau of Labor Statistics to go ahead with a weekly experimental survey of employment conditions. After one week of data showed some improvement, Hoover discarded any pretense of scientific method and declared, "The tide of employment has changed in the right direction."[10]

Clearly, it had not. As the situation worsened, Democrats and Republicans sparred over which numbers constituted reality. Various agencies were collecting information and providing different pictures. As Royal Meeker described it, given the sorry state of clear information, "At irregular intervals, which mark the end of business cycles, business smashes itself to smithereens, and the unemployment problem flames up with a terrifying menace which calls forth furious guessing and agitated oratory from everybody involved."

As of 1930, the government had rudimentary employment statistics based on census data and surveys of businesses. But there was no unitary unemployment number. Unemployment as a statistic is not simply the opposite of employment; it is a category that requires definition. The lack of unemployment metrics made assessing the damage of the economic crisis of the late 1920s almost impossible, and the perils of that lack became crystal clear in 1930. In response, Senator Wagner once again introduced a bill to authorize the BLS to assemble monthly information on "the volume of and changes in employment."

This time, with many now waking to the gap in knowledge and the liability that posed, it passed.

It's been said that accepting and acknowledging a problem is the first step toward solving it. Until 1930, the absence of clear and consistent information about employment and unemployment wasn't widely perceived as a problem. It wasn't that earlier crises had been so mild. In fact, the dislocations caused by nineteenth-century panics and recessions could be catastrophic by today's standards. It's been estimated that at any given point in the 1870s, as much as half the American workforce was unemployed, though without any reliable statistics, it's hard to know. If stevedores working the piers of New York City were idle, were they unemployed? Had they actually had "a job" and been employed, or were they simply transient labor with ebbs and flows in demand for their services? Those questions were never adequately addressed until the 1930s. Until the early twentieth century, significant economic hardship was so woven into human history and experience that it wasn't yet seen as an aberration. Only the combination of a severe crisis and the belief that such crises not only could but should be prevented by collective government action led to the creation of unemployment statistics. That then led to the demand for statistics for prices, production, and industrial output and for the entire panoply of modern indicators that have come to define our twenty-first-century world.

The moves during the Hoover administration to develop better and more accurate gauges did not benefit Hoover himself. Quite the opposite. By 1932, the BLS was surveying sixty-four thousand businesses—about the size of the current employment survey. While there was still no official unemployment rate or even a consistent metric for the size of the labor force, there was increasingly better information about just how many people had lost their jobs between 1930 and 1932. That information made it almost impossible for Hoover to argue that Americans should simply stay the course. Armed with hard numbers that painted a grim picture, Franklin Roosevelt and the Democrats in 1932 condemned Hoover as a man adrift and demanded a new approach.

With new estimates indicating that more than 20 percent of the workforce had lost their jobs, and with farm foreclosures adding substantially to the national misery, Roosevelt trounced Hoover to win the presidency in November 1932. At that point, FDR's governing philosophy—which had been vague during the campaign—emerged. Against Hoover's firm belief that the United States could not "legislate itself out of a world economic depression," FDR offered action. In place of Hoover's emphasis on voluntary efforts to redress collective suffering, FDR promised a government-led campaign akin to war. As we know, his victory ushered in a protracted period of aggressive government measures, beginning with a flurry of New Deal legislation in the spring of 1933. New Deal laws were designed to support farm prices and output, and they authorized direct government intervention in industrial America in order to restore confidence, generate activity, and create jobs. Equally vital for the future arc of American society was the rush of enthusiasm for better information and for statistics that would prove that these programs were working.[11]

Some of the impetus came from Roosevelt's inner circle, especially Harry Hopkins in his multitudinous roles, and from Frances Perkins, who had served as FDR's labor commissioner in New York State and was appointed labor secretary in his cabinet. But the New Deal also coalesced currents that had been swirling amorphously through the body politic for years. The most consequential was enshrining the idea that government had a constant and ongoing responsibility to lessen the pain of economic cycles and provide safety nets. That idea had already taken hold in parts of Europe, but it took the New Deal in the United States to implant similar views. The quest for accurate data to demonstrate that these new programs were having the desired effect was a less heralded—and given the less than scintillating nature of statistics, less immediately interesting—aspect of the New Deal. But in terms of the world we confront in the early twenty-first century, marked as it is by what the leading indicators tell us, the push for data and statistics was revolutionary.

The Bureau of Labor Statistics received a needed jolt with the appointment of Perkins and the surge of funding authorized by Congress. Perkins was that rare woman in high politics. She was the first woman to serve in the cabinet, and hence the first woman in American history to be in line for the presidency. She also served for the entirety of Roosevelt's three-plus terms and was deeply involved in many of the signal accomplishments of the early New Deal, including Social Security. Perkins navigated deftly but not always easily through the halls of power, and her New England upbringing ensured that while no one ever questioned her rectitude or integrity, few ever found her warm or charming.[12]

While the Department of Labor held cabinet rank, it was hardly a marquee role. Perkins changed that. With labor issues at the forefront of the emerging Depression and a commitment by Roosevelt to work with unions to forge a safety net, Perkins became a forceful voice in the 1930s. She appointed a respected statistician named Isador Lubin to replace the aged and retiring Stewart at the BLS, and Lubin oversaw the birth of what we now know as the unemployment rate. Of course, it was only the birth, because the government would not start compiling an actual number until the 1950s. Still, the change after 1933 was geometric compared with the arithmetic changes in the years before.

Perkins confronted a Labor Department of low morale and erratic talent. She immediately recognized the importance of a forceful mind and personality to head the BLS. Stewart had served admirably, but he had reached the end of his career. Perkins did not know Lubin personally, and she vetted him from a list of candidates chosen by the American Statistical Association. Her conclusion was that he, more than most, would "remember that statistics were not numbers but people coping or failing to cope with the buffetings of life." And nothing was buffeting people more than employment and its manifold challenges in the 1930s.[13]

Lubin may have looked and sounded like the right person, but the job he ended up doing was unlike the job his predecessors had done. Thankfully, he was up to the task. Creating what in time became the unemployment rate—that number with such consequence in shaping our policies and determining success or failure during elections—was no simple task of counting. You could count employed people, maybe, but what precisely did it mean to be unemployed? That was what Lubin and the BLS and multiple groups defined in the 1930s.[14]

Unemployment meant defining the difference between not having a job and wanting a job, between being part of the labor force and outside of it, and it meant first determining the size of that workforce at any given time. Starting in the 1930s and evolving continuously since then, the BLS defined unemployment. To be unemployed, you had to be part of the workforce, and to be part of the workforce, you had to be actively looking for a job. The statistical definition of unemployment is not the absence of a job; it is the inability to find a job when you are actively seeking one. Even that definition, of course, relies on individuals accurately conveying what they are doing to surveyors who ask. That is not always the case, of course. Someone might say that he has been looking for a job when he has not been and thus be counted as part of the workforce when he is not. Someone might also say that he has a job when he doesn't, whether from pride or shame. Over time the BLS developed multiple unemployment gauges, ranging from out of work, temporary work, and underemployment. But the initial challenges were already apparent in the 1930s.

In order to offset the inevitable problems of surveying only individuals, the BLS drew on two primary sources: (1) a survey of businesses and their payrolls and (2) intermittent Census Bureau surveys of households. The idea was that businesses would not misreport employees on payroll, but individuals might not accurately report their employment status. Not until the 1950s would those two sources be unified into one report, issued monthly. That is what we know today as the monthly jobs report. And not until 1959 were those numbers released with any fanfare to the press and public and then used as a regular reference point. Not until the end of the *1950s*. As we shall see, that means that the many supposed truisms about the relationship between the unemployment rate and success or failure in presidential elections ("No president has ever been reelected with the unemployment rate above 7.2 percent!") are based on barely more than fifty years of information—hardly a blip in time and not nearly enough to make hard and fast conclusions with any certainty.

In the inside-baseball world of statisticians, the most significant change in the 1930s was the widespread introduction of sampling techniques. When governments began to assemble the first wave of statistics, the assumption was that you had to count everyone and everything: people, prices, jobs, homes, and crops. But the modern field of statistics relies entirely on sampling, or counting only a fraction of whatever is being measured. Employment numbers today are based on samples and surveys of sixty-four thousand businesses and four hundred thousand households, which is less than a half a percent of the population.

The trick in sampling, however, is to make sure that the "sample set" is representative of the whole set. Obviously, a sample of prices or employment that used the Upper West Side of Manhattan; Palo Alto, California; Evanston, Illinois; and Austin, Texas as the sample set would provide an extremely distorted picture if used to determine the national number. So too would a sample based on Wichita, Kansas; Detroit; and Navajo County, Arizona. A sample of businesses that used General Motors, General Mills, and Sears, Roebuck and Co. as the primary set would also present a very skewed picture. A sample of a household with six people, including three wage earners, would show a much higher income than a household of six people with one wage earner. For the BLS and others government agencies in the 1930s and 1940s, figuring out the right sample was key to getting the national picture right. Sampling error was a major problem, and it remains one of the weak links in the ongoing attempt to define the world in numbers. From the 1930s on, much of the internal work of these agencies has been focused on refining sample sets and assessing whether they are sufficiently representative to draw national conclusions.

And there were also human errors, as there always had been. Business surveys today are usually sent out by mail (and increasingly by email) and then filled out by the companies surveyed. The household survey is conducted by telephone. But in the 1930s, surveys relied on surveyors, just as the census did. These were not the highest-skilled jobs, nor did they necessarily attract a high caliber of surveyors. Send out people with a list of questions and directives about whom to ask, and some of them will botch it. In one household survey in the 1930s, a BLS supervisor noticed that something was off; one interviewer had submitted results that showed remarkable conformity of occupations. On one of his surveys, a group of households had mostly bakers; another, mostly machinists. Such uniformity of occupations seemed statistically unlikely. When the surveyor was asked more deeply about how he'd gone about his work, he confessed that he had gotten bored and frustrated with the endless ringing of doorbells, with no one answering or people answering and becoming hostile or unresponsive. Finally, he just sat down on the curb and started to fill out the forms using his imagination, selecting different occupations at random.[15]

Many of the surveyors in the 1930s were hired as part of the relief programs of the New Deal. The Works Progress Administration in particular supplied surveying jobs to thousands of people. While the WPA fulfilled its goal of finding employment for able-bodied workers, its primary mandate was not to find people who were competent for these jobs. That quality of the surveys in the 1930s was therefore uneven, which only complicated an already complicated task. By the 1940s, however, the BLS and other agencies were able to hire permanent and trained staff, and that removed some of the most egregious problems. Budgets also went up. The overall expansion of the federal government and the mania for statistics created a critical mass in Washington, and across agencies, statistical groups worked together and transformed the landscape from erratic, unreliable data into the world of leading indicators.

There was one other issue: from the moment the government began to compile official numbers, some suspected that the efforts had ulterior motives. For the free-market right, the progressive ideology of Stewart, Frances Perkins, and so many others was suspect. The leaders of the Bureau of Labor Statistics were overwhelmingly in favor of giving labor more support and providing unemployment insurance (enacted in 1935 as part of the Social Security Act), minimum wage guarantees and more union leverage in negotiations with companies. These progressive impulses were vehemently opposed by the right. Insofar as the people responsible for creating the new numbers were advocates of New Deal government activism, they and their work generated resistance.

Government efforts to create official economic statistics also triggered fears on the left that the purpose was control rather than relief. Academics in the 1960s and 1970s, prone to mistrust government, cast parts of the New Deal and subsequent programs as efforts to contain the masses, which first required registering them and then folding them into government programs that made their actions traceable. In this view, which started as a left-wing critique but then dovetailed nicely with right-wing fears of overarching federal control, the creation of leading indicators was integral to establishing a too-powerful, overweening government that brought all aspects of life under its control.

The belief that the government is purposefully skewing the

numbers for its own insidious motives was woven into popular consciousness almost from the time that these numbers became central to public life. And while that suspicion certainly applied to the unemployment rate, it has been even more acute about inflation and gross domestic product, both of which were coming into being at the same time that the unemployment rate did. The 1930s were the crucible of the modern leading indicators. The invention of unemployment shaped the era and has marked ours, but nothing was more important to the rest of the twentieth century than the invention of gross domestic product, GDP, the indicator of all indicators and the single most important gauge of this entity we call "the economy."

3

NATIONAL INCOME AND THE MAN FROM PINSK

In 1968 the United States was roiling, torn by multilayered protests challenging the Vietnam War, assailing the still-prevalent racial intolerance that existed even as Jim Crow walls were being torn down, and demanding a more equitable balance between the sexes. Capturing that spirit with a passion for remaking America, New York senator Robert Kennedy, younger brother of a slain president, former attorney general, onetime Cold War crusader turned born-again reformer, called on Americans to rethink their metrics of success and demanded a new way to measure the collective good. In a campaign speech at the University of Kansas in March, the newly declared candidate for president was unsparing in his critique:

> Too much and too long, we seem to have surrendered community excellence and community values in the mere accumulation of material things. Our gross national product . . . if we should judge America by that, counts air pollution and cigarette advertising, and

ambulances to clear our highways of carnage. It counts special locks for our doors and the jails for those who break them. It counts the destruction of our redwoods and the loss of our natural wonder in chaotic sprawl. It counts napalm and the cost of a nuclear warhead, and armored cars for police who fight riots in our streets. It counts Whitman's rifle and Speck's knife, and the television programs which glorify violence in order to sell toys to our children.

Yet the gross national product does not allow for the health of our children, the quality of their education, or the joy of their play. It does not include the beauty of our poetry or the strength of our marriages; the intelligence of our public debate or the integrity of our public officials. It measures neither our wit nor our courage; neither our wisdom nor our learning; neither our compassion nor our devotion to our country. It measures everything, in short, except that which makes life worthwhile. And it tells us everything about America except why we are proud that we are Americans.

Kennedy would live only a few months before his life, his candidacy, and, for many Americans, hope for a different course for the future were cut short by an assassin's bullet in an industrial hotel kitchen in Los Angeles. Within a few years, the echo of his plaint that American society had become relentlessly focused on the material to the exclusion of a life well lived would fade. In the 1980s and 1990s and well into this millennium, Americans went even further down the road that Kennedy warned against. Perceptions of national strength were increasingly determined by the economy, and the economy, in turn, was measured by a limited set of numbers. Rather than a collective focus on less quantifiable but vital aspects of society, the determination of whether we are thriving or not came to hinge on the leading indicators: whether there is more income and more goods and services with each passing year, and whether individuals have more money and more stuff or lower wages and less ability to meet their basic needs.

And most of all, since 1968, Americans—and, increasingly, all countries throughout the world—came to rely on one synthetic, simple figure, the very number that Robert Kennedy had so questioned so eloquently and yet so ineffectively in the final days of his life:

Gross domestic product. GDP. No single number has become more central to society in the past fifty years. Throughout the world, GDP has become a proxy for success and for failure, for sentiment about the future and sense of well-being in the present. It has the power to win or lose elections, overthrow governments, start popular movements. A GDP that is growing in sync with expectations or exceeding them is a potent arrow, which deployed well can enhance a country's strength and power. A GDP that is contracting or failing to expand commensurate with hopes and dreams heats the social cauldron rapidly and often to a boiling point.

And yet a hundred years ago, it didn't exist. The vast preponderance of human history has unfolded without it. Empires and kingdoms went about their business with nary a number that captured their economic output, and Americans fought a revolution, a civil war, and conquered a continent without a measure of national income. Not until the early decades of the twentieth century did the impetus of the young economics profession to measure what had been unmeasurable intersect with the desire of governments and politicians to quantify the effect of their policies to produce the first pass at what became GDP.

Between the 1930s, when economists in both Great Britain and the United States turned their efforts to calculating national income, and the 1960s, when gross national product (GNP)—the precursor to GDP—assumed an ever-greater prominence in countries around the world, these figures were still largely wonky and academic. But because of a felicitous convergence of the marketing of the American dream in the 1950s and the demands of the United Nations that new countries measure their economies, GNP and then GDP became *the* litmus of economies everywhere. As Americans competed to prove that their system of free-market capitalism was superior to the Soviet system of state-driven Communism, GDP became even more important to national prestige and global image.

By the end of the twentieth century, GDP growth could determine the fate of nations and the arc of elections, along with its cousin the unemployment rate and inflation, which we will get to in the next chapter. Marlin Fitzwater, the sometimes avuncular, sometimes fierce press secretary to President George Herbert Walker Bush, detailed a meeting in 1992 during the heat of the campaign against Democratic nominee William Jefferson Clinton. Bush was briefed in late spring by his chairman of the White House Council of Economic Advisers and told that "second quarter economic growth would be lower than in the first quarter, maybe around 1.5 percent. The first quarter was 2.7 percent. The president's face went ashen. He slumped down in his chair. 'This is the worst news I've ever heard,' he said," and then proceeded to lose the election.[1]

Yet, much like the unemployment rate, GDP is a product of the 1930s. It is a relatively new invention, and while it has since burrowed deeply into our collective consciousness, it was created to meet specific needs at a specific time. In both Great Britain and the United States of the 1930s, the impetus was the Great Depression. Gross national product, GDP, and the national accounts on which they are based evolved because of the Depression and then were given added teeth with the onset of the world war of the early 1940s. The dual demands of war and Depression were the parents of GDP, and not even the most ardent creators of those massive sets of data imagined that they would become so central to every state in the world within a few short decades.[2]

Talk to a citizen of the United Kingdom—or rather one of its few citizens who live and breathe a passion for the origin of statistics—and he will tell you that GDP and national accounts were the brainchild of several great minds, most notably John Maynard Keynes along with the Nobel Prize–winning Oxbridge dons James Meade and Richard Stone. In the United States, however, most of the credit goes to another Nobel Prize winner, Simon Kuznets, one of the more innovative, eclectic, and influential thinkers—and a name that few outside of the economics profession even recognize.

Kuznets has been lauded as one of the giants of his profession, yet when he began the work that would culminate in the system of national accounts, only a few people cared. The very term *economics* wasn't coined until a London professor named William Stanley Jevons introduced it in 1879. The analysis of "political economy," which had been one of many subjects that historians and philosophers considered when they asked deep and important questions about the shape of society, was a respected endeavor. But Jevons wanted to establish a "science" of how a system called "the economy" functioned. All that he and others lacked, and lacked for many years, was reliable data and useful statistics. Theories they had in abundance, but hard facts and numbers—which they hoped would allow for the same level of scientific rigor that characterized physics—those did not exist.[3]

The absence of such markers deeply disturbed a young Kuznets. Born in Pinsk in the Russian Empire of the Romanov tsars in 1901, Kuznets grew up in a Jewish family of furriers who pushed him to erudition and sent him to college in the university town of Kharkov. But the 1917 Russian Revolution interfered, and the resulting civil wars made normal university studies impossible. Uninterested in those ideologies, Kuznets emigrated from war-torn Ukraine in 1922. Coming of age in a period of intense turmoil left its mark. Beginning his studies during a time when established ideas about social order were being violently upended, Kuznets was acutely aware of how the old order in Russia led the poor to suffer during periods of change because their thin or nonexistent margin of safety gave them little room to compensate when things went seriously awry. During the year he spent in

Kharkov, he began a lifelong quest to understand income distribution, who had it, who did not, and why.[4]

Arriving in New York, he was admitted to Columbia University, and in less than five years, he earned an undergraduate degree and a PhD. And then, as a young man barely in his late twenties, he was hired by the new National Bureau of Economic Research, which most Americans have never heard of but which came to play a pivotal role in everyone's lives as the official designator of economic cycles; it is the economists of the NBER who determine when recessions begin and when they end. But in 1920 the bureau was simply a small group of concerned professional economists who had worked in government during World War I and who saw the dearth of statistics as a crucial national weakness that government—the energies of the technocrat Herbert Hoover notwithstanding—was not about to address with any urgency.

Its head was an energetic Columbia economics professor named Wesley Clair Mitchell, who recognized the potential of his young Russian graduate student. Kuznets, doctorate in hand, promptly accepted Mitchell's offer of a job. Mitchell was adamant that economic theory was all fine and well, but absent rigorous gathering of data, which was then massaged into statistics, it was just so much philosophy, compelling to read—maybe—but impossible to prove. Economics then was still a branch of the humanities, closer to history and philosophy than to math and science. It was free from the intricate formulas that soon became its hallmark. Any lay reader today can pick up a copy of Adam Smith or of his influential contemporary David Ricardo and understand what is being written. The same cannot be said of someone picking up a copy of the journal of the American Economic Association in 2014.

Kuznets, following the lead of his mentors, was unimpressed and uninspired by words and rhetoric. He wanted hard facts and scientific methods. He wanted to answer key questions about the viability of national economies and policies. And he wanted data rather than gossamer webs of words. He believed that theory had a place, but only theory as defined as "a statement of testable relations among empirically identifiable factors." Not surprisingly, Kuznets was anything but a wordsmith, and most of his writings are well-nigh impenetrable to all but the most schooled economist. He excelled at rigorous collection, formulation and analysis of statistics, and therefore, privileged those skills over eloquent argument and graceful prose, qualities that he lacked either by temperament or because Russian was his first language and English a later acquisition.

One of the masters of his profession was another émigré, Harvard University professor Joseph Schumpeter, whose theories of economic cycles were then in vogue and continue to resonate today. It was Schumpeter who later coined the term *creative destruction* to characterize capitalism. Schumpeter's ideas were popular and catchy; Kuznets was unimpressed. It wasn't that Kuznets disagreed with the idea that economies evolve in waves, with periods of creativity and innovations punctuated by periods of collapse or contraction. In fact, he believed exactly that, and after he made his mark defining national accounts and GDP, he spent much of his subsequent career developing theories of economic development that embraced just such a theory of cycles and waves percolating throughout history.

However, Kuznets had little but disdain for the descriptive nature of Schumpeter and others who posited grand theories of human evolution without concrete facts to back those up. Some of this may have been professional jealousy; in the 1930s, Schumpeter was a sage at Harvard and the object of rapt students making pilgrimages to study at the foot of the master. Kuznets was two decades younger and working on a project that he knew was important but hardly the stuff of popular culture. Unlike Schumpeter or the vastly influential English economist John Maynard Keynes, who was then tilling similar fields, Kuznets believed that economics should above all be a science rather than a philosophy, and that made him a perfect fit for the emerging world of official statistics.[5]

Science meant data sets and methodical testing of theories rather than florid descriptions of history and the material evolution of mankind. Schumpeter and nineteenth-century practitioners of political economy were focused on identifying the formula for growth via a careful analysis of the past. Given the dearth of reliable statistics across centuries and cultures, that made eminent sense. But Kuznets was of a different mind. Instead of embracing the statistical vacuum, he was driven to fill it. That demanded consistent methods, meticulous definitions, and data that simply did not exist before the twentieth century.

Yet it wasn't just about numbers. Kuznets was deeply interested in grand narratives and all-encompassing theories of growth and development over the centuries. He would spend much of the later part of his career assessing growth; the effects on growth of technology, population, innovation; and even that loosest of all concepts, culture. Like Schumpeter, and like the great Russian thinker Nikolai Kondratieff—who remained in Russia in the 1920s and would later and inadvertently inspire generations of Wall Street traders looking for rhyme and reason in the endless chaos of financial markets—Kuznets identified waves of business cycles that lasted fifteen to twenty years and were primarily determined by demographics. He argued that population changes constitute inflection points because a growing population triggers public and private spending on infrastructure. When the population stabilizes, that spending ebbs, and economies contract. It was a descriptive theory, but always—always—his theories were grounded in empirical research and hard data.

Given his lifelong passion for finding the elusive formula for growth, it made sense that Kuznets approached the question of national income with such enthusiasm. From the late 1920s through the late 1940s, that was the abiding focus of his life. He began at the NBER as a recent PhD working for his mentor, but within five years, his work was catapulted out of obscurity. Just as the shock of the early 1930s propelled the American government to establish a statistic that determined how many people were unemployed, the wave of legislation ushered in by Franklin Roosevelt and the New Deal spurred an urgent interest in statistics that could measure the economy as a whole.

In Congress, Senator Robert La Follette Jr. of Wisconsin, who had also led the charge to create unemployment numbers, pushed for the establishment of national income accounts. While not the same as GDP, these accounts were the building blocks of understanding what the overall economy was producing and what consumers were earning. For statisticians, national income on the one hand and goods and services produced on the other were understood as roughly the same; neither was being measured with any regularity or consistency as of the early 1930s. Kuznets had made rapid and startling progress to systemize these accounts in his work at the National Bureau of Economic Research, but that was a far cry from an official calculus that could be used by the government to assess the depth of the Depression and to gauge whether government policies were having any positive (or negative) effect.

La Follette was the scion of a powerful Wisconsin clan that included his father, "Fighting Bob" La Follette, who was one of the lions of the Progressive movement and had served as both governor and senator from Wisconsin. The La Follettes were crusaders for reform and social justice. They were tireless opponents of trusts, of the vast profits of big business against the backdrop of widespread want, and of special interests corrupting what they saw as the true egalitarian democracy of America. They opposed the tilt of American foreign policy toward greater intervention in world affairs and viewed the League of Nations with deep suspicion. In multiple respects, they were heirs to Thomas Jefferson and progenitors of many of the protest movements of the second half of the twentieth century.

The younger La Follette was just as determined as his father, and he saw the lack of hard evidence and information about the state of working Americans as an impediment to change. His calls throughout the 1920s had gone unheeded, but the severe turn in 1929 led many others to pick up his initiatives. The rifts in the American and global economies were evident to the naked eye, but, absent reliable numbers, it was hard to justify any specific action. Without a clear diagnosis of what was happening, a credible prognosis was impossible. That explains La Follette's calls for unemployment data and his push for national accounts.

The ultimate goal for La Follette and for those who launched the New Deal was a full-bore public campaign to ameliorate unemployment and restart the industrial engine. To that end, La Follette convened hearings in the Senate in 1931 and took testimony from leading statisticians. To a man, they testified that the current framework was inadequate, not just for measuring employment and unemployment but for assessing the country's output and income. One witness, Frederic Dewhurst of the Department of Commerce, was asked if it would be helpful for the government and American citizens "to secure a complete picture of the economic situation." Dewhurst answered, "In my opinion, it would be most desirable. May I add that a statistician is prejudiced in that he always wants more statistics. Statisticians are never satisfied. But I am impressed constantly with the requests for information that we get in the Department of Commerce, so many of which have to be answered to the effect that we do not know. So often we have to say we do not know, and nobody else knows so far as we can tell."[6]

And so, in June 1932, La Follette introduced a resolution in the Senate calling for the establishment of official national income accounts, relying on the work of the National Bureau of Economic Research and Simon Kuznets. "I believe that the data to be compiled under the authorization of the resolution . . . will be of very great importance in helping Congress to determine policies," he said. The measure was passed, and the Department of Commerce was instructed to prepare estimates of "national income originating from agriculture, manufacturing, mining, transportation, and other gainful industries . . . and in the form of wages, rents, royalties, dividends, profits, and other types of payments."

Kuznets did not invent the idea of national income and GDP. Since the late seventeenth century, there had been periodic attempts in Europe to measure a country's output and income. The motivations then were either intellectual curiosity or the desire for control. The intellectual aspect was simple: understanding the workings of human society. In that sense, measuring the output and income of a state was part of the same drive as classifying all the animals and insects in the world or charting the heavens. The desire for control was also basic: as governments in Europe became more centralized, they sought new ways to draw revenue and manage the population.

In England in 1665, fresh from years of civil war and religious upheaval that had seen one king beheaded and another restored to the throne, Sir William Petty conducted an experiment in what he called "political arithmetick." As one of the founders of the Royal Society of London, Petty thought of himself as a practitioner of science and an enemy of "indefinite generalizations." He had traveled widely throughout France and western Europe, which may have been in the midst of its thirty years of war but still offered an enterprising and fearless young man an education in science, medicine, and human nature. He came back to England as a physician in the army of the lord protector Oliver Cromwell and then was appointed a tax collector. And that was what propelled him to measure England's output. Was the country richer and more powerful than its continental adversaries? Could the government obtain enough revenue in taxes to overcome a smaller population than France? His answer was a resounding yes. "A small Country and a few People," he concluded, "may by their

Situation, Trade and Policy, be equivalent in Wealth and Strength to a far greater People, and Territory."

Of course, the efforts of Petty were based solely on sketchy information from the governmental Treasury, tax records, and census records. His estimates were soon challenged as being overly optimistic about the state of England's wealth relative to France and other competitors. But while he may have been wide of the mark statistically, his work did succeed in establishing the principle that sound policy could be made only if rulers could gauge the actual wealth of the nation. At the end of the seventeenth century, another practitioner of political arithmetic explained why it was so vital: "A great statesman, by consulting all sort of men, and by contemplating the universal posture of the nation, its power, strength, trade wealth and revenue . . . and by computing upon the whole, shall be able to form a sound judgment, and to give a right advice: and this is what we mean by Political Arithmetic."[7]

The line from Petty and other seventeenth- and eighteenth-century minds to official statistics prepared by trained economists and statisticians was not straight. These initial efforts did not bear immediate fruit. In fact, only with the changes caused by the industrial revolutions of the nineteenth century did various people begin to revisit the question of accounting for national wealth and output. In Great Britain as well as in France, Germany, and Russia, a series of nineteenth-century individuals devoted years of their lives to the task of calculating national wealth. They were driven by a cocktail of curiosity and national pride, and by the desire to find the elusive formula to collective wealth and happiness. The motivations for measuring income have always been fused with the quest for happiness. That is why much of the earliest work was done by philosophers who saw "political economy" as one element of a larger puzzle of what makes one society secure and content and another weak and decayed. Then as now, the guiding assumptions were that the more prosperous and materially secure people are, the greater the likelihood that society will thrive.

By the late nineteenth century, those initial impulses were augmented by the availability of more data. Equally important, however, was the scientific imperative to rationalize that data. In Western Europe and in the United States during the industrial revolution, measurement was all the rage, in part from the belief that what could be measured could be tamed and shaped. The task then was to make sense of the sea of data and, hence, the evolution of a new profession of statistics.

Statistics represents the fusion of mathematics with the collection and analysis of data. Most of the people who conceived the leading indicators were not statisticians. They were thinkers, economists, and policy makers looking for answers to their questions. But the people who then refined and developed the actual numbers thought of themselves as statisticians. Early in the twentieth century, the field of statistics was still forming, but by midcentury, it had become its own distinct discipline, combining sophisticated mathematics, probability theory, and sampling methods, as well as accounting.

As we will see, today's leading indicators are firmly in the hands of professional statisticians, while the invention of those indicators was as much a product of economists and policy makers. That matters. The creators of these indicators were attempting to answer specific policy questions. In the case of the push for reliable national income accounts and GDP, the drive was to understand the nature of the Great Depression. That shaped what was measured and what was not. Statisticians tend to focus on how to improve measurement, estimation, sampling, and revisions, while leaving the policy questions to policy makers. Much like the military, they are concerned with implementation and execution, and less with grand strategy.

One of the key decisions facing Kuznets and his colleagues was whether to include domestic work in their calculations of national income. The argument for including housework is powerful: a goodly portion of society's material output stems from domestic work that takes time, provides vital needs, and enables other activity. The simplest example is cooking a meal at home. Shopping for food, preparing it for cooking, and then cleaning up after are imperative activities. We all need food, and without it, there can be no work, let alone life. Cleaning and caring for a home are also necessary, yet none of that domestic work is included in national income or GDP.

No one in the 1930s argued that domestic work was anything but central to the material well-being of society. And no one argued that housework was not a form of economic output. At the same time, almost everyone involved in crafting the numbers believed that these forms of work should be left out. The reason was simple: because these types of work are unpaid, they do not have a measurable cost. As Richard Stone, who was central to the creation of national accounts in Great Britain, remarked in his Nobel lecture in 1984, "Although household activities . . . take the form of production, as in cooking a meal or redecorating a house, their output does not have a measurable cost, since household members and amateurs give their services for nothing; these services are innumerable and unrecorded; in general, they are not very well defined and merge imperceptibly into the activity of living. This being so, until recently it has been agreed that household and amateur activities should not be included in production and should not be accounted for."[8]

The decision to omit such work was seen at the time as a necessary trade-off between the desire to measure all societal output and the limitations of collecting data. Because domestic work, hobbies, volunteering, and leisure activities are not easily measured, they were left out of the equation of national income and national output with the full recognition that doing so meant that an entire swath of human activity and societal well-being would simply not exist in the official statistics.

And so the work proceeded in the 1930s, leaving out a crucial dimension of economic life yet moving rapidly toward a new system of measuring consumption, production, and overall income. In addition to the issue of excluding domestic and leisure activities, there was the conundrum of how to account for government spending. Before the 1930s, government spending was not a substantial portion of economic activity, but with the expansion of the New Deal in the United States and numerous social welfare programs in Great Britain, that changed profoundly. The initial national income accounts did not include government as a separate category, because whatever businesses and individuals reaped from government spending would be captured by national income. If the government spent $500,000 on a naval ship, that would show up as business income. But the explosion of emergency spending programs meant that government outlays multiplied, and that, in turn, led to a push not just for national income accounts but also for what was first termed gross national product (which only at the end of the twentieth century was supplanted by GDP). The transformation of government into a substantial economic actor was driven not by the brilliant Simon Kuznets but rather the combined demands of a global recession and one man who trumpeted a solution, John Maynard Keynes.[9]

Keynes has since become synonymous with aggressive government spending in the face of economic downturns and the concomitant evaporation of demand for goods and services. "We are all Keynesians now" is the famous quote attributed to Richard Nixon, though it was actually uttered—in disdain—by that icon of the free market, Milton Friedman. The point was that after the experience of the 1930s, nations everywhere embraced the idea that government spending could—and must—counteract the excessive saving or hoarding of cash by anxious consumers during times of uncertainty. Keynesianism was in sharp contrast to the classical economic thinking of Adam Smith, David Ricardo, and their disciples, who believed that economic systems tend to function in perfect balance but are occasionally punctuated by times of crisis. In the classical view, the system then naturally corrects, and crisis and imbalance in due course give way to the natural state of full employment, perfect prices, and an exact match between demand and supply. Of course, such corrections can be damaging and painful, and at various moments in history, the system collapses before it has a chance to self-correct.

As Robert Skidelsky makes clear in his magisterial biography, Keynes had little use for neat theoretical models that were held up as perfect representations of reality but were in truth no more than Plato's shadows on a cave wall. Keynes's experience as an investor and businessman in England, having run companies and earned and lost fortunes in the stock market, made him acutely sensitive to the outsized roles that human behavior and irrationality played in determining outcomes. In his view, there was nothing self-correcting about societies gripped by economic panic and fear. He was also adamant that the scientific urge to quantify and to reduce the world to what could be measured and tested confronted serious limitations when it came to the workings of society. Economists from the dawn of the profession were characterized by a belief that society could be understood as a machine. Keynes saw things differently.

Like many of his English contemporaries, Keynes was trained at Cambridge University with a healthy respect for mathematics and models. He was particularly drawn to probability theories, which may account for his propensity to gamble in the stock market. While he had an upper-class education, he had been raised with middle-class means. In 1919 he opened a fund focused on trading currencies, and he did what George Soros would do decades later, but not quite as well. Some of Keynes's bets paid off handsomely, but he took on too much leverage. When the British pound failed to rally as he expected in 1920, the entire fund was wiped out. Keynes kept moving forward, however, and by 1927, he had rebuilt a nest egg of about $2 million in today's dollars. By 1930, he had lost almost all of it, victim of a global slump in the commodities that he had bet on. Within five years, he reversed his losses yet again and had over $25 million.

Keynes the investor shaped how Keynes the economist thought. Though he was adept at math and models, in the end, he saw economics as an art of description rather than as a science. In his experience, people are not rational actors. They save when they should spend, panic when they should hold fast, buy when they should not. They yearn for safety and clarity about the future and in the desperate urge to avoid confronting uncertainty make even worse decisions. Keynes rejected the classical and neoclassical economic models that put full faith and credit in the invisible hand of the markets. Instead, he came to believe that the only agent capable of guiding the market and steering it when it went off course—as it always did—was government. And so, he became the prime proponent of government spending as the only reliable tool to compensate for recession and depression.

His ideas evolved over decades. They formed out of the crucible of his personal experience in the markets and his service in the British government, most crucially in the Treasury during World War I. Keynes was born in 1883, so by the time of the Great Depression, he had been honing his views for years. But as influential as he was in the halls of Parliament as a voice for government action, he was acutely aware that better data would vastly augment the case for spending and would also allow policy makers to modulate their spending more precisely.

Convinced that economic contractions were the result of a collapse in demand, Keynes advocated tactical spending to stimulate demand and provide enough short-term security to coax consumers out of their foxholes. He called this "cheap money, wise spending." The goal for government, then, was to figure out just how much it needed to spend. Keynes argued that the government had to allocate enough to bridge the gap between what consumers were spending and what they needed to spend if the economic system were to remain healthy. Without reliable data and consistent statistics, however, officials could only guess how much was enough. You knew a recession when you saw one, usually, and you knew if tax revenues were drying up because of less trade, production, and consumption. But if you were the prime minister of Great Britain or the president of the United States, how could you figure out how much extra spending was necessary? If the gap between actual demand and actual production was $1 billion, then you needed to spend at least $1 billion to bridge it (and probably more to jump-start activity). Then, to assess if that $1 billion in spending was having the desired effect, you needed hard data about subsequent developments in order to determine whether it was having the intended outcome.

National income accounts were a start, but because the initial calculations did not include government expenditures, other numbers were needed. In 1934 a man named Clark Warburton, who like Keynes was deeply involved in the calculus of national income and who later became one of Keynes's dogged critics, proposed the creation of a "gross national product" statistic that would include government outlays. His motivations were to find better gauges, not to implement Keynesian economics, but by the late 1930s, as the policies of the Roosevelt administration became increasingly focused on spending, the need for a statistic that justified that spending became acute.[10]

The New Deal did not begin as a Keynesian program to spend and spend. It was instead an ad hoc series of programs designed to halt the collapse of the banking system and get people back to work. By FDR's second term, however, the idea that the federal government could and should incur deficits to offset the worst of the crisis was more widely accepted. Roosevelt himself started to explain and defend his programs by using national income accounts as proof that the policies of his administration were working. In a major campaign speech

in Pittsburgh in October 1936, running against the Republican chal-
lenger Alfred Landon, Roosevelt asked people to elect him to a second
term because of what he had done to raise national income above its
perilous lows in the early 1930s when Hoover was president.

> During the four lean years before this administration took office,
> national income had declined from eighty-one billion a year to
> thirty-eight billion a year. In short, you and I, all of us together, were
> making forty-three billion—spelled with a *b*, not an *m*—forty-three
> billion dollars less in 1932 than we made in 1929. Now, the rise and
> fall of national income—since they tell the story of how much you
> and I and everybody else are making—are an index of the rise and
> fall of national prosperity. They are also an index of the prosperity
> of your government. The money to run the government comes from
> taxes; and the tax revenue in turn depends for its size on the size of
> the national income.

As a result of his decision to use deficit spending to address the economic catastrophe, Roosevelt claimed, national income rebounded
sharply. "It was thirty-eight billion in 1932," he told the crowd in
Pittsburgh. "In 1935 it was fifty-three billion, and this year it will be
well over sixty billion. If it keeps on rising at the present rate, as I am
confident that it will, the receipts of the government, without impos-
ing any additional taxes, will, within a year or two, be sufficient to
care for all ordinary and relief expenses of the government—in other
words, to balance the budget."

Only because of the work of Kuznets and others could Roosevelt
make these assertions and cast the work of his administration in such
terms. The use of statistics to support political claims was a great
boon to policy makers in these years and transformed economic arguments from pure ideology into at least partial fact. Of course, soon
enough, ideology would again rule the day, and data would become

a handmaiden of partisan arguments about what to do. But what changed permanently was the need of even the most partisan policy makers to defend their economic policies with statistics.

Still, Roosevelt could point only to the growth of national income as evidence that government policies were working. In 1937 activity contracted sharply once again in the face of spending cuts. FDR and his advisors believed that deficits should be temporary measures to be paid off as soon as feasible, but the premature curtailment of government spending in 1937 hobbled the precarious recovery. That reaction—spending cuts leading to recession—could itself be evidence of the link between government action and national income, but there were no reliable, consistent numbers to prove that and silence critics. National income reflected the effects of government spending but did not actually break out government outlays as a separate category of economic activity. If, say, the government spent $1 million on the Works Progress Administration, and the WPA then hired ten thousand people to renovate a public park, that would show up in the national income accounts as income to those ten thousand people and to the tree farmers and landscaping businesses that won contracts. But there was no distinct line for government spending in these initial national income accounts.

Starting in 1939, Roosevelt began to cite national income statistics in his annual report to Congress on the state of the union and the economy. But there was still no GNP figure. Those who advocated for more expansive government spending needed a statistic to demonstrate a conclusive link between government spending and overall economic prosperity. The unemployment rate was one hook on which to hang those arguments; gross national product was another. GNP was much like GDP except that it included the value of all production owned by Americans, whether that production was done in the United States or not. The goods produced by a furniture factory owned by an American businessman operating in England would be included in

GNP. But not in GDP. Conversely, a factory owned by a Japanese or Chinese company in Tennessee today has its output included in US GDP but not in GNP. Given that the extent of these foreign ventures was minimal in the 1930s, gross national product was the preferred metric, and not until 1991 did GDP fully supplant GNP.

The move to develop GNP was driven first by politics; it was then propelled by the demands of war. Keynesians in the Roosevelt administration wanted to prove that public works projects and other big government programs were imperative to economic health during times of duress. But what catapulted this obscure number to the center of public policy was not the Depression but the next great global cataclysm, World War II.[11]

In 1940, in response to the German invasion of Poland in September 1939, as well as the continued militarization of Japan and its ongoing war in China, the United States ramped up military spending. In 1941 Roosevelt, having been elected for an unprecedented third term, asked Congress to spend $25 billion on the military; that was nearly two-thirds of the entire federal budget. These ballooning expenses led to concern about how much could be spent on defense without critically undermining an already tenuous domestic economy. Could the United States ratchet up defense spending without triggering shortages in vital goods along with massive inflation and scarcity? National income couldn't measure that. Gross national product, with its breakdown of the overall value of goods and services by sector, could.

Kuznets was again called upon to answer these question. In 1942 he began work for the US War Production Board, which was the agency responsible for putting the American economy on a war footing and marshaling the might of domestic manufacturing to produce the tanks, planes, and guns that turned the United States into the "arsenal of the world" and eventually led to the defeat of the Axis powers. The administration, however, was deeply concerned that too much redirection of manufacturing would cripple consumer demand for goods such as cars and would lead to shortages, rationing, and skyrocketing prices. Both would have dire effects on the domestic economy and thereby undermine the war effort.

FDR solved some of the issues by instituting price controls. To keep people from behaving in ways that would collectively send the economy into a tailspin, the government also developed numbers to measure the cost of goods and inflation. That mattered because of the fear that people would hoard goods and save excessively from fear of future inflation. By instituting price controls and disseminating statistics about inflation, the government hoped that people would be reassured that the prices for basic essentials such as food, clothing, and shelter would remain stable.

Then, in 1942, to solve the central question of whether the United States could devote the vast majority of its government spending and its private industry to the war without upending society, economists and statisticians finally unveiled what had been years in the making: gross national product. GNP provided a way to calculate precisely how much the government could spend and how much it could increase taxes to pay for defense. GNP wasn't a weapon, but it helped win the war.

As in the actual fighting of the war, the Americans and the British worked closely on the development of all of these numbers. Keynes once again proved vital. He argued for the concept of "an inflationary gap," which was a way to use national income and GNP figures to measure how much excess demand for goods there was relative to production. If consumers had $70 billion in income, which was the rough calculation in 1942, and there was only $65 billion of goods produced according to GNP figures, then in theory that would lead to inflation, as more people and more money chased scarcer products. To prevent that from happening, government would have to either tax more or adjust price controls. On the flip side, these figures allowed the federal government to measure the effects of the war on the domestic economy.

The astonishing success of the United States in fighting, financing, and furnishing the war over the next three years banished the Great Depression to the annals of history. Eight years of fervent New Deal efforts had barely stabilized America. Three years of war transformed the country into a global economic powerhouse. And the ability of government bureaucrats, following the lead of Kuznets and Keynes, to measure and then recalibrate policies transformed these statistics from areas of academic concern into pillars of what Henry Luce, who was to become the leading acolyte of these numbers as metaphors for American power, called "the American Century."

The success of managing the war economy was heralded as one of the great triumphs of human ingenuity and skill. The people who staffed the agencies responsible along with the leaders of myriad businesses that coordinated their efforts with the government saw that triumph as a product of sheer will, national character, and science. The end of the war, as we all know, was ominously punctuated by the development of the first nuclear bombs by thousands of scientists and engineers working in secret for the Manhattan Project. The culmination of those efforts was celebrated by most, save for the one scientist who led the work, J. Robert Oppenheimer. Witnessing the explosion of the first bomb at the test site of Alamogordo, New Mexico, in July 1945, Oppenheimer was led to utter a passage from the great Hindu text the Bhagavad Gita, "I am become Death, destroyer of worlds." He understood what had been unleashed, even if many of those around him cheered.

The story of the atom bomb and its consequences have not lacked for discussion in the years since. But the same impulse to control what had been seen as the uncontrollable and to leash forces that had been a threat to human society animated the development and deployment of official statistics in the 1930s. The goal was to tame the unruly beast that was economic life, the sharp, wrenching, and often destructive ups and downs, booms and busts that characterized human history.

What had been mysterious and opaque was suddenly cast into what seemed like sharp focus, and that, in turn, gave people the hope that they could at last steer the economic ship with precision and thereby end once and for all those destructive cycles.

Understandably, the conquest of the economy with hard data and new statistics was far less touted than the conquest over the Axis powers. But in terms of how people came to view the present and future and how they defined power and success, the invention of these indicators was just as important. The war was crucial, but it was in the years after the war—when the ideological battle with Communism heated up even as the Cold War pushed direct military conflict to the sidelines—that these indicators were woven into every nook and cranny of economic life and popular culture. This happened not just in the United States but also in the world at large, born on the wings of the globalizing impulses of the United Nations and the proselytizing nature of American capitalism. Trade, employment, and GDP were key elements, but soon enough there was a proliferation of indicators as both government and the private sector rushed to create numbers that would capture what was happening in all aspects of economic life.

Yet at the outset, national accounts, GNP and GDP were limited in what they measured. They were designed to assess prosperity, but with the understanding that multiple aspects of life were being left out or not fully valued. It wasn't just domestic work and hobbies that were omitted. It was the very way that output was gauged as a net positive regardless of the nature of that output. As Alan Greenspan, one of the earliest acolytes of the new system of indicators that emerged from the ashes of war and depression, observed, if residents of the southern United States buy lots of air conditioners, which they do, to offset the crushing heat of summer, that will show up as a positive for GDP (assuming those air conditioners are made in the United States, which would have been the case until late in the twentieth century and is no longer). So too will the money that people spend on electricity bills. Vermont, with less arduous heat, likely sees fewer purchases, and thereby would show a lower GDP than Alabama, at least insofar as air conditioners are concerned.[12] But such numbers say nothing about the relative prosperity of the two states or about the overall quality of life in either place.

Kuznets and his cohort understood full well that what was included and what was not would have a significant impact on conclusions drawn. They understood as well that it was imperative that anyone using these numbers recognize the limitations. But as the numbers became touchstones of public policy and media reference points, those subtleties were lost.

World War II was the last great conflict of the twentieth century. What followed was a global competition defined not by the battlefield but by numbers—numbers meant to demonstrate the superiority of capitalism and its ability to provide prosperity, power, and, yes, happiness. For a while, the leading indicators seemed to prove just that, until late in the century, when social mores and the nature of production began to change radically even as the indicators developed in the 1930s did not. How those indicators came to rule our world is a story tied to the end of the war, to a world exploding with new nations and new alliances, and to a man who saw the power of those numbers to capture the imagination of millions.

4

THE INVENTION OF THE ECONOMY

"During the past dozen years or so, we have been watching, in the US, something close to a miracle . . . [The United States] has become—incredibly—a nation with full employment, sensationally booming production and the widest distribution of plenty ever known anywhere . . . The once sick American economy has become the wonder of the world."[1]

So began an article in the widely popular *Life* magazine that appeared in a 1953 issue entitled "The American and His Economy." *Life* was part of a suite of magazines published under the aegis of Henry Luce, who as much as any individual helped shape postwar culture, one that trumpeted American affluence and ingenuity, condemned Communism as immoral and ineffective, and used statistics that had not even existed a few decades earlier to bolster the case for the American way.

If there was a high priest of the gospel of American economic progress in the twentieth century, Luce was it. And while his magazines eventually included not just *Life*, but *Time* and *Sports Illustrated*, it was *Fortune* that became the house vehicle for American economic exceptionalism. Conceived as a celebration of capitalism, *Fortune* was launched inauspiciously in 1930, just as the Depression was quashing the giddy and perhaps naïve utopianism of the 1920s. But the publication was able to retool under Luce and become an organ of sharp, intelligent, and even academic commentary about the nature of business and how companies were facing the challenges of the era.

Luce's partner, Briton Hadden, was skeptical that *Fortune* could succeed, but he died before Luce could prove him wrong. Both men were true blood Wasps: Hotchkiss for boarding school and then Yale University class of 1920; well bred but not rich; ambitious, elite, and yet deeply respectful of merit over birth. Luce had the more atypical upbringing, having spent his youth in China with missionary parents in Shanghai. That instilled a lifelong passion for all things Sino and later led Luce to become one of the more vehement critics of American policy toward Chiang Kai-shek when the generalissimo was driven from China in 1949 by Mao Tse-tung's Communist masses. His childhood rival turned publishing partner Hadden died prematurely at the age of thirty-one in 1929. Had he lived, he would have seen Luce's vision of *Fortune* vindicated.

Perhaps befitting his background, Luce brought a missionary zeal to his ambition for America. The perils of the economic crisis of the 1930s, followed by the military crisis of the 1940s, transformed Luce from an aggressive publisher into a leading champion of what might loosely be called the "American way" of free-market capitalism, democracy, and the fight against Communism that defined American foreign policy from 1945 through the late 1980s. And Luce was the American way preacher—or at least his publications were, suffused with common sensibility, yet deeply informed; arrogant about the ability of America and Americans to solve any problem and confront any crisis, yet curiously insecure and unsure whether they would indeed rise to the occasion. The mix of preening certainty and nagging insecurity may explain the hyperbolic nature of much of what Luce and, by extension, *Time* and *Fortune* published, as if an excess of rhetoric was needed to force Americans to answer the call of the better angels of their nature.

Of course, one could debate what Luce and company understood as better angels. He had no truck with much of the New Deal and detested the efforts of FDR and his administration to bring big business to heel and insert the government as an aggressive agent of economic activity. Luce disliked Roosevelt deeply, and the feeling was reciprocated. Yet both were proponents of America's involvement in the fight against Germany and Japan long before many Americans were, and in spite of their mutual disdain, they both were advocates of America playing an outsized role on the world stage.[2]

Fortune conceived of business as the foundation of twentieth-century "civilization," and Luce was not shy about using such terms. With the advent of the New Deal, however, came a shift in public awareness of how business, government, and labor interacted to produce either crises or opportunities. There had always been sharp disagreements over the roles of government and business in American society. The Progressive movement had been one iteration of that conflict, which in turn had raised the question of the fate of labor. Out of that cauldron came a variety of new laws to guard labor and tame business, along with those first efforts to create statistics that would—in theory—replace endless ideological jousting with solid data.

Luce, however, was an ideologue of the best and worst sort. He had strong passions that dictated his agenda, and he was prone to filter reality through the prism of his beliefs. After the war, those beliefs in American world destiny and in the incomparable superiority of American capitalism compared with Soviet Communism dictated a relentless elucidation of America's economic strengths. That meant long—and by today's standards, dense—articles in *Fortune* by serious economists such as John Kenneth Galbraith and Daniel Bell explicating the strengths and challenges of the new economy that emerged from the ashes of war. And such explication was necessary, because as *Fortune* itself announced in 1946, there was no question that an economic boom had begun, but the causes were unclear. "What's happening to the economy? Something, but no one knows precisely what."[3]

That is where the rage for data and statistics that characterized the New Deal era in the United States entered a new phase. Before, the push for indicators had come largely from academics, civil servants, labor leaders, bureaucrats, and a few elected officials such as Senators Robert Wagner and Robert La Follette. After the war, the demand for indicators became more widespread, with businesses and the media hunkering for as much as they could get. Some of the impetus was a direct reaction to the Soviet mania for numbers as proof that its system of state-driven production was superior. The Soviet government was endlessly touting its industrial production in terms of millions of cars made, thousands of tons of steel rolled, acres sown and harvested, weapons produced and deployed. But the American passion to hone and invent indicators was also fueled by an innovative spirit that sought to understand the nature of the American system, as well as by the continued desire to tame and ultimately control unruly patterns of boom and bust.

If the statistics invented before 1945 dealt with the twin crises of depression and war, the world after was marked by how to measure affluence.[4] It was also marked by a remarkable transformation in how not just Americans but also people throughout the world came to define themselves. For thousands of years, the basic question of how society was faring was answered in terms of military might and enough—just enough—food and security to keep people alive and perhaps content. As we have seen, the pre–twentieth-century efforts to measure national economic activity hardly left their mark on public consciousness; as dedicated as Ethelbert Stewart and his cohorts were, they toiled largely in the shadows of a larger culture that was focused on conquering territory and advancing science and industry.

But the emergence of the United States as a global force unparalleled and nearly unrivaled in material might catapulted obscure economic indicators into central, abiding elements of national life. No "man on the street" would have given a thought to gross national product or national income in the 1920s or at any point before then, and not simply because that number didn't exist. People wouldn't have thought of their nation or their society or their own lives in terms of the collective material production of their country. And they would not have marked success or failure by a series of indicators.

That changed markedly after World War II, for two reasons. Though the basic contours of unemployment, GDP, and inflation (as we will discuss later) were formed in the 1930s, not until after the war did they coalesce into simple, straightforward statistics that could be tracked, issued, and debated on a regular, ongoing basis. In essence, the numbers were invented in the 1930s but marketed only after 1945. And with a few leading indicators in hand, people went about doing what they always do: they invented more.

Marketing was crucial; without that, the numbers might have remained useful but obscure. The proliferation of indicators after the war was driven in part by government, in part by industry, and in part by media outlets such as Luce's *Time* and *Fortune*, along with *BusinessWeek* and newspapers across the country. Private indicators were developed by professional associations such as the Institute for Supply Management, academic institutions such as the University of Michigan, and nonprofit organizations such as the Conference Board. Meanwhile, the Census Bureau, various Federal Reserve bank branches, the Bureau of Labor Statistics, the Bureau of Economic Analysis, and others continued their statistical work, and so the indicators evolved in scope, scale, and complexity. The final element was the vast proliferation of information collected, collated, and analyzed by newly created global agencies such as the United Nations and the World Bank, of all which developed a hunger verging on a fetish for data and statistics that has lasted till today.

But it wasn't simply the efflorescence of indicators that mattered. It was their movement to the center of American culture and of societies throughout the world. The years after the war saw these indicators go global, care of the adamant efforts of the United States to demonstrate its superiority. They went global as well because of the particular need of the emerging international community for common standards and common metrics to assess whether or not the world was on a constructive economic trajectory. For many in these years, the world war that consumed so many lives was seen as a product of stagnant, bankrupt economic philosophies and systems. Preventing a new collapse and insuring that the people everywhere were each year more able to meet their material needs was understood as central to peace and security.

These forces combined to create what we now know as "the economy." Before there were metrics and indicators, "the economy" didn't exist. No, economic activity wasn't invented in the middle of the twentieth century. But this thing called "the economy" was. Until the 1940s, there was no "the economy." People did not use the term and they had only just begun to think of the material affairs of a nation as a coherent and cohesive subject that could be defined, measured, and tracked over time. Look up "the economy" on Google's comprehensive Ngram Viewer site. Ngram is a digital repository of all texts ever written before the advent of copyright. Until the mid-1930s, the term *the economy* appeared hardly at all; after that, its usage soared. In short, the leading indicators invented "the economy."

Evolving as it did when it did, the economy as a concept is inseparable from the nation-state. The numbers that allowed the idea to become ubiquitous were national statistics developed first by governments to measure their own domestic societies. Just as thinkers and economists had tinkered over the centuries with measurements of output in order to rank their national strength compared with other nations, the initial impetus for these numbers was for governments to understand what was happening domestically. Circumstances in other countries were of limited interest, except to assess whether adversaries and allies were rising or falling. As a result, in the 1930s, there were no international statistics of output and employment. The numbers stopped at each country's borders. And even as those borders have become less significant and more porous, that has changed only marginally.

As we shall see, even today, in a world that is unarguably global and more like a three-dimensional chessboard of countries, companies, and individuals, almost all indicators are based on the idea that an economy is a closed system with physical boundaries that define a nation-state. We have precious few truly global indicators. After all, who would collect them and who would pay for them? And as a result, our indicators are limited to states. That may have made sense before World War II, but it has made less and less sense with each passing decade since. An analogy would be if US economic information was assembled state by state, with fifty different GDP numbers, with trade between Alabama and Mississippi or between New Jersey and New York adding or detracting from the growth and output of each state, and the only national figures the product of just adding up all fifty states.

Prior to the later decades of the twentieth century, you could make a strong argument that the preponderance of economic activity was contained within national boundaries, even if those were porous, and that while the nation-state as the primary economic unit raised issues, it was better than no unit. Economics as a discipline emerged in the nineteenth century just as the nation-state did; hence, economists took the state as a closed system that defined this thing called "the economy." Well into the late twentieth century, economic activity was deeply constrained by geographic borders and by the efforts of governments to control what went on inside those borders. Currency rates were zealously guarded by governments, and gold acted as a common denominator to value those currencies against one another. Tariffs and taxes, even if they were relaxed in the name of free trade, were barriers that states erected to defend themselves or keep out competition. Central banks were (and in most respects still are) national entities established by national governments to manage national economic affairs and the printing of national money.

So for economists and statisticians in the first half of the twentieth century, it made some sense to define "the economy" as a closed system that began and ended with national borders. Yes, the state wasn't the only economic unit, and while it suited economists to model reality as if states were hermetically sealed units, there was also trade and flows of money and people. Nonetheless, economists developed theories that treated a national economy as a closed system that will always, in the end, result in equilibrium. Classical economic theory dictated that forces of supply and demand govern economic life, and that the two eventually find their perfect balance. Prices, wages, production—all will balance out in the end: that is why the system of accounts developed by Kuznets and others had two sides of a ledger: production and income, inputs and outputs, each of which must precisely match the other. It was a purely scientific approach to an economy, like a vacuum chamber where no matter can be destroyed and none created.[5]

The invention of "the economy" with numbers to measure it was a vast improvement over what prevailed before. It gave governments a way to measure and assess what was happening and a means to test whether policies were doing good or causing harm. It gave society a greater degree of confidence (sometimes false) that people need not be at the mercy of mysterious and dangerous economic storms. The overdependence on indicators that evolved over the final decades of the twentieth century and into the twenty-first is a core issue of this book, but that isn't an indictment of the creation of these indicators in the first place. To repeat an earlier analogy, the tools of the Renaissance navigators—that astrolabe and rudimentary compasses—were a far cry from the high-tech systems of today and in many cases were woefully inaccurate and even fatal to the brave seaman who relied on them. But compared with navigating by the stars, sun, and moon as the only reference points across thousands of miles of uncharted oceans, they were invaluable. The same is true of the national indicators invented in the early and mid-twentieth century; they were an unequivocal improvement compared with what came before.

In 1945 there were a few select indicators disseminated largely within individual governments, especially the United States, Great Britain, and the Soviet Union. Twenty years later, indicators were everywhere: in public, in politics, in business, and increasingly in our everyday lexicon. They were also global. By the late 1960s, every country in the world kept national accounts and published GDP figures according to standards set by the United Nations. If they didn't, they faced immense pressure from the World Bank, the UN, and the US government. The global proliferation of indicators was less dramatic (and not nearly as scary) than the proliferation of nuclear weapons that took place in the same period, but in terms of everyday life for billions of people, it was no less—and perhaps even more—momentous.

Today it seems so commonplace to speak of different countries in terms of their GDP or income or trade. Much of the friction between China and the United States in recent years revolves around trade statistics and GDP figures. Much of the concern about the passage of the North American Free Trade Agreement (NAFTA) in 1994 focused on the effects on employment, unemployment, trade, and wages. These issues aren't abstract. They generate public passion. And how people feel about these issues is almost entirely a product of the leading indicators and what partisans say that they say.

Yet in 1945 it would have been hard to imagine a world so suffused with these numbers. None of the people who created them intended for them to become such prominent societal markers. Even so, that is precisely what happened. It happened because of the likes of Luce, and it happened as well because of the United Nations.

While the post–World War I League of Nations had been a first stab at weaving an international community in order to prevent catastrophic war, the United Nations was the version 2.0 that was supposed to correct the deficiencies of the League—one of the most glaring of which has been the absence of the United States as a member. The UN would be a forum for collective action and collective security, with both a General Assembly and a Security Council of elite states empowered to act as custodians of global peace.[6]

It is hard to overstate the idealism inherent in the creation of a multinational forum for peace and prosperity. Rather than a zero-sum world characterized by a state of near-constant war punctuated by lulls of peace, the UN envisioned the possibility of a state of near-constant peace interrupted only by "just wars." And unlike the League that preceded it, the UN took a hard-edged approach to the reality of states as possible aggressors and rulers as potential tyrants. Collective security, overseen by the most powerful, would be a tool not just to advance peace but also to enforce it.

"The United Nations," announced then-president Harry S. Truman, "is designed to make possible lasting freedom and independence for all its members." Such rhetoric was typical of the times. Said Ralph Bunche, the African-American Nobel Prize winner who was one of the architects of the UN, "The United Nations is our one great hope for a peaceful and free world."[7] The United Nations charter, hammered out over a period of less than a year and signed on June 26, 1945, outlined a comprehensive vision for international security and an elaborate structure to protect it. Because the formation of the UN was followed so quickly by the deterioration of relations between the

United States and the Soviet Union, the security dimensions of the organization assumed more prominence than originally envisioned. The result was decades of focus on the machinations of the Security Council, and the waning of the UN as a respected force in international affairs as it proved unable to overcome the animosity of its most powerful members.

The creation of the UN was followed in 1948 by the Universal Declaration of Human Rights, which is remembered—when it is—for its lucid defense of political rights for all citizens of the world. Those included freedom of expression, freedom from arbitrary arrest, the outlawing of torture, the rule of law, and the right to worship according to one's faith. What is less recalled, however, and was relegated to the sidelines quickly afterward, were entire sections dedicated not to political rights and freedoms but to economic ones.

These economic rights, characterized at the time as human rights on par with freedom of religion and the rule of law, included the right to sufficient food, shelter, clothes, leisure, health care, and a safety net for unemployment, disability, disease, and old age. The UN itself was organized not just with a General Assembly and a Security Council but also with an Economic and Social Council that would monitor global economic activity. The goal was to protect and promote economic security, and the Economic Council was seen as parallel to the Security Council. The great powers would guard international security through the mechanisms of the Security Council and the nations of the Economic Council would protect and promote global growth.[8]

The pressures of the emerging Cold War, however, pushed economic rights to the side. For the next decades, the struggles that rent the globe were defined almost entirely in terms of political philosophies, with the Western world focused on the repressive political systems of the Soviet Union, China, and various states governed by military dictators. Economic issues weren't forgotten, and the United States and international institutions spent billions in aid to developing countries in order to raise living standards and to prove the superiority of free-market capitalism over state-dictated Communism. But the primary focus of these years was the contest between the United States and the Soviet Union, with the UN Security Council often at the center of international crises.

And yet at the United Nations itself, economic development and economic rights remained powerful issues, and one of the first things the new organization did was to formalize a standardized system of national accounts that could be applied to every country in the world. The result? Before the late 1940s, only a few countries had even a rudimentary map of their national economic activity. Within a few decades, every nation in the world was measuring output, income, and national wealth in the same way. With that came comparisons and rankings, and those ubiquitous lists of countries ordered by size of economy. With that as well came a global pecking order defined not by the size of armies or the number of nuclear warheads but by new ideas such as per capita income and GDP.

The United Nations was created with remarkable speed. For an organization that in later years came to be marked by a bloated bureaucracy and stunning inefficiency, it was born lean. The basic outlines were determined at the end of 1944 by China, the Soviet Union, the United Kingdom, and the United States, and then the organizational charter was hashed out in a few months in San Francisco before being formally adopted in the summer of 1945. The first meeting was held in October 1945, barely a year between idea and reality. And that December, a committee of "National Income Statistics" met and presented its findings to the UN Statistical Commission.

This emerging statistical framework received precious little attention, and, honestly, why would it? Statisticians meeting to discuss formulas for global national accounts was hardly the stuff to make a reporter's career or win an election. The subject wouldn't even make a compelling essay for *Fortune*, lacking as it did the ideological debates of growth versus austerity, Keynesian spending versus free-market solutions, Communism versus capitalism. Yet the work of this quiet and obscure committee of statisticians, reporting to the equally obscure and quiet Statistical Commission, would ultimately shape the way billions of people came to understand their lives and measure how well their respective countries and governments were meeting their hopes, needs, and expectations.

Most of the people who toiled in these fields did so in relative obscurity. But one did not, and like Simon Kuznets, he became an icon in his field and would eventually win the Nobel Prize in Economics for his pioneering work in giving shape to the system of national accounts. Richard Stone was the quintessential Englishman, born on the eve of World War I, the only son of a London barrister who dutifully followed his father's educational footsteps as a prep student at the old palace of schoolboy prestige, the Westminster School. Stone promptly failed to live up to modest expectations. In 1930 his father was appointed as a judge in Madras, India. In Stone's later recollection, said father asked the school headmaster what to do with Richard. "If I were you," the headmaster replied, "I should take him with you; he doesn't seem to be much good here." And so, as Stone told an interviewer toward the end of his life, he "went to India and had a good time."

That sojourn to the fading heart of the empire gave Stone an appreciation of the wider world, but he soon returned to England to enroll at Cambridge University "in accordance," he recalled, "with [my] father's plan." At Cambridge, he learned Roman law, studied Greek and Latin, and then, in the first act of rebellion against his father's wishes, he switched from law to economics, and thereby did both the profession of law and that of economics a great service.[9]

His economics education in those years was not suffused with numbers and equations. The profession still leaned toward the humanities and required a deep immersion in the works of not just Adam Smith and his *The Wealth of Nations*, but also the essays of Sigmund Freud on the nature of human psychology and the corpus of Karl Marx and Vladimir Lenin for an understanding of how the emerging Communist world analyzed the problems of economies and their solutions. Stone was drawn to economics for the simple reason that the Great Depression was unfolding around him, challenging the conceit of the early twentieth century that society could be understood as a machine with officials and wise men pulling their levers for the greater good. He acquired as a mentor and a friend Colin Clark, a young lecturer focusing on national accounts who also liked to take Stone on canoe trips. And in that cozy, bucolic world of high table and punting, pub crawling, and long winter nights, Stone also attended seminars led by the master Keynes.

Stone graduated, married, and found a job at Lloyd's of London assessing insurance contracts for international shipping. That was interrupted by the outbreak of war, and Stone was assigned to the ominously named and hastily convened Ministry of Economic Warfare. Whether his temperament was too genial or the job too insubstantial, he transferred to the economic unit of the War Cabinet to work on national income accounts. There he began to collaborate with Keynes, and along with his colleague James Meade, took the first stab at creating a system of accounts comparable to what Simon Kuznets was doing across the Atlantic at the same time. Having refined the British system, Stone ventured across the ocean to meet with his counterparts in Canada and the United States to harmonize efforts and create common standards.

The drive to unify standards only accelerated with the end of the war and the formation of the UN. Stone spent several weeks at the Institute for Advanced Study in Princeton, New Jersey, and while his work there may not have had the impact of physicists such as Albert Einstein—who were then grappling with the forces unleashed by the splitting of the atom—the long-term effect on how people throughout the world understood the risks and opportunities that life presented them was just as pronounced. Fast-forward seventy years, and people are wracked with anxiety and animated by the hope of how their economic lives will unfold; except when a power plant fails or a rogue state threatens war, they rarely give nuclear weapons or nuclear power much thought.

It wasn't just the United Nations that spurred the development of uniform international standards for national accounts. It was also the nascent European organizations formed after the war, infused with American aid that flowed from the Marshall Plan in 1948. Though announced with great fanfare by President Harry Truman as an act of both generosity and national security, with few strings attached, the plan that passed the US Congress was not unconditional. To continue receiving aid, European states had to meet certain benchmarks of growth and development. That then made it necessary to measure the effects of the aid on economic activity.

The institutional imperatives of the United Nations as well as the Marshall Plan demanded the creation of international systems that would promote and safeguard economic development around the world. Stone may have come across as the most genial of Englishmen, tweedy academic that he was, yet he was deeply affected by the twin blows of depression and war that had nearly taken down in a decade what the nations of Europe and the world had spent centuries creating. Like many of his colleagues, he believed that a new statistical framework was a vital tool to ensure that never again would the world flirt with utter darkness brought on by fear, scarcity, and ignorance.

Stone spent the decades after the war shuttling between Cambridge and various positions at the United Nations and other institutions. Sponsored by Keynes to be the first head of the Department of Applied Economics at Cambridge, Stone fused academic theory with real-world applications. He understood that for a truly international set of standards to work, there would need to be a better grasp of the vast differences in levels of development around the world. In 1950 he went to Nigeria (then a British colony) to work on national accounts there. As he observed later with typical understatement, "This work gave rise to many problems that were new to us." The level of detail available to the British government about factory production in Manchester or to the American government about spending in Cleveland simply didn't exist in a land of hundreds of tribes, where little was written down except for what British colonial administrators recorded.

Nonetheless, a system emerged, one that was meant to work for all societies, from Nigeria to Norway, from Argentina to Australia. Much as Kuznets did for the United States, Stone labored with like-minded statisticians and economists from around the world to refine the double-entry framework of national accounts that tallied the total outputs and inputs of a nation. To complicate matters, Stone adopted a different methodology than Kuznets had, and that led to a divergence between precisely how the United States compiled accounts and how the rest of the world did until the 1970s. But all of the templates shared a basic approach to assessing the economic output of a nation, and the result was the publication by the UN of *A System of National Accounts* in 1953.[10]

That system transformed the way people everywhere understood the material ebbs and flows of society. All of those stops and starts, from Chinese emperors employing armies of meticulous mandarins to record crops and weigh bullion in the treasury, to Romans tabulating the tribute of Gauls and barbarians, to the haphazard efforts of medieval and Renaissance scholars to calculate the wealth of nations, and through the nineteenth and early twentieth centuries' attempts to describe economic life using numbers and statistics—all of those came together in the national accounts promulgated by the United Nations. These accounts constituted a map of national economic activity that could be used by every country in the world—and were. They treated an economy as a mechanical system of inputs and outputs, production and consumption, exports and imports. The national accounts could then be used by policy makers to hone policy. Rather than being at the seeming mercy of economic cycles that were as little understood and just as difficult to prepare for as the weather, governments around the world embraced the national accounts in the hopes of banishing the destructive economic forces that had kept humans from achieving their full potential.

And, yes, the language and the goals were that utopian. These statistical innovations were seen as the key to end poverty, alleviate want, end a history of scarcity, and produce abundance. Growth would not be guaranteed, but it would be given more than a fair chance against contraction. The core belief in these years was that societies could be delivered from want, whether by remaking the social order through Communist revolution or refining it through democratic capitalism. The multiple development agencies and United Nations initiatives to address the challenges of disease and hunger stemmed from a similar conviction that out of the horrors of war could come progress and healing. Statistics collected universally, compared, and collated would allow governing institutions to judge whether their efforts were succeeding.

The United Nations was central to the global spread of these indicators, but it was not the only force propelling the diffusion. The World Bank and the International Monetary Fund—both created at the same time as the UN and meant to finance governments and projects around the world, with an eye toward ending poverty and generating sustainable economic growth—had an insatiable hunger for statistics. Businesses in the United States clamored for their own bespoke numbers to guide spending and hiring plans. Media outlets started to latch onto a few simple, round numbers as part of the evolving story of economies. Soon the numbers were more than just guides, more than tools for governments and bureaucracies. They became a language that people used to discuss what was happening to "the economy." As anxiety over the economic future started to mount, these numbers assumed ever more prominence. They became, in short, part of society's gestalt.

5

THE ECONOMIC GESTALT

To recap what we have seen so far: the first leading indicators were driven by the needs of government. They were truly macro statistics, meant to give shape and form to the big picture. Unemployment, national income, gross national product, trade, and agricultural output, and, as we shall get to, inflation—all were markers that defined "the economy." They were not, however, designed to help individuals navigate their economic lives. After all, no one has a personal unemployment rate of 7 percent. Our own unemployment rate is either zero or 100 percent, though possibly it could be in the middle if you are working only half as much as you want. And national income, while deeply useful for policy makers to assess the potential output of the system, says very little about the lives lived by citizens individually. By the mid-1940s, therefore, a matrix of indicators revealed much about the economic activity of the nation but very little about the economic lives of people.

The initial wave of indicators led to the emergence of

macroeconomics as a major academic discipline. It also allowed for the economic policy making of Keynes along with other approaches, including state capitalism practiced by the Communist countries during the Cold War. Fast-forward to the present and this way of viewing economic policy, government, and the state through the lens of economic indicators is so embedded in the way we live and how governments govern that it's nearly impossible to imagine a world without them. The leading indicators are fused to policy and to the way that we collectively discuss "how we're doing."

Yet there are other types of leading indicators that weren't created by government. While most of the macroeconomic leading indicators were developed just before and during World War II, many others were created in the years just after the war. These were focused not on systems and states but on people and industries. They were invented not by bureaucrats or academics drafted into government service but by an eclectic mix of economists, psychologists, statisticians, marketers, and executives.

Once again, economics is a profession grounded in the belief that "the economy" is a machine and a closed system. The more clearly that machine is understood, the more its variables are precisely measured, the more we will be able to manage and steer it as we choose, avoiding the frenetic expansions and sharp contractions. With better indicators would come better policy, and with better policy, states would be less likely to fall into depression and risk collapse. That was certainly the hope of Keynes and his many disciples.

Classical economics and Keynesianism can be remarkably bloodless. Money in, money out. Keynes himself, however, wasn't. He deeply respected the animal spirits of the multitudes that shaped behavior and drove outcomes. Kuznets also recognized that the shape of national accounts—by leaving out housework especially—privileged the macro and neglected the micro; or to put it another way, the national accounts focused on states and systems and ignored people.

The resulting statistics were both helpful in smoothing the extremes of the business cycle and rather hollow when it came to assessing how actual people were experiencing this rather abstract thing called "the economy."

Some economists, however, recognized that people were, at the very least, an important variable. If Kuznets and Keynes were avatars of the most macro of indicators, George Katona was the godfather of the most micro. And not just the most micro, but also the fuzziest, softest, squishiest, and elusive: consumer sentiment, a measure not of large impersonal forces such as output and trade but of something much more emotional, personal, and harder to capture with numbers: what people felt about their economic lives and what they believed the future had in store.

Few economists gravitated toward these questions, but then again, Katona wasn't really an economist. Born in Budapest in 1901 to a Jewish family in the twilight of the Austro-Hungarian Empire, Katona's background shared some similarities with Kuznets: both Jewish, both educated in European universities before emigrating to the United States, and both drawn into the nexus of policy and economics before becoming giants in their respective fields. Unlike Kuznets, however, Katona was most interested in the tangled area of human psychology and behavior. He saw the world not as a mechanical system to be charted but as the product of shifting human attitudes. Kuznets wanted to create a template to measure the economy; Katona strove to build a database of desires, inclinations, fears, and hopes that dictated individual economic behavior and that predicted whether someone would buy a car or a washing machine or instead save their money out of an excess of caution or a surfeit of prudence.

At the end of World War I, Katona enrolled at the University of Göttingen, which had been founded two centuries earlier by the Hanover elector turned English king George II as a haven for the spirit of free inquiry of the Enlightenment. Katona's PhD in experimental psychology was fully in that tradition; it was a new discipline that attempted to validate theories of human behavior through intensive study of . . . actual human behavior. The cornerstone of the discipline was to test hypotheses about human actions by studying subjects in simulated situations in controlled settings or through intensive surveys and questionnaires. In time, these experiments became the foundation of "behavioral economics," which examines the connection between human psychology and economic behavior. If traditional economic theory enshrines the notion that we are all rational actors, behavioral economics embraces the idea that we are not.

After finishing his academic studies, Katona moved first to Frankfurt and then Berlin, where he witnessed the rise of Weimar Germany and its unraveling in a haze of hyperinflation and the ascendant Nazi Party. Katona worked both as a journalist and a bank analyst, and in these years he also delved into Gestalt psychology. While that term would gain pop-culture status in the United States in the 1960s and 1970s as a path to self-discovery, in the 1930s it was just another branch of academic psychology. Gestaltism held that humans are wired to identify structures first and then proceed to organize their thinking and actions. When we look at a building, we see one unified structure first, not an assortment of floors, windows, carapaces, and masonry. We crave order and meaning, and so find it.

Katona was less interested in the academic understanding of human behavior and more compelled by solving social problems that arose because of human behavior. The gravest of these was inflation in Germany that led to the breakdown of social order. That breakdown, the end of Weimar and the rise of the Nazis and Adolf Hitler, compelled Katona to leave Germany in 1933 for the United States, which was then witnessing not inflation but deflation and the collapse of demand that characterized the Great Depression.

For much of the 1930s, Katona combined his interest in human psychology with his fascination with markets. He had worked for banks in Germany, and in New York he joined the faculty of the eclectic New School for Social Research while also working as an investment advisor. His joint passion for economics and psychology were fused once again with the outbreak of World War II and the direct involvement of the United States in the conflict after December 7, 1941. Having witnessed the corrosive effects of inflation in Germany, Katona—who became a US citizen in 1939—was deeply concerned that mobilization for war would lead to inflation in America, as goods were rationed for the war effort. In his book *War Without Inflation*, he argued that inflation was as much a product of consumer expectations as it was of the typical factors that economists emphasized, such as money supply. In order to prevent consumers from assuming that inflation would rise, Katona concluded, the government had to create "a gestalt," which would temper those fears and instead create expectations of price stability.[1]

While Keynes would have appreciated this emphasis on human emotion and perception as a key factor in shaping economic trajectories, for most economists this hybrid approach, with its focus on emotions and behavior, was alien and unwelcome. That "rational actor" principle dictates that individuals utilize all of the information at their disposal in order to maximize their self-interest. The idea has its foundations in the classical economics of Adam Smith and David Ricardo, but it was given much fuller form as economics blossomed as a discipline in the twentieth century. Either way, the rational actor concept stood in stark opposition to the views of Katona, who saw individual decisions as flowing from a myriad of causes, including not just the desire to maximize gain but also the interplay of complex and powerful emotions ranging from fear, to greed, to hope.

After a brief wartime stint in the Agriculture Department, where he continued his work on consumer psychology, Katona's views crystallized. He hit upon what he believed was a key yet overlooked driver of economic activity: consumer attitudes. The first set of leading indicators measured actions, not feelings; for Katona, that was a glaring omission. He took his training in psychology and extrapolated that how consumers felt would drive what they spent. What they spent would then determine if economic activity expanded or contracted and thus impact everything from production, to output, to inflation, to employment. There was thus a direct connection between feelings and action, and if policy makers did not account for that, policy would be flawed. However, if you could reliably measure sentiment, Katona theorized, you could gauge more effectively not only what was happening in the present but what was likely to unfold in the future.

At the end of the war, Katona ended his government stint and was wooed by the University of Michigan. Along with several of his growing staff, he relocated to Ann Arbor. Michigan had recently created a Survey Research Center and was searching for a dynamic head. Given Katona's fervent commitment to building a database of consumer attitudes and the university's willingness to foot the bill, it was a good home.

The relationship proved to be immensely fruitful for both. Katona's work morphed into the first consistent surveys of consumer sentiment along with an index that crafted a numerical score from those survey questions. The higher the index, the more optimistic consumers were said to feel; the lower, the more pessimistic. That index, so easy to grasp and so simple, emerged as a mainstay of social and media commentary and became a marker for arguments about whether "the American consumer" was feeling good or bad about that new and amorphous statistical entity called "the economy."

The consumer sentiment surveys began life as the outgrowth of one man's passion to link attitudes and economic behavior. They ended the century as a data set sold by one of the largest information companies in the world. Katona remained in Ann Arbor until his death in 1981, and the university then expanded and further commercialized his work. Over the decades, Michigan profited immensely from the center's research, both literally and figuratively. Selling the indices proved to be increasingly lucrative as the twentieth century progressed, and Katona's efforts along with other substantial statistical endeavors such as the World Values Survey branded the University of Michigan as a global leader in these fields. There is an entire substory that could be written about the marriage of Katona and the University of Michigan, and about the beginnings of commercialized social science research that created income streams for higher education in much the way that the physical sciences did. Eventually the index was licensed by the global media conglomerate Thomson Reuters, which now sells it to businesses, investors, and media outlets worldwide. And big business it is. The release of these numbers can move markets, which is why hedge funds and traders pay significant sums to have an early read on the data.[2]

The commercialization of private indicators stands in contrast to the public funding of the statistics discussed so far. The federal government pays for the staffs that compile GDP, unemployment, inflations, trade, and other statistics via the budgets for the Departments of Labor and Commerce. Labor houses the Bureau of Labor Statistics (which assembles unemployment and inflation data), while the Commerce Department's Bureau of Economic Analysis calculates GDP and various trade figures. State governments have their own statistical offices to measure state output and employment. But following the model of Katona and the University of Michigan, private sources of data emerged, not as a public service but because the data and the statistics proved to be a lucrative business.

Katona's first major question was to ask what effect the end of World War II and the demobilization of millions of troops would have on the US economy. The fear was that the war's end and the transition from a wartime economy back to a more free-market system would lead to the end of price controls, which would then trigger a spike in inflation and a drop in production. It would be the worst of all possible worlds. First there would be a sudden uncorking of years of pent-up demand by Americans who had saved and denied themselves luxuries as well as necessities during the war. But then there would be an insufficient supply because the nation's factories wouldn't be able to shift production quickly enough from tanks and ammunition to cars and appliances. There would also be the added burden of high unemployment, as millions of soldiers returned from war and millions of women employed during the war went back to housework.

As it turned out, these fears were unrealized. Instead, the US economy boomed. Inflation, though it went up significantly in 1945 (more than 8 percent), did not accelerate to destructive levels as it had in Germany in the interwar years. Nor did American consumers open their wallets and flood the country with too much money too quickly. Instead, after a brief transition period, the nation experienced robust and stable growth.

Katona's contribution to this issue was to argue that inflation was the result of consumer expectations, and not just a product of money supply or demand imbalances. When people believe that there will be significant inflation, they adjust their behavior. "Increased worry about inflation [would induce] American consumers to reduce their discretionary expenditures and increase their rate of savings," he explained.[3] And, in fact, that seems to be what happened as the war ended. Inflation concerns were widespread; American consumers did begin to spend more freely with the war's end, as predicted, but not too freely because they were worried about inflation. That, in turn, kept inflation in check just enough to limit the damage. Katona had identified a link between sentiment and behavior, and between consumer feelings and tangible economic outcomes at a macro level.

The surveys developed by Katona at Michigan started with the presumption that what people believe about the state of the economy intimately shapes their spending decisions. If you can measure what consumers feel, you can predict whether they are more likely to spend or to save in the months ahead. "The better off people feel, the more they spend," Katona quipped, "and the worse off they feel, the less they spend."

Katona did not in these years actually use the word *economy*. He spoke instead about spending, savings, and sentiment, and about the accuracy of those in forecasting future activity. The surveys began in 1946, and from the first batch of several hundred responses to multiple questions, Katona concluded that the prospects for future spending by consumers were bright. The basis of his conviction was the prevalence of optimism about the future, which spanned the spectrum from unskilled workers to professionals and executives. That optimism, Katona believed, would lead to a protracted period of steady spending rather than fear-based saving, while concerns about inflation would act as a check on runaway spending. The result would be a long-term sweet spot for America.

The initial surveys were widely used by both academics and officials, especially at the Federal Reserve Board, whose mandate was—and is—to contain inflation. These initial surveys were conducted annually and consisted of hourlong interviews with three thousand "spending units," which was an ungainly term for a family that spent its resources collectively. Katona's researchers preferred to interview the husband, on the assumption that he would act as a patriarch dictating the major family expenses. If the husband wasn't around, the wife might be interviewed provided that she had full knowledge of the family's finances.[4]

You could easily criticize Katona's assumptions. Did husbands really make final spending decisions, especially for the many households where women controlled domestic purchases and were in charge of the home? But at least the methodology was clear and consistent, and the researchers were committed to sampling properly, touching major geographic regions as well as carefully balancing urban and rural areas. Then in the early 1950s, Katona introduced a new feature:

the index of consumer sentiment, which has been kept ever since. The index generated one number to determine overall sentiment, and it was based on six questions asked of five hundred people. Before long, that was reduced to five questions—the same five of which are still asked today, by both the University of Michigan and the Conference Board, which began its own consumer confidence index in 1967.

These questions are basic and could be understood by just about anyone:

1. Would you say that you are better off or worse off financially than you were a year ago?

2. Looking ahead, do you think a year from now you will be better off financially, or worse off, or just about the same?

3. Now, turning to business conditions in the country as a whole, do you think that during the next twelve months we'll have good times financially or bad times, or what?

4. Looking ahead, which would you say is more likely—that in the country as a whole we'll have continuous good times during the next five years or so, or that we will have periods of widespread unemployment or depression, or what?

5. Generally speaking, do you think now is a good or bad time for people to buy major household items?

While some of the language has been moderately tweaked, those questions remain the backbone of the consumer sentiment index. From the answers, a scale was created, and the surveys now use 1966 as an arbitrary benchmark of 100; in the years since, the index has been as low as 50 and as high, in the heady days of the 1990s, as 110.

These surveys quickly entered popular consciousness. Michigan gained a competitor with the Conference Board in 1967, but that only served to amp up the profile of both. News outlets found these reports attractive because they gave a monthly number that served as a launching point for articles and commentary about how Americans were feeling. The indices were also complemented by polling data assembled by firms such as the Gallup Organization that asked specific questions: "How do you feel about the Soviet Union?" "Should America be fighting a war in Vietnam?" "Do you approve or disapprove of the president's performance?" In a society that increasingly marked its success or failure by its economic success or failure, sentiment indicators gained more traction with each passing year.

And yet, even as the profile and awareness of these indices increased, economists in general accorded them less weight and even less respect. Katona believed that these gauges weren't just useful as descriptions of attitudes; he thought they could help forecast the near economic future. He also argued that what economic models treated as soft—emotions, attitudes, and individual opinions—were crucial variables that the economics profession was arrogantly ignoring.

Not surprisingly, Katona was almost immediately questioned and challenged by the academic establishment. The Federal Reserve Board convened a committee in 1955 to investigate whether the Michigan surveys and the index really did predict how consumers would behave. Chaired by Harvard economist Arthur Smithies, and with the participation of future Nobel laureate James Tobin, the committee concluded that no, the surveys did not accurately forecast what people spend or save. Nor did any academic study establish a conclusive or compelling connection. Katona pushed back, accusing his critics of misusing the information. He said that the surveys couldn't be judged simply by "reinterviewing" people a year later to see whether their behavior corresponded to their answers. Instead, they were useful in toto as indicators. Any one family or set of families might behave very differently than they had said they would, but combined, the surveys would form a gestalt, a complete picture of sentiment, that would then play out in the overall behavior of consumers as a group.[5]

Yet even on that score, the preponderance of subsequent research failed to demonstrate a clear and reliable connection between the surveys and future spending or savings. And not for lack of studies. In fact, generation after generation of scholars have attempted to find the elusive link between consumer sentiment and consumer spending, or to prove decisively that no such link exists. After all, what thornier issue than whether what people said they felt at a specific time in response to a limited set of questions actually foretells how they will behave?

Say that someone answers that she thinks she will be worse off in a year. Then she is reinterviewed a year later, and, lo and behold, she has curtailed spending. The temptation is to say that the survey predicted it. But what if she spent less because of illness, or because of sudden job loss, or because of the unexpected birth of a child? Or because of sudden macro scares or political drama, like the Cuban Missile Crisis, the assassination of Martin Luther King, or 9/11? Those may impact decisions far more, making a correlation between what people said they would do and how they subsequently behaved look like causation, when it wasn't. When surveyed families didn't behave the way they said they would, some researchers yelled "Gotcha!" thinking they had exposed the surveys as worthless. Yet there, too, the logic proved slippery. The behavior itself may have made it appear as if there was no link between sentiment expressed and future actions, but often the only reason that behavior changed unexpectedly is because the world did as well. A family surveyed in the summer of 1962 may have felt good about its economic prospects and fully intended to spend more in the months ahead; then the Cuban Missile Crisis happened. That may have been a failure of politics, but it was hardly a failure of sentiment surveys.

Katona responded to his critics with a combination of defensiveness and evasiveness. His contention was that attitudes clearly shape individual behavior in some way, and so they must also shape collective behavior in some way. Knowing more about what people felt about the future was better than knowing less, even if hard and fast conclusions were not feasible. Still, the lack of a firm connection led the Federal Reserve to cease funding the surveys and led as well to the community of economists to shift its attention elsewhere.

Not for the last time, the skepticism of professional economists was in inverse proportion to public interest. In fact, Katona's work proved so successful in attracting attention and funding that it was emulated by other institutions. The Conference Board index that began in 1967 tried to distinguish itself from the Michigan studies by enlarging the sample size to five thousand families, and rather than reinterview some of those, it started afresh with a new group of five thousand the next period. In 1987 *Money* magazine and ABC News joined forces to produce a weekly consumer confidence index. These all garnered attention, especially from the media, from investors, and from the world of economic forecasters.

Even though no one could quite prove that indices predicted anything, few were willing to dispose of them altogether. As Katona argued, separate from the controversy over whether the surveys predicted behavior, they did shine a light into the murky psyche of individuals. The interest in knowing what people think ranges from the prurient to the pragmatic. Most of us have a deep and abiding interest in peering into the bedroom of our neighbors. The sentiment surveys, like so many other surveys of values, sexual habits, religious beliefs, and opinions about pressing issues, were of interest because they said something interesting about how people were emotionally experiencing this thing called the economy.

Because the studies showing that there was no simple link between attitudes and actions did not and could not prove that there was *no* link, Katona and his emulators could continue to argue that there was.[6] All that the many studies demostrated is that it is almost impossible to say with any certainty that when people are pessimistic about the future they spend less and save more, and that when they are optimistic they spend more and save less. The only expectations that showed consistent correlation with future behavior appeared to be car buying and intentions to purchase large durable goods. There, at least, multiple studies showed that people who said they were likely to buy a car in the coming months were, in fact, more likely to buy a car in the coming months than people who said they weren't likely to. The reason? Unclear here as well. It may be that for big-ticket items that require some planning and research, people's stated intent is the necessary first step toward actually doing it, and without that stated intent, they are unlikely to make a purchase. After all, few people can or do buy a car on impulse, with a "Hi there, I was just passing by and decided to pick up that Tesla."

And yet Katona and others who crafted these indicators could always point to times when the indices did presage a slowdown or were confirmed by later weakness in other indicators. People en masse feel pessimistic for many reasons, some economic and some not. People are seasonally pessimistic in February, perhaps because the combined weight of holiday spending, too much exposure to family madness, and the depth of winter in most parts of the country leave people feeling gloomy and grumpy. Then as spring ripens and summer emerges, they become more optimistic, with confidence peaking in August coincidental with vacations and beach and easy weather.[7]

People also respond to external shocks, and that sometimes forecasts future behavior and sometimes not at all. In recent memory, consumer confidence slid in April 2001 to an eight-year low after the sharp collapse in the stock market bubble and the recession that followed; that April reading did indeed signal tough times ahead, which was the case even without the attacks of September 11. On the flip side, the Michigan index plunged in the fall of 1990 after the Iraqi invasion of Kuwait, yet spending picked up notably after the success of American forces in early 1991. At times consumer pessimism in aggregate is a function of consumers reading the tea leaves of economic trajectories earlier or more intuitively than the static indicators on which forecasters rely. Consumers are acutely sensitive to shortened work hours, fewer shifts, impending layoffs, quiet stores, and management anxiety. They identify these ebbs and flows in real time; they also quickly notice tighter credit or higher rates from their local bank. As a result, sentiment gauges are right just often enough to make them compelling and wrong far too frequently to make them reliable.

Sentiment metrics also filled a glaring hole in numbers such as trade, agriculture output, unemployment, and GDP. They provided a human element to what were otherwise impersonal measures of impersonal systems. Unemployment figures are just numbers, but the pessimism of a family expressed in a survey conducted by Katona's staff spoke to the larger questions of happiness and satisfaction and whether the state and society are structured to maximize those. The surveys speak to how secure people feel, and that, in turn, raises the question of whether the systems in place societally are succeeding in providing the most potential to the greatest number. People argue still about what the actual goal and metric of societal success should be, and these surveys surely do not answer that. They did and do, however, provide a subjective perspective about how the larger indicators intersected with the lived experience of actual flesh-and-blood people.

Katona remained active to his death in 1981. In his later years, he delved ever more deeply into the relationship between expectations and inflation, and tried to untangle the complicated nexus of expectations, attitudes, and material affluence. He challenged the presumptions of advertising that consumers could be manipulated into making purchases, and he used years of survey data to argue that people were smarter, more nuanced, and more balanced in their behavior and thinking. They were not just maximizing their economic interests; they looked to enrich their lives through culture, art, education, and leisure. Katona viewed the tapestry of America through the rose-tinted lenses of an immigrant who had left a collapsing Europe where fear ruled the day, and his hopeful stance allowed him to identify signs of stability and balance during periods such as the 1970s, when more hyperbolic assessments of consumers and society were common. Such attitudes were in short supply then, as they were in the United States in the opening years of the twenty-first century.

The evolution of sentiment as a quantitative measure and the attempts to tie that number to spending, savings, and future growth broadened the scope of the indicators available in the middle of the twentieth century. Having been dominated by big synthetic indicators compiled by government in order to help policy makers assess policies, the economic landscape was rapidly populated by privately assembled metrics that took a decidedly different angle. New metrics were invented by businesses and professional associations that were just as desirous of clarity about the marketplace as government officials were of clarity about the overall health of the economy.

Some of the private metrics stemmed from the Great Depression. The influential Institute for Supply Management monthly manufacturing survey, the purchasing managers' index, or PMI has evolved over the years to become one of the most prominent private indicators of economic activity. It began during the 1930s, in part as a response to the urgings of Herbert Hoover. Not only was the president dismayed by the lack of clear and consistent information on employment and national output, he was also frustrated by the absence of reliable real-time information from industry. He suggested to the US Chamber of Commerce, which was then and now one of the largest voluntary associations of businesses in America, that it take the lead in coming up with surveys and data. It did, but its efforts to muster a consistent set of several hundred companies came to naught.

It fell instead to the National Association of Purchasing Agents (NAPA) to pick up the slack. In the first decades of the twentieth century, manufacturing had been rationalized and revolutionized by the scientific methods of Frederick Taylor. But supplying factories with the needed parts and raw materials had remained a more informal skill, with the fate of enterprises left to the touch and feel of purchasing agents who had to anticipate prices, supply, and demand correctly or else doom their company to failure. With little transparency, these agents used informal networks to gauge prices and supplies. While these personal surveys could be extremely valuable, they were limited in scope and only as reliable as the people they sampled. These personal networks, however, dictated how business was conducted and how it always had been. Traders had traded not just goods at port but also stories, information, and intelligence about what was going on in distant cities, who was buying what, who was winning, who was losing, what was in, what was out.

As the Depression deepened, however, it became clear that using informal networks and informed gossip gleaned from trade associations was no way to run a business or an economy. The slew of failed enterprises and bankruptcies was testament to that. Word of mouth also led to destructive feedback loops. Recognizing the imperative of more rigorous data, NAPA committed itself to a survey of current business conditions, using the agents as the primary source of information. Agents were asked about new orders and whether they were going up, down, or staying the same. They were asked about inventories and backlogs and commodity prices, and about hiring plans and whether deliveries from suppliers were arriving in a timely fashion.

Eventually, these questions were scored, and a formula was created to combine the answers into one synthetic number, just like the sentiment index. Though the war interrupted the survey (and would have led to distorted data to boot, given government price controls and supplies being requisitioned for the war effort), the surveys continued after the war and became a primary source of information for business conditions. The ISM index (as it is now known) has an unusually high correlation with GDP, and it remains one of the few leading indicators that does indeed foreshadow whether and how much overall output is expanding or contracting.[8]

In the last decades of the twentieth century, indicators proliferated. Home building surveys were the purview of the Commerce Department and the Census Bureau, but these were augmented after the 1970s by surveys of existing home sales conducted by the National Association of Realtors and a housing market index compiled by the National Association of Home Builders (NAHB). The Census Bureau itself broadened the scope of its surveys and its methods to be more responsive to the needs of businesses. Census surveys started to address everything from construction to retail sales to small business creation. The various Federal Reserve bank branches have also been active in building databases. The New York, Philadelphia, and Richmond, Virginia, branches began to conduct surveys and issue monthly reports on industrial production and capacity utilization nationwide.

In response to the proliferation of indices, the Commerce Department in the 1960s tried to combine both public and private indicators to create a mega-index. It published a regular digest of all the indicators, and grouped them by whether they were leading (suggestive of future trends), coincident (providing a snapshot of the present), or lagging (measuring recent trends but not necessarily predicting future ones). The most important lagging indicator was and is unemployment. The unemployment rate says nothing about the future rate, only about what has already happened. It also "lags" the overall downturn in other indicators, such as production. A "leading" indicator foreshadows changes in other indicators; for instance, building permits or manufacturing orders are leading because when they tick up, construction activity and production are likely to as well. If, however, building permits suddenly grind to a halt, it's likely that many other indicators will soon register a slowdown, from construction to the prices for commodities.

In 1995 the Commerce Department sold its indicator series to the

Conference Board, which ever since has published its index of leading economic indicators and marketed it as a vital tool for economic forecasting. The index consists of ten indicators assembled by government and by private institutions such as the University of Michigan, and it integrates the performances of stocks in the S&P 500 index and the money supply information provided by the Federal Reserve. And just to confuse matters, the board's index of leading indicators consists of both leading and lagging indicators as defined by economists. They are "leading" in the sense of "major." These categories notwithstanding, it is from this series—first assembled by the Commerce Department and continued by the Conference Board—that we get the umbrella term "the leading indicators."

Defining an indicator as lagging, coincident, or leading is connected to another vital notion: the business cycle. Indicators are lagging or leading based on where economists believe we are in the business cycle: whether we are heading into a recession or emerging from one. Just as the indicators were formulated only in the twentieth century, the concept of a regular "business cycle" is also a recent invention. We now treat it as a law of economics, but if so, it is a new law and tested only over a few decades.

In 1946 two economists at the National Bureau of Economic Research, where Kuznets and other influential minds got their start, published a book titled *Measuring Business Cycles*. Arthur Burns and Wesley Mitchell are famous names in the annals of economics, but at the time, they were at very different stages of their careers. Mitchell had founded the bureau and hired Burns just as he hired Kuznets; he was at the end of a towering career marked by both his organizational abilities and his mentorship. In 1946, Burns was in his early forties, another immigrant from Eastern Europe, also Jewish, born in Galicia, who found a home in America and turned to economics as a discipline.

At the epicenter of the wave of government and macrostatistics then being created, Mitchell noticed certain patterns that seemed to repeat over the years and which the new data might be able to fore-cast. He had been mulling the question of whether there was, in fact, a business cycle that had consistent characteristics over time even as the particular details might change. Could there be a common and repeated pattern that people had missed simply because there hadn't been adequate information? Could it be that there was a business cycle that saw ebbs and flows as predictably as the life cycle of a person, from birth to death?

Even as late as the mid-1940s, with the immense work done to define national income, prices, employment, and production, there was scant ability to compare changes over time. As Burns and Mitchell explained in *Measuring Business Cycles*, "The longest record of cyclical fluctuations in economic activities are the contemporary opinions of journalists. They show that men whose business it was to report the condition of trade were impressed by the alternations of prosperity and depression long before the concept of business cycle had been for-mulated. They indicate what years were deemed good and what years bad by contemporaries, and thus are helpful in identifying successive business cycles and in making rough measures of their duration."

It's rather extraordinary how the economics profession has evolved in the years since two leading economists at one of the pre-mier research institutions of the day credited journalists with what was then the best understanding of business cycles. The work done by Mitchell and Burns turned the business cycle from something that journalists observed into a statistical construct that could be treated as a "law" of macroeconomics.[9] Their work also significantly raised the profile of the NBER for one reason: the organization became the self-appointed yet officially sanctioned entity that declares when there is or has been a recession in the United States. In recent years, that determination has often been made in retrospect, after all the relevant indicators have been assessed in final form. The recession of 2000–01, for instance, wasn't officially declared until after it had ended. But the power to "call" a recession is immense and has obvious consequences for society as a whole.

The regimentation of the business cycle as a key aspect of an economic system has dramatically shaped how we now understand our lives. The language we use reflects that. In the media and politics, we speak of recessions and recoveries, of heading into a recession or out of one, into an expansion, or headed for a slowdown. All of those terms are based on the basic (and unchallenged) notion that economic activity for the economy as a whole follows cyclical patterns that can be measured, and that those patterns are familiar over time. The very familiarity and even predictability of those patterns supports the idea that businesses and government, as well as individuals, can take measures to offset the worst effects, or at the very least prepare for them and keep them as short and as shallow as possible. Codifying business cycles spoke to a conviction that what had been mysterious and powerful—those economic shifts that caught statesmen and citizens unaware and unprepared—could instead be tamed, described, charted, and mastered.

The concept that an economy (1) is characterized by regular cycles that (2) follow familiar patterns (3) illuminated by a series of statistics that (4) determine where we are in that cycle has become part and parcel of how we view the world. It shapes capital spending and hiring plans by large companies; it influences whether an entrepreneur will start a small business and whether the loan officer at a bank will fund it. It shapes investment advice and how huge pension funds and individuals plan for retirement.

But as these pages have tried to show, the idea of a business cycle—so obvious, familiar, and assumed in our world today—is a very new one and did not gain widespread acceptance until after World War II, when Burns and Mitchell published their book. The concept of the business cycle then provided even more validation to the indicators. Within a few years, it was as if those ideas and those indicators had been around forever. They were reported widely and used intensively throughout government and industry. Magazines such as *Time*, *Fortune*, and *Newsweek* started to run regular stories about cycles, as did major newspapers such as the *New York Times* and the *Washington Post*. Industry associations didn't just create their own metrics; they also created an entire framework to assess current conditions in light of the business cycle. The presumption was clear: if you identified the cycle correctly, you could anticipate the next tic up in demand or the next leg down.

By the 1970s, these concepts had permeated not just business and politics but also the entire culture. By way of the UN and the World Bank, many of them were exported throughout the world, just as national accounts and GNP/GDP were. The proverbial "man on the street" began to frame social issues and challenges in terms of what was happening with "the economy." And in the 1970s, the leading indicators challenged multiple presidents, may have led to the defeat of one, and raised the profile and power of economic statistics to new heights. The main culprit? Inflation. And Arthur Burns, who had made a name for himself defining the business cycle, found himself at the center of the Nixon administration, being undone by his own creation.

6

INFLATION: FROM LEADING INDICATOR TO GOVERNMENT CON

"Arthur Burns," declared the *New York Times* in August 1974, "is a prophet without honor." Strong words for a reserved seventy-one-year-old academic turned policy maker, but these were trying times. President Richard Nixon, whom Burns had supported and who in turn had supported him, was on the verge of resigning in disgrace before Congress went ahead with his impeachment trial. The country was experiencing rapid and what felt like runaway inflation, which had just passed 11 percent and was higher than anyone could remember. The war in Vietnam appeared lost; confidence in America was shaken; and the economic growth engine, so potent since the end of World War II, was sputtering, with many doubting that it would ever rev again.

Succeeding Nixon, President Gerald Ford made inflation public enemy number one in a major speech delivered before Congress on October 8, 1974. Called the "WIN speech"—for "Whip Inflation Now!"—it saw Ford announce, "Our free enterprise system depends on orderly capital markets through which the savings of our people

become productively used. Today our capital markets are in total dis-
array . . . Prudent monetary restraint is essential. You and the American people should know, however, that I have been personally assured
by the chairman of the Federal Reserve that the supply of money and
credit will expand sufficiently to meet the needs of our economy and
that in no event will a credit crunch occur." Suddenly, the Federal
Reserve and its reserved chairman were thrust to the epicenter of US
politics. Within a few years, the mandate of the Fed, established in
1913, was expanded not only to include price stability and the over-
sight of banks but also to ensure full employment as well.[1]

By 1974, inflation had not been an issue in America for generations, but it had never faded as a potential danger in the minds of
central bankers like Burns. As counselor to Nixon during the 1968
presidential campaign, Burns named inflation the biggest threat to
prosperity—and that at a time when inflation was muted and the
economy seemingly strong. Even in the United States, which had
experienced a Great Depression but not the hyperinflation that had
so impoverished Germany and parts of Europe earlier in the century,
inflation held a special place in the circles of economic hell. Yet fears
were most acute among central bankers, and America was no exception.

But vigilance, alas, wasn't sufficient. Burns served as Fed chairman
for eight years, yet combating inflation proved beyond his capabilities.
In the decades since, there has been no end of debate about what triggered the "Great Inflation" of the 1970s, nor about what the Federal
Reserve or Congress might have done differently to alter the trajectory. Unlike his academic peers, who had included Simon Kuznets,
Wesley Mitchell, and Irving Fisher, Burns became a policy maker at
a crucial time, and his economic orthodoxies, right or wrong, proved
no match for the hurly-burly, messy realities of America in the 1970s.

Not since the 1930s had the politics of the economy been so
prominent. The inflation of the 1970s became the lens through which

most major debates occurred. The fact that the first wave of inflation had been seemingly triggered by international events helped bridge domestic and foreign policy and made inflation the galvanizing issue for three presidential administrations and propelled Ronald Reagan into the executive office in 1981.

The Arab-Israeli War of October 1973, known as the Yom Kippur War, led the oil-producing Arab states to impose an oil embargo against Israel's Western allies, the United States above all. The spike in inflation that began in 1973 followed the oil embargo and its soaring energy costs. The spike also came on the heels of the momentous decision by Nixon to take the United States off the gold standard in 1971. Because either of these events was on its own sufficiently disruptive to shake the equilibrium of prices, many argued both at the time and since that the Great Inflation of the 1970s was the product not of inept policy by central bankers following economic orthodoxies but rather the result of global forces beyond the control of bankers and economic policy makers. The critique of the policy makers—voiced particularly by Milton Friedman, the Chicago University economist who was the scourge of easy money bankers everywhere and always—was that the government had created too much money. According to accepted economic theory, inflation was first and foremost a product of the money supply, which the government controlled. Even if foreign crises precipitated bad economic policy decisions, it was those decisions that were to blame. Regardless of cause, however, the inflation of the 1970s returned economic policy to a level of prominence last seen during the Great Depression, when many of the indicators that would then be used as reference points in the 1970s were invented.

No one questioned that there was high inflation in the 1970s, but many wondered both what was generating it and how high it actually was. The first question was one of economic theory; the second one of how the statistic called "inflation" was calculated. And if those issues weren't intractable enough, there was an additional twist: throughout this period, the agency responsible for calculating prices, the Bureau of Labor Statistics, was engaged in a multiyear internal debate about whether it was overstating inflation. The result, ultimately, was a new formula that showed, not surprisingly, that inflation wasn't quite so high as had been thought and not as severe as people experienced in their everyday lives.

There were two forces at work: one was what that proverbial man on the street experienced when he bought groceries, or a car, or filled his tank with gas. The other was what the consumer price index said each month. The former was the lived experience of prices; the latter was a statistic, an indicator, that we call "inflation."

Like the other leading metrics discussed so far, "inflation" was a product of the early twentieth century. It emerged somewhat earlier than national accounts and just a tad after unemployment statistics rose to the fore in the days of Ethelbert Stewart. The modern concept of inflation was an outgrowth of government efforts to measure prices, which stemmed from the same Progressive impulses to assess whether the industrial system was allowing most citizens to meet their basic needs. There had been a few initial efforts to measure prices in the late nineteenth century, and the BLS had done some preliminary surveys of prices in a few cities in 1907 and again in 1912. Then in 1916 the reformist-minded BLS commissioner Royal Meeker authorized a survey of the expenditures of more than two thousand families in the District of Columbia in order to answer a simple question: "What does it cost the American family to live?" That, in turn, led to the first official "cost of living" index published in 1918.[2]

Refinements to the index, however, were slow to evolve. The one group adamant about better gauges was organized labor. Unions had started to demand that any wage agreements be pegged to the cost of living, arguing that a "living wage" was, by definition, a wage that one could live on. The only effective way to demand a certain wage that would meet basic needs was to have a neutral party compile an index that determined what those needs cost. Hence, the work of the BLS, and, hence as well, the start of decades of dispute about whether the consumer price index did, in fact, accurately report what those costs were.

By the mid-1930s, the BLS was still using the basic methodology of 1917, with quarterly surveys of a basket of consumer goods taken in cities across the country. A comprehensive survey of family expenditures between 1934 and 1936 covered 12,903 white families and 1,566 African-American families in forty-two cities. The New Deal Works Progress Administration also conducted surveys. The demand for these metrics intensified during the war, in light of government price controls and wage freezes. After the tribulations of the Depression and the wage controls demanded by the war, labor leaders believed that the American working class was bearing the brunt of economic hardship. George Meany of the American Federation of Labor, who would continue that harangue over the coming decades, charged that the BLS and the government, in league with big business, systematically and purposely underestimated the cost of living. Meany accused the Roosevelt administration of manipulating the numbers. Having failed to keep down the cost of living, FDR (in Meany's eyes) had an interest in snookering the American people and convincing them that the cost of living was less than they thought. "We are led," declared the implacable labor leader, "to the inescapable conclusion that the bureau has become identified with an effort to freeze wages, to the extent that it is no longer a free agency of statistical research."[3]

Thus began a long and tortured legacy of how citizens relate to official government statistics. No number has been the subject of greater controversy and antagonism than the consumer price index (CPI), which is the source of the official inflation statistic. The CPI was the direct successor to prewar cost of living indices, and was christened in 1945 as the "consumer price index for moderate income families in large cities." Ever since, it has engendered dark conspiracy theories about government officials purposely understanding the cost of living in order to pay citizens lower Social Security benefits and allowing corporations to underpay workers. By the early twenty-first century, the CPI affected the government benefits of nearly eighty million people. And given that cost-of-living adjustments in wages and benefits are often pegged to inflation, the CPI may be the leading indicator that most directly impacts our everyday lives.

It was never intended to carry such weight. Speaking in 1952, the deputy commissioner of the BLS responded to the criticisms of the agency's work and placed those in the context of a vastly changed landscape. People were beginning to use indicators in ways that few professional statisticians or economists had anticipated, and as we saw, the sudden ubiquity of these numbers and the way they were being disseminated in popular culture transformed what had been modest indices for use by government or academics into social, political, and cultural touchstones. The commissioner warned that the statistical profession was "scarcely prepared, and certainly not organized, to meet the serious responsibilities placed upon us by the new use of statistics."[4] If both government and private compilers were to retain credibility, they had to be rigorous about methods and responsive to critics.

Part of the challenge lay in the nature of the numbers themselves. Price indices were more complicated than employment numbers or national accounts because they contained variables that changed more rapidly and varied widely by region. The cost of a loaf of bread in New York City differed greatly from the cost in Peoria, Illinois, and that loaf could fluctuate dramatically over the course of a year, depending on the price of wheat, the cost of shipping, and whether wages held constant. Creating a representative sample of prices and making sure the resulting inflation gauge is fair has been one of the great challenges in the era of the leading indicators.

Inflation as an indicator had its origins in the work of one of the titans of the economics profession, Irving Fisher. Born in 1867 in Saugerties, New York, a minister's son imbued with a firm sense of black and white, right and wrong, Fisher became an economist just as the profession was coalescing. As an undergraduate and then graduate student at Yale in the 1880s and 1890s, he didn't learn what we now know as economics, because there was as yet only the most rudimentary sense of what that even meant. As we saw the American Economic Association was founded in 1885, but that was far from the profession that emerged in the twentieth century. Fisher studied mathematics and philosophy, and his thinking was intimately shaped by the physics professor Josiah Gibbs, who enjoined his students to genuflect to Newtonian laws of thermodynamics. Fisher was the first person to receive an "economics" PhD from Yale, and he defined the new discipline not in terms of the humanistic observations of Adam Smith, David Ricardo, and John Stuart Mill, but rather in terms of laws based on theories that could then be proved by data. His imprint on subsequent generations of economists could hardly have been greater.[5]

Discussing how inflation came to be measured necessitates diving into some professional weeds. It requires us to look at how economists and statisticians think, and their thinking is often expressed in jargon, mathematical formulas, and language that is incomprehensible to the rest of us. In short, some of the following discussion will not make for good cocktail party chatter, unless that cocktail party is hosted by statisticians. And even then . . .

Fisher believed that economic patterns could be observed and quantified just as scientific phenomena were. He also believed that humans are driven to measure the world, and that the instinct to figure out issues such as the cost of a loaf of bread was no different and certainly no simpler than measuring the distance between the Earth and the moon or trying to calculate the summer equinox. Like his longtime colleague Wesley Mitchell of the National Bureau of Economic Research, Fisher tried to steer the emerging field of economics in the direction of science and engineering: figure out how the mechanism works and then adjust it accordingly for maximum social benefits.

Fisher gravitated toward that view of economies as mechanical systems, and he extended that to all aspects of his life. He had a passion for cars (the ultimate machine of its day) and for exercise equipment (which he took to after he nearly died of tuberculosis), each of which allowed human beings to transcend their physical limitations. Similar limitations existed for how any one individual or government approached economic affairs. They needed tools to understand the workings of a system, and the tools for economies were better data, more rigorous math, and coherent statistics. Human beings may not have understood or identified the architecture of economies in the past, but with scientific methods combined with mathematical formulas, they could in the future. And for Fisher, rigorous indices would make that possible.

In many ways, Fisher and Wesley Mitchell were professionally intertwined. As part of the first undergraduate class at the newly created (by Rockefeller money, no less) University of Chicago in 1892, Mitchell was fascinated by Civil War price movements, which marked him as a young man of unusual passions. He then became fascinated by the problem of creating reliable indices, especially for questions that depended on survey data. Surveys always had a human element and, therefore, all the attendant messiness of whether questions were asked correctly, answered honestly, and compiled wisely. Mitchell served during World War I on the price section of the War Industries Board, and that gave him an acute appreciation for the difficulty of determining actual prices in real time. Throughout his long academic career and his short public one, he sought better data and better methods for collecting it. He was passionate about the National Bureau of Economic Research because he knew that no one person, no matter how brilliant, could possibly analyze the workings of complicated, multilayered systems. You needed multiple minds tackling the problem from multiple angles. That, again, was a very scientific approach: break down the problem in manageable components and get brilliant people to figure those out. That was how J. Robert Oppenheimer later approached the task of building the bomb during the wartime Manhattan Project, and it was how Mitchell hoped to find the master key to the business cycles that he, along with Arthur Burns, spent so much effort delineating.[6]

Like Mitchell, Fisher shared an interest in the historical movement of prices; his doctoral dissertation was titled, "Mathematical Investigations in the Theory of Value and Prices." That, in turn, became the first undergraduate course he taught. In the 1920s, though he was safely ensconced as a tenured professor at Yale, Fisher created the Index Number Institute in response to what he saw as the limitations and deficiencies of the work of the BLS. He was particularly interested in how wholesale prices moved, as these were the costs borne by operating businesses. Consumers struggled with both limited information (in the years before you could price check on Amazon.com or the web) and limited options (when you couldn't easily just order anything from anywhere and have FedEx deposit it tomorrow at your doorstep). But companies and their purchasing managers had better information than consumers about prices, whether of iron ore (for steel production) or wheat or ball bearings. Hence, the prices they paid tended to be closely tethered to the "real" costs of goods. Fisher also grappled with the mathematical challenges of index construction, and he invented formulas to inch closer to his own personal Holy Grail, "the ideal index."

The primary challenges were where to start and how to track changes in a manner that would allow someone over the course of years to compare apples to apples, literally and figuratively. A price index that starts with one hundred goods, for instance, is fine as long as there is no change in those goods over time: no additions, no subtractions. But life doesn't work that way in modern societies, or we'd still be including buggy whips in the consumer price index. New products constantly appear, so you need an index that can add those without showing sudden jumps in the cost of living. Old products drop out, but usually over a period of years, which could create the misleading impression of decreasing costs of living when the only reason for the decline is that people are buying less of a specific product that is in the index but not spending less overall.

Fisher and Mitchell both approached the task of creating the ideal index as an issue of scientific measurement. Mitchell was the more applied of the two, Fisher the more theoretical. In describing his approach, Fisher used the analogy of many different weights being placed on a bar resting on a fulcrum; the average weight would be when the bar was balanced, and that would be the average price of a basket of differently weighted goods. After testing hundreds of different formulations, Fisher concluded that the "ideal" index would be a combination of constant weights and "chained" weight. Constant weights meant that the basket of goods was set, and then amended periodically as new goods entered and old ones dropped out. A "chained" index was more fluid and adjusted more frequently to account for the simple fact that as prices fluctuate, so does consumption. The most obvious modern example is what happens when the price of gasoline goes up. In a fixed index, the sharp rise in prices at the pump translates into an equally sharp rise in that component of the consumer price index. But in real time and real life, people and businesses respond to rising gas prices in a whole series of ways, from buying less gas, to driving less, to carpooling more and finding other ways of fueling their needs. When the price of beef goes up, they shift to pork. This behavior has been called "the substitution effect." The problem is that it's easier to compile a fixed index because that only demands collecting a representative sample of *prices*. A chained index is much more difficult; it requires not just prices but also data on the actual quantities people are buying.[7]

These debates were not settled at the time. True, few people think in terms of chained or unchained indices. Fewer care much about the contrast between the Laspeyres index (which has fixed weights and was named after the nineteenth-century French statistician Etienne Laspeyres) and the Paasche index (which is more akin to chained and was named after the nineteenth-century German economist Hermann Paasche). And only devotees celebrate Fisher's solutions as the perfect compromise between these alternatives. Fisher himself recognized from the get-go that fixed baskets based on arithmetic formulas would always show rising prices, whereas a "chain-weighted index" would show a lower level of inflation. His argument that you needed a blend of both became more obviously correct as the twentieth century wore on. The will-o'-the-wisp of finding an index that accurately measures the cost of living has been the source of intense controversy ever since.

Measuring inflation juxtaposed the academic and scientific impulses of Fisher with the pragmatic and hard-nosed impulses to measure the world embodied by Mitchell. It was propelled by the political needs of government to assess whether citizens were earning a living wage and the demands of organized labor that businesses pay them enough to live decently. The net result was the first CPI issued by the Bureau of Labor Statistics in 1945, which adopted the simpler fixed basket and not the more accurate but complicated and impractical methods proposed by Fisher. Even though the BLS approach led to chronically higher reported inflation than the alternative approaches (given that it made no allowance for the substitution effect), it still attracted the ire of labor leaders such as Meany and has ever since. Critics claimed that the survey sample was questionable and the sample set rigged, concentrated as it was in urban areas (and the CPI has always emphasized urban consumers). They also charged that the BLS did not sufficiently distinguish between various levels of income, with the result that "official" inflation and costs were always less than what millions of people experienced daily.

The work of Fisher and Mitchell on indexes was a central aspect of the invention of the economy that was under way in these years. Using statistics and math, they took the messy, chaotic real world and tried to make sense of it through "ideal indexes" and "business cycles." Later observers remarked that Fisher, Mitchell, Burns, Kuznets, and many others suffered from "physics envy." They wanted to capture the inner workings of the world of economic affairs with the same level of precision they thought that physicists possessed. And they wanted not just to describe the economy. They wished to shape government policy. After the war, governments everywhere—in the United States, of course, but also in Europe and throughout the Soviet bloc—internalized the view that among their primary responsibilities were governing the economy and satisfying the material needs of citizens. Emulating Keynes, economists seized the opportunity and entered the political fray as counselors and increasingly as policy makers themselves.

These economists were real people with real ambitions. The indexes designed to guide policy, however, were abstractions. The CPI was underpinned by surveys of thousands of families (and today the number is seven thousand families each quarter and another seven thousand keeping meticulous diaries of what they have spent), but the index itself was a mathematical model managed by statisticians. What could be measured was measured but what couldn't be wasn't. A commercial object with a price could be measured. But as Robert Kennedy observed about GDP, that left out swaths of life. It left out the qualitative questions of how people decided what to buy and what not to buy, what constituted a need versus a desire, and how consumers adjusted spending in light of changing prices. Those questions—touching on subjective experiences and decisions—were considered beyond the reach of statistics. Just as national income accounts left out housework because it was deemed too difficult to quantify, so were personal and emotional responses to prices. How individuals balance needs, wants, and desires was omitted from the economic calculus.

Fisher and Mitchell and an entire professional cohort seemed untroubled by these omissions. The economics profession that evolved in the twentieth century veered increasingly away from descriptive approaches, such that the "softer" methods of the George Katonas of the world were looked at askance. Not until late in the century did the field of behavioral economics emerge as a semi-respectable discipline, after decades of disdain and dismissal. And so, when the crisis of the Great Inflation hit in the 1970s, economists in the mold of Fisher and Mitchell—who lived and breathed models and theory—were at the helm, and none more so than Arthur Burns.

Burns served as chairman of the Federal Reserve for eight years, and his tenure is not remembered fondly. As an economic advisor to Richard Nixon during the 1968 presidential campaign, he had been forthright about his concerns over inflation. Nonetheless, the actual surge in inflation that occurred after 1973 was steeper and proved to be more intractable than Burns or most policy economists had anticipated. To reiterate, part of the problem was diagnosing causes. Was inflation the result of the spike in oil prices after the Arab embargo? Was it a delayed reaction to the end of the gold standard brought about by President Nixon's August 1971 decision to suspend the redemption of dollars for gold and institute wage and price controls? Was it the consequence of too much money in circulation? Was it because the Fed bowed to Nixon's emphasis on full employment even at the expense of some inflation, which once unleashed became uncontrollable? There were people arguing for each theory, and no one really knew.

Yet inflation became a political and social challenge bar none as the decade wore on, confronting three presidents—Nixon, Ford, and Carter—and three Federal Reserve chairmen, with Burns lasting until 1978. Burns epitomized the economist turned policy maker. Yet in Washington, he remained too much of an academic to be trusted by politicians and too political to be trusted by academics. His ineffective efforts at the Fed to curb inflation did not win him many allies, even as no one else proved able to solve the issue. And it didn't help that the Great Inflation ebbed and flow, spiking in 1974, and abating in 1976 before spiking again and rising even higher after 1977, along with a sharp rise in food prices and yet another energy shock after the 1979 Iranian Revolution and a global disruption to oil supplies. Because of these erratic patterns, for a brief period in the middle of the decade, Burns believed that inflation had been tamed. We know now that it was not.[8]

The effect of the 1970s inflation was to make Americans more attuned to the way that official economic indicators shaped policy and to how those indicators often painted a different picture than the one they were experiencing in their everyday lives. Inflation was eventually corralled by the aggressive tactics of Fed Chairman Paul Volcker, who raised already high interest rates not by stops and starts but in leaps, from 11 percent at the time he became chairman in 1979 to 20 percent in 1980. The result was a shock to the economy, a defeat for Jimmy Carter to Ronald Reagan in the 1980 presidential election, a sharp recession in 1981, and then a long boom with low inflation for decades after. Whether Volcker's actions were the primary cause of that cascade of events, they were certainly part of the mix that produced one of the longest boom periods in American history.

Even so, the searing effects of soaring inflation didn't fade from collective memory. In almost every country in the world that has experienced sharp inflation, the fear leaves scars, whether Weimar Germany in the 1920s, or Latin America in the 1970s, or the United States during the same period. One consequence of the seventies was to propel government indicators such as the CPI to the center of political and social concerns. That also led to a much wider debate over whether the numbers being assembled did, in fact, measure prices and inflation accurately.

For most people living through the seventies, their experience was of rapidly rising costs for basic necessities such as gasoline and food, higher borrowing costs that made it difficult to purchase a home, and middling overall economic growth, which meant that there wasn't much in the way of higher wages to offset these increased expenses. The United States was also beset with a general malaise about the country and the world in the wake of the Watergate scandal that drove Nixon from office and the inglorious end of the Vietnam War that had already divided the nation. The rest of the Western world wasn't faring much better, with equally high inflation and violent clashes between workers and the state in England and less than stellar economic performance in Western Europe.

The response of the federal government, however, was to question whether inflation was as severe as it had appeared. Economists and government statisticians were concerned that the measure of prices using a fixed basket of goods was overstating inflation, even as most people in their daily lives were certain that official statistics were understating it. The response of the BLS was to experiment with new ways to calculate the index. The Bureau of Economic Analysis also joined the fray and developed a chain-weighted analysis of prices. The desire to jigger the numbers was not some dark plot. It stemmed from the impulse to improve; the indicators were devised in the twenties, thirties, and forties based on available information and keyed to a particular economy. But nothing is static, and as the economic system evolved, the people compiling the numbers understood the need for those to evolve as well. Some change was embedded in the numbers themselves: the composition of the basket of goods used to determine prices shifted organically as new goods appeared and then showed up in surveys of purchases. Other changes, however, wouldn't be reflected unless there was an effort to integrate new forces.

As Janet Norwood, the commissioner of the BLS, testified in the late 1970s, inflation was a number no one liked. "Some people would like an index that doesn't go up so much, and other people would like an index that goes up more. And when they don't have that which they want, they feel there must be something wrong with the indicator itself."[9] The same could have been said for almost any number, any indicator, but the consumer price index was notably controversial.

The Bureau of Labor Statistics evaluated and refined its methods constantly. It did so not just with inflation and CPI but with every metric. Employment measures came under renewed scrutiny in the 1970s as well, especially with a stagnant economy and soaring costs. New job categories had emerged, particularly in the service sector, that weren't adequately captured in earlier surveys. There was also the dramatic movement of more women into the workforce. States, in turn, kept their own unemployment records, and these were not always consistent with the methods used by the BLS. That led to conflicting local and national data, which complicated how billions of federal dollars would be spent on training, how those would be allocated, and where they should go. In 1978 Congress passed the Full Employment and Balanced Growth Act, which set a target of 4 percent unemployment and moderate inflation. Of course, like many pieces of legislation before and since, it left vague how those targets were to be achieved. But the passage of the bill made better calculations of both numbers that much more imperative.

The primary professional criticism of inflation numbers in the 1970s was that they overemphasized the rising costs of volatile components such as energy and food and overstated the impact of rising prices on both the system as a whole and on individual families. Because energy costs spiked sharply and quickly after the Arab oil embargo in 1973, it appeared that inflation had jumped. Of course, it did jump, but critics rightly pointed out that those prices also receded quickly after the crisis abated. If government spending, wages, and pensions were keyed to inflation, there was a danger that these would go up and down so much as to make it impossible for any person or business to have any certainty about costs and spending. As the *New York Times* put it, "Since the index has been overstating inflation, it has triggered billions in excessive increases in wages and pensions. Thus the index not only measures inflation but contributes to it."[10] That spoke to the long-held belief, which George Katona documented so well, that inflation is not simply a function of government monetary policy. The 1970s brought the realization that sentiment combined with statistics could create dangerous feedback loops. As the CPI went up, government spending increased. Increased prices triggered increased wages, which then led to higher reported inflation, which then continued the toxic cycle. The result was runaway inflation.

The specific solution to the volatility of food and fuel prices was a new index called core CPI, which was CPI minus food and energy costs. It was unveiled in 1977. In the years since, people have derided core CPI as "inflation minus whatever gets more expensive," but the point was to separate volatile prices from less volatile ones, so that government policy and employers weren't reacting to spikes like yo-yos. As the BLS explained, "food and energy prices are more subject to significant shocks than prices of other goods and services. Inflation due largely to higher food and energy prices might have different policy implications than broader inflation." As core CPI became the preferred metric for policy makers at the Federal Reserve, the Congressional Budget Office, and elsewhere, it marked yet another wedge between popular perceptions of "the economy" and what the leading indicators indicated.

There was also the tricky problem of housing. Homes are one of the major consumer expenses, but they are not bought and sold with the same frequency as food or appliances or cars. Nonetheless, a significant portion of the inflation index was housing—as much as 25 percent, in fact. Until the 1950s, the CPI tried to incorporate housing as part of the cost of living by using rental prices. Given that home ownership was less widespread early in the century (around 45 percent of the population owned their home between 1900 and 1940, with the rates then climbing to about 65 percent in 1980), you had to include rents in the index as well as home prices. But rent-control laws were also widespread earlier in the century (and survive today only in select pockets such as New York City); that meant that rental costs were kept from rising at the rate of inflation. In response, the BLS changed its formula and started using home prices instead of rent.

By the 1970s, however, with rising interest rates and high inflation in the overall economy, the housing component of the CPI began accelerating substantially more than other components of the index. Each element of housing triggered other increases: rising mortgage costs made interest payments higher; general inflation led to asset price inflation; higher prices for homes led to bigger mortgages. Given higher interest rates, that led to higher monthly payments. Yet the index did not take into account the fact that as housing prices went up, fewer homes were bought and sold and more people began to rent. In short, because the basket was fixed while home prices and mortgages were anything but, the inflation index showed higher housing inflation than many people were actually experiencing, especially if they already owned their home and had minimal or no mortgage payments. Added to the mix was the entire issue of expected inflation, which in the case of housing led to higher sale prices and steeper mortgage rates.

After repeated calls to alter how housing was measured, in 1983 the BLS again changed its methodology. Here's where it starts to get truly arcane. Instead of using home prices (what was called an "asset price" method), it began using rents again. It also broadened the scope of its surveys to encompass fifty thousand units spread out over ten thousand distinct areas of the country. The BLS then added a new twist called "owner's equivalent rent," which is the theoretical rent that homeowners would have to pay if they rented the home they owned. The result of this switch was a noticeable reduction in measured inflation. When the new formula was applied retroactively to the 1970s, the revised numbers using owner's equivalent rent showed that instead of inflation rising 188 percent between 1967 and 1982, it increased 165 percent—still considerable but unquestionably lower.[11] But the fact that the revised index showed more moderate inflation fueled the popular belief that the government was systematically lowballing inflation in order to reduce federal outlays for Social Security and give companies a justification to pay workers less.

Though inflation had been officially tamed by the aggressive measures of Paul Volcker at the Federal Reserve, and though the overall economy was, statistically speaking, booming, many in government still believed that the CPI was exaggerating price increases. Those concerns in the late 1980s and early 1990s were confined largely to policy wonks and academics, but they burst into wider view when Alan Greenspan, then the new and dynamic head of the Fed, testified before Congress in 1995. In his quiet, professorial tone, he stated, "The official CPI may currently be overstating the increase in the true cost of living by perhaps half a percent to one and a half percent per year . . . If the annual inflation adjustments to indexed programs and taxes were reduced by one percentage point . . . the annual level of the deficit will be lower by about fifty-five billion dollars after five years." As a result of Greenspan's testimony, Congress appointed a commission chaired by Michael Boskin, Stanford professor, conservative economist, and former chair of the Council of Economic Advisers under President George H. W. Bush. And that commission, to little surprise but considerable controversy, concluded that Greenspan was right.[12]

Few questioned the comprehensiveness of CPI: it surveyed forty-four metropolitan areas and tracked 207 different goods. Yes, housing represented a huge chunk, but then again, surveys of consumer expenditures showed that housing expenses were a huge chunk of most people's budgets (usually around 35 percent). It was the methodology that was at fault. The Boskin commission and Greenspan emphasized the problem of a chained index and the inordinately long time it took to integrate new products, new services, and improved products and services.

The BLS responded to these critiques by adjusting yet again the way that CPI was calculated, moving toward what Irving Fisher had advocated decades earlier and blending its fixed basket based purely on arithmetic formulas to one that took a more geometric approach. In making the changes, the BLS hoped to better account for that "substitution effect," whereby consumers adjusted their behavior in response to changing prices (for example, buying wheat instead of corn products if corn prices spiked). The bureau also began to factor product improvements into its assessment of prices through a process called "hedonic" adjustments, which we will get to in a moment.

No, this is definitely not the stuff of scintillating cocktail chatter. If your head is spinning from this endless array of measurements and changes to how we assess inflation, consider for a moment that the discussion so far barely scratches the surface of jargon and complexities. There are multiple variations of CPI, ranging from the most commonly used one for all urban workers (CPI-U), to one for urban wage earners and clerical workers only (CPI-W), to one for the elderly (CPI-E). There are cost-of-living indices, which are similar to but not the same as the CPI, and which economists called "cost of goods" indexes. Cost of living measures what it actually costs people to meet their needs, versus CPI, which is an index of prices. Then there are CPI-U-X indices—five of them—which test various ways to account for owner's equivalent rent. There are multiple formulas for hedonic pricing, and then there are the indicators of inflation kept not by the BLS but by the Bureau of Economic Analysis and derived from the national accounts and the GDP figures. The BEA inflation indicator is known as the price consumption deflator, a chained index that often does a better job of capturing consumer behavior and, hence, was the preferred measure of inflation for Alan Greenspan and others who yearned for alternatives to basic, arithmetic CPI. Finally, there were the numerous revisions to methodology and survey size, along with regular statistical adjustments and "smoothing" the numbers to compensate for "seasonal effects" such as high retail sales over Christmas.

In short, there is no simple thing called "inflation." Yes, there is a number reported monthly and collected assiduously from thousands of surveys of households across the country. But that indicator is only one of multiple gauges meant to capture prices and costs of living. As we've seen, CPI itself has been revised and criticized countless times, and continues to be. The mutability of the number fuels popular beliefs that these figures are gamed in favor of those who have power and resources (government and business). Writing in *Harper's* magazine in May 2008, Kevin Phillips described the legacy of suspicion surrounding official inflation figures, saying, "Since the 1960s, Washington has been forced to gull its citizens and creditors by debasing official statistics: the vital instruments with which the vigor and muscle of the American economic are measured. The effect, over the past twenty-five years, has been to create a false sense of economic achievement and rectitude, allowing us to maintain artificially low interest rates, massive government borrowing, and a dangerous reliance on mortgage and financial debt, even as real economic growth has been slower than claimed."

The critics were hardly confined to the lunatic fringe who believed that the entire fiat currency system was a proverbial house of cards ready to collapse at any moment and bound to eventually. In 2003 University of Chicago professor Austan Goolsbee claimed that the US government was "cooking the books" in the way that it measures economic trends. The influential bond manager Bill Gross of Pimco, which manages trillions of dollars of assets for individuals and institutions, wrote in 2004 that CPI was essentially a government con job:

> My quarrel, though, is not just with those who are fixated on the core CPI or the core PCE, but with those who support what we know as hedonic adjustments. Talk about a con job! The government says that if the quality of a product got better over the last 12 months that it didn't really go up in price and in fact it may have actually gone down! Why, we could be back to Bernanke deflation real soon if the government would quality adjust enough products. For instance, prices of desktop and notebook computers declined by 8% a year during the past decade . . . but because the machines' computer power and memory have improved, their hedonically adjusted prices have dropped by 25% *a year* since 1997. No wonder the core CPI is less than 2% with computers dropping by that much every year. But did *your* new model computer come with a 25% discount from last year's price? Probably not. What is likely is that you paid about the same price for hedonically adjusted memory improvements you'll never use. Similarly, government statisticians manipulate the price increases for cars and just about any durable good that comes off an assembly line but find it difficult to extend that theory to underwear or a pair of shoes. Perhaps that's next. Talk about Uncle Sam getting into your shorts![13]

As the indicators developed totemic status as absolute markers of what was going on, they were assessed not in terms of their methodological rigor but for their social and political consequences. On that score, many found them at best inadequate and at worst destructive. Few if any of the leading indicators were invented to help the "average" person navigate the world. They were created to empower officials and give policy makers clarity. They were not designed to give Mr. and Mrs. Smith insight. Once these metrics became part of our collective culture, however, Mr. and Mrs. Smith took great interest in what the numbers said, and often found that the numbers reflected their own experiences hardly at all.

The disconnect between CPI as a leading indicator and how the average person experiences or understands inflation exposed the limitations. The indicators may have measured the economy, but they could not determine whether the economic system was meeting citizens' needs and expectations. How individuals experience "the economy" is distinct from how statisticians measure the economy. The indicators were invaluable tools in the first half of the twentieth century, especially in contrast to the complete absence of such indicators for most of human history. But by the end of the twentieth century, the gap between what these numbers say and what many people and businesses experience was growing untenably wide.

There is no right or wrong in this story, but if you want to understand just how wide that gap has yawned, the evolution of "hedonic pricing" would be a good start. A legitimate attempt to integrate the effects of technology on costs, hedonic pricing exposes just how far statistics can be detached from experience. And while experience of individuals is often subjective, that experience shapes whether the bulk of people believe that their system is working. The path from hedonic pricing to the question of happiness may not be straight, but it is a path that affects all of us.

The leading indicators were meant to measure the health of the system, but along the way, they became referendums on whether people are content and satisfied. On that score, the indicators have been found wanting. How we got here is one story; what we do about it is another. These metrics began as guideposts to help policy makers and businesses understand what was going on. By the early twenty-first century, however, they were used to justify trillions of dollars of government spending and business investment. In fact, it is now almost impossible for government to spend money, for businesses to plan ahead, and for individuals to make decisions about investing and retiring without reference to these numbers. Rather than taken as guides, they are used as inputs into a system that is assumed to operate like a machine: calibrate the inputs correctly and you can, with reasonable accuracy, predict the outputs. It all seems very neat, and it is. It is also, with disturbing frequency, wrong.

7

DIMINISHING RETURNS

On a chilly day in February 2009, newly elected President Barack Obama stepped up to a podium in Mesa, Arizona, outside the local school. He had just assumed office under unenviable circumstances. Panic gripped the global financial system, and the United States was at its epicenter. Millions of people had seen their homes foreclosed, and millions more were in limbo. The BLS reported in December that the US workforce had shed nearly 700,000 jobs, and about 650,000 more were said to have evaporated in both January and February—numbers that would later be revised even higher. These numbers were not greeted with measured reaction. In fact, with the twenty-four-hour news cycle now augmented by the instantaneity of the web, it's fair to say that never before had employment numbers released by the BLS received such intense attention and been used to make such sweeping conclusions about the state of the economy.

Obama and his new team of economic advisors already knew that the situation was parlous. They had known for months, and they had been planning a strategy. As it turned out, as bad as they thought it was, it was worse, but they wouldn't know that for many months. The data available in the fall of 2008 and the early weeks of 2009 showed an economy contracting. The figures for the third quarter of 2008 initially came in at about -0.5 percent, but by the time Obama's team was grappling with what was happening, the situation had deteriorated significantly, with the fourth-quarter GDP contracting almost 9 percent.[1] But at the time, the data showed that fourth-quarter output had shrunk about 4 percent—bad but a different kind of bad than twice that pace. That divergence between what the numbers said and what was actually happening would have more than minor consequences.

Obama greeted the crowd, which was hopeful of some help yet suffering from the collapse of the local housing market and with it a local economy several ticks worse than the national average. Arizona, along with central California, Las Vegas, and Florida, was ground zero for the housing bubble. Obama did indeed promise help. "Yesterday, in Denver, I signed into law the American Recovery and Reinvestment Act, which will create or save three and a half million jobs over the next two years—including seventy thousand right here in Arizona; right here doing the work America needs done. And we're also going to work to stabilize, repair, and reform our financial system to get credit flowing again to families and businesses."

The American Recovery and Reinvestment Act was a stimulus bill totaling $787 billion, give or take. It was one of the largest such bills ever passed, rivaling even the heralded New Deal. The actual figure was the product of two months of intense debate, first among Obama's own inner circle and then with Congress. As Obama spoke that day in February, the unemployment rate, the one calculated by the heirs of Ethelbert Stewart and Herbert Hoover, was hovering in the range of 8 percent. But many people felt that the official number was too low; that it understated the pain and the insecurity caused by the financial meltdown of 2008. And many took comfort in the promise that with the massive commitment of $787 billion by the federal government, the job loss would be stemmed, and the jobs would come back.

That is also what Obama and his team hoped and believed. The size of the bill was based, initially, at least, on the calculations of a team of economists and economic policy makers that included Christina Romer at the Council of Economic Advisers, Larry Summers at the White House National Economic Council, Timothy Geithner at Treasury, Peter Orzag at the White House Office of Management and Budget, and Obama's chief of staff, Rahm Emanuel. The team was assembled quickly and most had not been intimately involved in the strategy of the campaign. It faced a rapidly unfolding crisis and understood the need to act. The question was what to do and how much to spend.

The $787 billion figure—later revised higher—emerged from a relatively simple calculus: how much money was required to close the gap between what the economy was producing and what it could produce. Closing that gap was supposed to reverse the decline in employment, because employment was perceived as connected directly to the expansion or contraction of GDP. Calculating the size of the gap required at least two data points: the actual size of the economy as determined by GDP and the potential size of the economy. The potential size is tethered to another concept, that of the "natural rate of employment." The equation goes something like this: if the economy is at or near full employment, it will generate its full potential output. And when economic activity is heated, the "output" gap can even be positive; that is, the economy can, statistically speaking, generate more activity than its "potential." That, in turn, is supposed to lead directly to inflation.

The problem is that there is no consensus about how to measure the output gap. While official GDP figures provide an agreed-on measure of actual output, quantifying "potential" or "full" output is a good deal trickier. In fact, it's an inherently unknowable number. Obama's team had to compile various estimates. Christina Romer was well versed in the concept, but the White House also took the temperature of the Congressional Budget Office and its team of economists, as well as a host of other sources ranging from the Federal Reserve to the White House's own OMB staff. Estimates about the size of the output gap ranged from -1.0 percent to -4.2 percent.[2]

The Depression-era ideas of Keynes had long since become the central operating framework of both the American government and most governments in the Western world (Germany being a notable exception). Faced with a gap between what the economy was producing and what it could produce optimally, policy makers believed that government should spend. For the Federal Reserve, that meant monetary policies such as lowering interest rates and keeping the cost of capital low; for Congress, that meant fiscal policy and increasing the budget. It wasn't enough just to calculate the size of the output gap and then spend an equivalent amount. Government spending is believed to have a "multiplier effect," which means that a dollar of stimulus spending can have more than a dollar of consequence, depending on whether it is in the form of tax breaks, grants to states, or direct spending. If activity is contracting rapidly, it might be necessary to spend even more aggressively.

Assessing how much to spend depends on multiple calculations and reams of data. Yet the Obama team couldn't possibly calculate the output gap with any certainty, given how fluid and chaotic the economy was at the time. The data they had were provisional, and no official indicators can capture economic activity in real time. An output gap of -1.0 percent leads to a very different stimulus plan than -4.2 percent, and the difference is in the hundreds of billions of dollars, if not more.

As Obama scrambled to manage both the transition to the White House and an economic crisis that was spiraling down with little regard for the niceties of election cycles and presidential handovers, his economic team was trying to devise a plan that could be put to Congress and implemented quickly. In a heatedly debated internal memo in December, Romer suggested that it would take a massive sum to close the output gap. "An ambitious goal would be to eliminate the output gap by 2011—Q1 [the first quarter of 2011], returning the economy to full employment by that date," she wrote. "To achieve that magnitude of effective stimulus using a feasible combination of spending, taxes, and transfers to states and localities would require a package costing about $1.8 trillion over two years." However, as Ryan Lizza of the *New Yorker* and Noam Scheiber of the *New Republic* each reported, those figures never made it into the final memo, nor were they submitted to the president.[3] Political considerations, driven by the assessments of Larry Summers and Rahm Emanuel about what Congress could stomach, pushed the figure down below $1 trillion dollars, to its eventual number just shy of $800 billion.

The passage of the stimulus bill of 2009 was, to say the least, controversial. The unemployment rate did not dip below 8 percent until the middle of 2012. While President Obama had hedged in saying that the stimulus would "create or save" three and a half million jobs, most people focused on *create* rather than *save*, because you can measure jobs created, but there is no reliable way to count jobs saved. It may be, as most economists concluded, that the spending of 2009 did indeed prevent much sharper job losses and further economic contraction. But that can never be proved conclusively. In the unfolding of human history, you know only what happened. There are no test cases for what might have been.

We know now that the spending did not reduce the unemployment rate as quickly as promised and that the unemployment statistics did not show three and a half million new jobs created. In fact, between February 2009 and the end of 2012, barely two million new jobs were added to the employment rolls, as determined by the Bureau of

Labor Statistics. As to whether three million jobs were saved, there is no statistical way of proving that, even if it is true.

All of these plans rested on economic indicators. It's remarkable how much the US government, which at the turn of the twentieth century had almost no capacity to measure economic activity, is now shaped almost entirely by a set of numbers that were invented barely fifty years ago. The stimulus bill of 2009—one of the largest government initiatives of recent memory—was designed entirely within a framework of statistics and models that rely on them. The assumptions were and are entirely mechanistic and mathematical: "the economy" has a measurable amount of output and a set level of full employment. When those are in balance, there is low inflation, sufficient supply and demand, and stability. When they are not, all hell breaks loose.

You would never know reading the memos that framed these plans just how new these concepts are. In 2008–09 policy makers such as Romer, Summers, Geithner, and presumably Obama himself weighed a variety of actions, just as Arthur Burns, Paul Volcker, and Alan Greenspan had at various points between 1960 and the early 2000s. No one thought that the economy was simple or solutions to the problems easy. Yet they all accepted the basic assumptions that there was such as a thing as a national economy that could be tweaked, shocked, shaken, and stimulated back to health. They based that assumption on a set of data stretching back only a few decades, and on statistics that were then put into charts and tables to highlight patterns and suggest cause and effect. How could you say that if you spent X dollars, that would create Y number of jobs? By compiling data on federal spending since the Great Depression and then juxtaposing that with the number of jobs that were subsequently created. Since there was no consistent method for compiling unemployment statistics until the 1940s, and since there was no way to measure output and GDP until then either, and since there was no coherent theory of government spending until Keynes and others developed one, all of these models used to determine trillions of dollars of spending rested on tenuous foundations.

Keynes was a driving force behind the development of national accounts. Because the implementation of his theories required better statistics, he was partly responsible for setting a course that led directly to the miscalculation of the Obama stimulus. That isn't an indictment of Keynes or the bill, though many do, in fact, indict both. Many others believe that the stimulus did considerable good, and if nothing else, it halted the rapid deterioration. But it was clearly miscalculated in the basic sense of the word; the assumptions and formulas did not play out as anticipated. But while Keynes would undoubtedly have supported similar measures, he was always attuned to uncertainty and to the very fact that these complex systems can't fully be captured by simple numbers. That is why he constantly urged nimbleness and creativity rather than doctrinaire approaches.

For a brief period in the mid- to late twentieth century, it may have been true that the indicators measured "the economy" accurately and that, in turn, gave policy makers the means to maintain growth and stability. Though economic policy broke down in the 1970s, as we saw, it could be argued that it collapsed because of an unusual convergence of external shocks. But there are two other factors that profoundly undermined the ability of these indicators to map the world: technology and globalization.

The world best captured by the indicators was one of industrial nation-states with high levels of control over trade and currency and a domestic market of consumers and workers separate and distinct from consumers and workers in other countries. That is not the world of the late twentieth and early twenty-first centuries. The statistics of the twentieth century have become increasingly detached from the world as it is and ever more likely to mislead.

Take the problem of inflation. Alan Greenspan's 1995 testimony that inflation was being overstated only made public what had long been known within professional circles: the statistical framework was showing signs of age. Greenspan was not yet being heralded as the maestro and master of economic progress, nor was he yet being dismissed as out of touch with the housing bubble that would lead to the financial crisis of 2008–09. He was one of the wise men of economic policy, and by the time of his appointment as Fed chairman, he had already accomplished more than many do in their entire careers. He had run his own economic analysis firm and then served as one of Nixon's primary advisors. He understood the way that government statistics were compiled as well as anyone, and he intuitively grasped—even before he was able to marshal his considerable staff of economists at the Fed—that economic activity in the 1990s was not being measured adequately.

Greenspan, trained as an academic, spent most of his career in business and then government, but he retained the air of a slightly detached professor. His early attraction to the theories of Ayn Rand may have shaped his sense that the world could be defined and molded by acts of extraordinary individual will. Without overdoing the influence of Rand (and, indeed, she would be delighted at just how much influence she is reputed to have had), the belief that reality is constructed by human systems should be more central to how we understand the leading indicators. They are numbers we made up, nothing more and nothing less.

In arguing that CPI was overstating inflation, Greenspan was implicitly acknowledging that gaps can and do exist between what the numbers say and what is actually happening in the real world. Leave aside for the moment the problem of how the numbers create a feedback loop that alters the world they are purportedly measuring; the numbers often fail to keep pace with change.[4]

The world in 1995 was substantially different from the world in 1935 or in 1955, yet the way that inflation was calculated had not changed commensurately. In 1935 rural electrification was still a challenge in the United States; Europe was only a few years away from a continental war that destroyed cities, obliterated infrastructure, and killed tens of millions of people. In 1995 Netscape was about to go public; the World Wide Web was soon to permeate all corners of life; life expectancy had increased everywhere; and the forces of globalization were reaching a scale significantly larger than at any point in history. In 1935 farming and manufacturing were the predominant sources of jobs and income. In 1995 farming had shrunk to a fraction of the population in the developed world, and manufacturing had been losing jobs since the 1970s. Instead, service jobs, ranging from information technology to consulting to entertainment were becoming the norm. Our statistics, however, were still focused on manufacturing, marked by nation-states, and defined by a largely male workforce.

The statistical cognoscenti understood that as the economy evolves, measurements needed to evolve as well. Yes, the physical world hasn't changed substantially in the past hundred years. But the political and economic systems have morphed dramatically, and arguably were (and are) changing even now at a more rapid clip than at any point in human history. By the 1990s, that meant that even statistics of relatively recent creation—say, fifty or sixty years—were in danger of becoming anachronisms.

It's not as if the people charged with assembling these statistics were unaware of the fluid nature of economic systems. To the contrary. Statisticians and economists who work in the US government and in governments throughout the world have always been well aware of changes in the economic system. The basket of goods that constituted the first consumer price index in the 1940s is a very different basket with different weights than its counterpart today. Then, food was the dominant component. In 1950 the average family spent more than 22 percent of its disposable income on food; today that figure is 11 percent.[5] Items such as bread and meat thus figured more prominently in decades past. So did clothing. Typewriters were in that basket midcentury; computers weren't. Telephones were; smart phones, not so much.

As we've seen, those changes are eventually reflected in how inflation is calculated. The basket of goods, even a fixed basket, adjusts over time as new goods creep into consumer surveys and old ones drop out. But larger changes can be reflected only if the way that the data is analyzed changes as well. As the sad deaths of the rotary-dial phone and the Betamax demonstrate, different goods enter the surveys and others exit based on technological changes and lifestyle shifts. But the improvements in an item are invisible. A car is a car is a car, no matter when it was made. Or is it?

People (or at least the types of people who think about these things) have long understood that the same item—a car—might appear to be the same item in 1950 and 1990 and 2010, but has, in fact, become a different machine over time. Unless efforts are made to account for the way "a car" has changed, the increase in the price of a car will reflect only that the same item—a car—has become increasingly more expensive. Calling those price increases "inflation" is correct in that a car that costs $3,000 in 1960 and $20,000 in 1990 has indeed become more expensive. In terms of the costs of living, the rise in sticker price matters. But that is not the only aspect of cost of living. The same car in 1960 might have gotten a fraction of the gas mileage, which means that it consumed more fuel, and, indeed, we know that for all the volatility in the price of gas, the percentage of the average household budget spent on gasoline has not changed between 1970 and 2011 and has remained about 3.5 percent. Fuel efficiency is a major reason, as well as antilock brakes and temperature controls for air-conditioning and heat, and yet you'd never know that just by looking at the price of a car. You might have spent much more on a car in 1990 than in 1960, but you also consumed less gas. Your "cost of living," therefore, did not go up in sync with the cost of the car.

The recognition that inflation as calculated might mask substantial

changes that lead to miscalculation of the cost of living was the impetus for hedonics, that methodology for factoring in product improvements that is at once so innovative and so controversial. Greenspan's
testimony emerged from years of mulling the connection—or lack
thereof—between economic statistics and the world as it actually
functions. Greenspan understood that economic statistics don't just
measure the economy, they define it. And if the way the system is defined remains static even as the system itself is fluid, then there will be
a disconnect between the numbers and the real world.

In Greenspan's view, the 1990s presented a number of conundrums. Economic growth as measured by GDP was expanding at a
very fast clip, faster than at most points in the twentieth century. Unemployment was low, and yet statistically there was minimal inflation.
There was also very low productivity, yet companies were reporting
record profits and record margins. That didn't make sense to Greenspan, nor to many others. With high growth and tight labor markets,
economic theory said that there should be higher inflation, unless
there was also higher productivity. Productivity is a relatively simple
concept: it is a measure of how much output is produced per unit of
input. Or, to put it more simply, how much stuff a person or machine
produces in an hour. The only way, according to the theory, that
growth could be strong and unemployment shrinking with low inflation were if each worker produced more output with the same amount
of labor and income. Otherwise, goods would be scarcer, wages higher,
and demand stronger, and voilà; inflation. But in the mid-1990s, productivity growth as measured by the Bureau of Economic Analysis
was muted and not strong enough to explain why there was so much
growth yet so little wage and price inflation.

Greenspan's answer was that there must be something wrong not
just with how inflation was measured but also with how productivity was computed. In his view, the math just wasn't adding up. So he
tasked the considerable staff of economists at the Fed to figure out

the problem. They turned to an academic concept called "multifactor productivity," which tries to capture output per hour that isn't explained by labor or capital alone. If labor and capital don't account for all observed output, then the only possible explanation is technology. In the 1990s, that meant information technology, personal computers, the Internet—none of which existed when inflation, productivity, and the whole suite of indicators were invented.

For much of the 1990s, even as the Internet boom seized popular imagination with utopian dreams of endless prosperity and the end of the business cycle, and even as the stock market soared and Washington ran a budget surplus, economic indicators showed only small gains in productivity. Everybody, it seemed, knew that the brave new world of computers and connectivity was changing the way we all worked and played. Everyone assumed that these new communication and information tools were making it possible to work more effectively, manufacture more efficiently, play more extremely, but no one could prove that. Now that most workers had a computer at their desks, were they analyzing sales figures more quickly? Or were they spending more time surfing sports scores on ESPN.com? In short, the statistics were saying, "What Internet revolution?" even as swaths of society were living it.

The economists of the Federal Reserve responded to Greenspan's conundrum with alternate statistical methods and formulas designed to capture the influence of information technologies. New multifactor productivity calculations showed that the economy was becoming more efficient after all. Technology was allowing labor and capital to boost output. The new way to calculate productivity closed the gap between what was obvious to most people living in the economy day to day and what the statistics said was going on in the economy day to day.

The greater use of hedonic calculations was more controversial, though in truth, the amount of work that hedonic calculations required meant that only television sets, a few items of clothing, and some appliances were "hedonically adjusted." Hence, for all of the furor that hedonics generated among those who believed that the government systematically low-balled inflation and that hedonic adjustments were the newest form of manipulation, the actual percentage of such adjustments was too small to be the deep, dark cause.[6]

Greenspan's brilliant insight that the indicators were not keeping up with the pace of change should have been a wake-up call that our collective ability to measure and then steer "the economy" was decreasing. Instead, legions of sophisticated statisticians and economists set to work on how existing statistics could be improved, either by better methodology or by better underlying data. The central belief that more data and better statistics would allow us to manage the economy better was never deeply challenged, especially since the 1990s were so prosperous. The recession of 2001 was rather mild, and the stock market collapse of 2002 unfolded against a backdrop of the war on terror in the wake of the attacks of September 11. In essence, the conviction that the leading economic indicators are vital tools to steer the economic ship only deepened even as the fissures between what the indicators indicated and what reality reflected began to widen and proliferate.

Yet as multifactor productivity and hedonics show, the only way that the changes in the economy could be captured by the mid-twentieth-century indicators was to move toward ever greater complexity. There has always been an inverse relationship between the simplicity of our statistics expressed in one headline number and the vast amounts of data and mathematical formulas that go into their formation. That "simple" GDP number is the product of thousands of data points and thousands of people assembling information. The same is true for inflation, for unemployment, and for all the leading indicators.

The complexity of "the economy," the continual refinement of the indicators, and the sheer newness of these numbers all combine to make governing the economy far more challenging. But the need to present policy and justify it using the indicators forces a level of certainty and simplicity that flies in the face of that complexity. That doesn't work as science; it doesn't even work for the discipline of statistics. No scientist could claim that a hypothesis is proved by the fifty or sixty data points that economic policy makers have at their disposal when assessing questions such as the relationship between government spending and unemployment.

Take the following: there have been eleven recessions in the United States since the end of World War II. Eleven. To conclude with any certainty that we know the connection between government spending during recessions and subsequent employment and economic growth—which is what the stimulus bill of 2009 and all government spending plans do—is to ignore the fact that eleven is not a large enough set from which to draw any firm conclusions. When statisticians, trained in math and probability theory, try to assess likely outcomes, they demand a plethora of data points. Even then, they recognize that unless it's a very simple and controlled action such as flipping a coin, unforeseen variables can exert significant influence.

To supplement limited data, statisticians employ "regression analysis." The various scenarios sketched out in December 2008 by Obama's economic team were based on regression analysis. ("If we spend $600 billion, it will have this effect on output and employment; if we spend $1.8 billion, it will have this effect.") Yet even this analysis is only as good as the inputs, and, once again, they were few and limited. As we've seen, it's not just the recent invention of GDP, unemployment, inflation; it's the recent invention of the entire concept of a business cycle with recessions that can be measured and "called" by the National Bureau of Economic Research, that brilliant child of Wesley Mitchell and others.

Of course, these uses of official statistics fit into a Keynesian framework that governments can and should adjust policies to moderate and alleviate downturns. That notion is rejected by another school of economists, many of whom claim inspiration from the Austrian Friedrich August Von Hayek, and most of whom look to Milton Friedman, the longtime University of Chicago professor, as a godfather. It's not that free-market purists reject indicators as useful. They just don't believe that governments are good stewards. They trust instead the market, which is best governed by the laws of economics rather than the whims of central bankers and the passions of politicians. Unlike Keynes, Friedman believed that the Great Depression was a failure of economic policy—specifically, misguided decisions by central banks—and not a market failure. He dismissed the idea that only government could secure the conditions for full employment, and he excoriated those who believed they could accurately calculate a "multiplier effect" for government spending.[7]

It's often said that Friedman's thinking won the day under Ronald Reagan and that "free-market" economics became the dominant theme in government and in the Republican Party. That had a parallel in the United Kingdom in the 1980s under the Tory government of Prime Minister Margaret Thatcher. But while those philosophies animated those parties, none of these governments ceased to be Keynesian. None ceased to function as if "the economy" could be measured, and none abandoned the precept that it is a primary role of government to ensure economic security. As we've seen, that view was embedded in almost every bureaucracy in the world. It was woven into the framework of the United Nations and into almost every nook of global governance. Milton Friedman's famous line "We are all Keynesian now" was a testament to the prevalence of those beliefs, even if Friedman himself rejected the core tenets.

Just as the indicators went global with astonishing speed, they also became enmeshed in every decision that government, industry, and individuals made. Like vines, they became entangled with vital areas of public (and even private) life. Take government budgets. As bureaucracy expanded in the twentieth century in the United States, Europe, and, indeed, throughout the world, governments needed better accounting of what they were spending and what the long-term consequences of such spending might be.

In America, that took the form of the creation of the Congressional Budget Office (CBO) in 1974. Given how ubiquitous and central the CBO has become to government policy, it's surprising how recently it was created. The White House Office of Management and Budget was established only in 1970, but that was simply a new name for an older organization, the Bureau of the Budget, which was created in 1921 to help the president with his constitutional duty of submitting an annual budget to Congress. The role of the CBO is different. It was set up as an independent watchdog of government spending, at a time when both inflation and spending were viewed with grave concern. The CBO is responsible for analyzing the effects of spending and of commitments to spend on the long-term federal budget. As the federal government began to rely on deficit spending in the 1980s, the Congressional Budget Office was anointed the official keeper of budget statistics, along with the OMB. That was formalized in 1985, when the rising public anxiety about mounting deficits—a foreshadowing of much higher levels of concern after 2008—led to the passage of a bipartisan bill to keep the deficit in check.

That bill, known as Gramm-Rudman, mandated that the CBO "score" all proposed legislation. If this all seems a bit thick and wonky, its real-world consequences have been anything but. One of the core functions of the CBO is to estimate how much the government will spend on health care and Social Security. Though the CBO is staffed by nonpartisan economists and accountants, its analysis is based almost entirely on guesstimates about the future rate of inflation, the future rate of growth, and the future rate of employment—all of which are inherently unknowable and each of which determines how much revenue the government will collect in the form of taxes. This is an almost impossible task. Add in the fact that ten-year projections, by law, must assume *no* change in congressional policy about taxes or new programs, and you begin to glean why we do such a poor job mapping future trends for government spending.

And a poor job we do. In 2003, just before the passage of the bold Medicare act that enshrined Part D, the new prescription drug benefit, the Congressional Budget Office estimated that it would cost $395 billion over the coming decade. In March 2005, the CBO announced that, instead, that figure looked to be $593 billion, a 50 percent difference. The reason? More people joined the prescription plan than initially assumed. A decade later, in February 2013, the CBO announced that its assumptions about the long-term effects of the Affordable Care Act of 2010 (known as "Obamacare") had *overestimated* the costs by about $200 billion because of incorrect assumptions about how quickly heath care costs would rise. As one scholar put it, scoring a program like this, or, for that matter, the 2009 stimulus bill, demanded "assumptions that could keep an army of economists busy debating and fine-tuning" along with "data sources that could employ surveyors, demographers, and marketers for years." In the end, these predictions are at best an "educated best guess."[8]

The budget process also contorts the way spending decisions are made. There are strict rules for how the CBO can score the consequences of proposed government programs. It can, for instance, project costs based on the assumed rate of inflation and whatever Congress has budgeted. Its ability to score projected savings, however, is highly constrained. So too is its ability to score social benefits that will likely result from certain types of spending but are not easily linked to the spending. For example, if a highway bill authorizes $10 billion for infrastructure improvements in Los Angeles, the CBO can score that as $10 billion of costs added to the federal budget. But if that $10 billion leads to fewer automobile accidents and shorter commute times, both of which would save billions of dollars that could be spent productively elsewhere, the CBO has absolutely no way to account for that. Such limitations make it nearly impossible for Congress to invest for the future and very easy to cut costs or spend only in the short term. The 2009 stimulus bill, passed in the heat of a crisis, was a rare exception.

The CBO is only one example of how indicators are plugged into policy and then determine how vast sums are—or are not—spent. We also saw earlier how inflation predictions emerging from the work of the BLS can shape assumptions about the long-term viability of Social Security payments and the short-term cost of unemployment benefits.

The most significant projection, of course, is what the rate of growth will be, which means how much GDP will expand or contract. That is also the most significant projection for global agencies such as the International Monetary Fund, the World Bank, the UN, the Organization for Economic Cooperation and Development (OECD), the Association of Southeast Asian Nations (ASEAN), the Communist Party of China, and the Inter-American Development Bank (IDB), to name a few. All of these organizations, along with every sovereign nation on the planet, measure GDP, and they all do so according to common standards for national accounts defined by the United Nations.

The UN System of National Accounts standardizes human commerce and economic activity. It provides everything from the official definition of "a transaction," to the meaning of a "household," to the difference between market activities (buying and selling goods and services) and nonmarket activities (volunteer service, domestic work). The tables and reports run into the hundreds of pages, yet the overarching goal is both stunningly ambitious and relatively straightforward. The system seeks to answer the basic questions of "Who does what?" and "Who has what?" And then some. As the introduction to the most recent UN report states, the goal is nothing less than to answer conclusively "Who does what, with whom, in exchange for what, by what means, for what purpose?"

This system anchors a dizzying global array of indicators, providing the raw inputs into everything from the CIA's *The World Factbook* to UN agency predictions. The World Bank alone publishes thousands of monographs and studies every year that tabulate and describe commercial life globally, from calorie consumption in schools, to climate change and its effect on poverty in North Africa, to rates of violence in the twenty-first century. In fact, take any international agency, and you will find reports laden with statistics and tables. The System of National Accounts, so novel and monumental in the 1940s, spawned a world that is now so data rich that no one could possibly absorb it all.

The keepers of the national accounts try, however. In 1993, after years of effort, the UN revised the national accounts methodology to amend the deficiencies of the original 1950s system. In 2008 there was another revision. These are massive undertakings, involving dozens of nations and thousands of ideas. One of the major changes in the national accounts in 2008 was a better way to include intellectual properties. We all recognize that information technology has been ever more central to our lives, from smart phones, to iPads, to the massive data centers of Google and Amazon.com, to our own online lives. Yet traditional metrics designed in the mid–twentieth century weren't designed to measure these activities. Nor were they designed to account adequately for valuable intangible assets such as leases or licenses for intellectual properties. A company such as Qualcomm gains most of its revenue from licensing its patents, which is a different business model than Ford manufacturing Model Ts or pickup trucks. The 2008 reforms also began to account for those activities that were purposely left out of the initial accounts and of GDP: the informal economies of housework, leisure, and cash transactions, none of which exist in official statistics but all of which are woven through our lives. The UN revision also supported those efforts at the Bureau of Economic

Analysis to revise its own accounting of the US economy that led to that hitherto uncounted $400 billion of GDP a year.[9]

The System of National Accounts is perhaps the most influential set of numbers in the world, yet few have heard of them. They are the bible of global economic indicators. But while few know how the numbers has been internationally standardized, we all have become increasingly aware of the numbers themselves. Take the monthly jobs report. As we've seen, until the late 1950s, unemployment statistics were quietly released by the Bureau of Labor Statistics, with little fanfare and occasional coverage by the print publications of the day. A truly bad or stellar report might rate a quick column in Luce's *Time* magazine, or *Newsweek*, and perhaps a mention on the business pages of the *New York Times* or the *Wall Street Journal*. In 1956, as Dwight Eisenhower was running for reelection, the Republican Party platform briefly touted the high levels of employment that his administration had achieved. But there is no comparison between the amount of attention these numbers received then and the amount they receive now.

In fact, the entire process of officially releasing the numbers has become an elaborate exercise. As brilliantly described by *Washington Post* reporter Eli Saslow, the release of the monthly unemployment report on the first Friday of each month at BLS headquarters in Washington has about the same level of security as a meeting at the White House or at the CIA. "In a windowless room in the Labor Department, 40 economists and journalists prepare for the report's official release. They studied the contents of folders labeled: 'Confidential Data: For those with authorization, access and need to know.' They receive the report 30 minutes early under strict supervision. Their computers were connected to a central switch, ensuring they couldn't publish anything until 8:30." In the mid-2000s, concerned that the report might be leaked prematurely, the BLS consulted with the same security experts that advise on how best to guard the codes to the American nuclear arsenal.

Within the BLS, procedures are just as stringent. The staff members responsible for compiling the numbers encrypt their computers and store the data into secure locations every time they get up to use the bathroom. The janitors and custodial workers don't even empty the trash in the week leading up to the release. Only the White House receives an early copy of the report, in a locked and guarded suitcase, Thursday evening, twelve hours before the report is issued to the public the following morning.[10]

The level of security stems directly from the level of scrutiny these numbers now receive. Wall Street traders started to trade on these numbers aggressively by the 1970s, and that made having an inside edge highly lucrative. The current state of lockdown is designed to prevent leaks that someone could take advantage of, as well as to prevent partisan media outlets and political camps from being able to spin the numbers to their own advantage. The same procedures are increasingly copied at other government statistical agencies, from the Department of Agriculture and its monthly crop report, to the BEA and its quarterly GDP release to the Federal Reserve and its monthly meetings announcing interest rate policy. Well into the 1970s, no one even reported on the monthly decisions of the Fed. You knew whether the committee had decided to raise, lower, or maintain rates based on whether they went up, down, or stayed the same in the weeks following the monthly meeting.

The 1990s saw an explosion of outlets that covered "the economy." Much of that was fueled by the Internet boom that saw millions of people begin to day-trade and many millions more drawn to the spectacle of new technology companies such as Yahoo! and eBay. As the mantra of the New Economy became louder, hunger for data grew accordingly. The changing media landscape, with twenty-four-hour-news channels augmented by websites, also demanded more fodder. Regularly released government indicators along with numerous private statistics proved to be perfect pegs for stories. That may seem like a minor development in the greater scheme of things, but in terms of how these numbers became more prominent, it was significant. In the 1960s, few outlets discussed job reports; by the 2000s, hundreds did, and job statistics became a regular point of reference for larger debates about the health of the overall system and where it is headed.

And so indicators have proliferated and our culture fetishizes them. Old indicators have morphed as statisticians and economists struggle to keep pace with societal change. New ones, such as home sales, muscle their way into the national conversation.

Nothing matters more than GDP. Even that is new. In 1991, after years of debate and study, the Bureau of Economic Analysis shifted from gross national product to gross domestic product instead. GDP had always been included in national accounts, but it was seen as having secondary importance. Now we speak of GDP as *the* leading indicator: the Zeus of the statistical pantheon. Public debates about the economy in every country in the world today are framed by whether GDP is growing or contracting and by how much. It is a convenient reference point for news and for politicians. After all, it's one number, rarely more than three digits, and almost anyone can grasp that if that number goes up, it's good, and if it goes down, it's bad. As goes GDP, so goes the nation, whether that nation is the United States or China.

The difference between GDP and GNP is that GDP measures only goods and services produced within the United States, whereas GNP includes all goods and services produced by US nationals regardless of where in the world production occurs. As we discussed in Chapter 4, if Toyota, a Japanese company, operates an auto factory in Tennessee (as it does), that counts as part of GDP, but not of GNP. And if Nike makes shoes in a factory it owns in China (as it does), that counts as part of GNP but not of GDP. The rationale for the official shift to GDP is that it relates more closely to the other indicators of the domestic economy, such as prices (inflation) and employment, as well as to nongovernmental statistics such as home sales and consumer sentiment.

The difference between GNP and GDP for the United States has not been huge. Many American companies, institutions, and individuals invest abroad or own assets abroad, just as many foreign entities invest and own in the United States. Over the past decades, those have tended to balance out. For the United States, therefore, the difference between using one or the other isn't that consequential. Yet there is potentially an issue in using one *rather* than the other. To grasp the overall picture, both are needed. In the past two decades, for instance, the scale of multinational business outside the United States has expanded, which has led to a booming of corporate profits. That fact cannot be reflected in US GDP numbers, even if a company such as Nike is profiting domestically because of it.

And neither figure accounts for the changed way that many companies function. Since the official switch was made, there has been far more sourcing of American manufacturing to other countries, rarely via American companies directly owning manufacturing plants in those countries. That does not show up in GDP, nor does it show up in GNP, since it is production owned neither by US entities within the United States nor by US entities in another country. Not only that, but when those goods get shipped back to the United States to be sold by the company that sourced them, those goods register as imports, which then acts as a drag on GDP because GDP treats imports as a subtraction from the domestic product of the country.

In other countries, the gap between GNP and GDP is already large; some countries receive extensive foreign investment but produce little domestic output. Think of resource-rich nations in Africa, which get billions in investment from mining companies but whose citizens have remained poor (until recently) and without substantial means to invest abroad. GDP is high; GNP, much less so. Even here, however, the problem isn't just the differences between the two numbers. It's that privileging one over the other rather than blending them invariably creates distortions.

Simon Kuznets understood early on that the fetish for simple, round numbers would be a major problem if these indicators started being used for social and political problems that they were never intended to solve. As he put it in his typically complicated prose, "The valuable capacity of the human mind to simplify a complex situation in a compact characterization becomes dangerous when not controlled in terms of definitely stated criteria. With quantitative measurements especially, the definiteness of the result suggests, often misleadingly, a precision and simplicity in the outlines of the object measured. Measurements of national income are subject to this type of illusion, and resulting abuse, especially since they deal with matters that are the center of conflict of opposing social groups where the effectiveness of an argument is often contingent upon oversimplification."[11]

Kuznets may not have been the world's best wordsmith, but he nailed the problem. And he would recognize in today's world the consequences. These numbers have turned into absolute markers of the human condition when they are simply statistical descriptions of specific systems. The issue of national GDP in a world that is ever more international and porous is one of the greatest challenges—one that Kuznets would have recognized and one that we need to look at in more depth.

8

WHERE'S WALDO?

And now we return to the question posed at the beginning of the book: What if you were told that one of the core assumptions that we make about our economic life is wrong? What if that assumption has colored one of the most important bilateral relationships in the world? What if you were told that there is no trade deficit between the United States and China?

"Every once in a while a revolutionary product comes along that changes everything. It's very fortunate if you can work on just one of these in your career . . . Apple's been very fortunate in that it's introduced a few of these." With these humble words, Steve Jobs launched the Apple iPhone to a packed and rapt audience in January 2007. The sleek device did not just catch the imagination: its sales soared to more than ten million in 2008, twenty million in 2009, and nearly forty million in 2010. Within a few short years, the iPhone became ubiquitous, a symbol of cool and cache, not just a phone but a totem of the next technology revolution and a symbol of American innovation and success in the midst of a devastating financial crisis that led many to doubt the viability of the American system. There was just one small problem: the phone was made in China.

On the eve of the 2012 elections in the United States, Americans appeared deeply divided on many major issues. Consensus about health care and how it should be paid for, about debt and the size of deficits, about immigration and its reforms (or lack thereof)—well, good luck if you could find any. Supporters of Mitt Romney kept little company with supporters of Barack Obama, to the point that Republicans and Democrats relied on separate but not very equal polls.

Yet there was at least one thing that most Americans agreed on: China. More specifically, most Americans agreed that China was a threat to the United States, that its currency had been systematically undervalued, and that, as a result, American jobs had been lost and manufacturing imperiled. Throughout his campaign, Mitt Romney vowed that one of his first acts as president would be to label China a currency manipulator, and the Obama administration was only slightly less adamant about the dangers posed. And the primary reason for these concerns was the large amount of US debt held by the Chinese government (in excess of $1 trillion) and the large trade deficit that had been growing every year to reach nearly $300 billion in 2012 and climbing even higher in 2013.[1]

And the iPhone, that icon of innovation, the child of that most American of all innovators and entrepreneurs, Steve Jobs, was adding to that deficit. Every time a new phone rolled off the factory floors of Foxconn Technology (Apple's main contractor in China) in Shenzhen and was shipped to the United States to be unloaded by massive cranes at the Port of Long Beach, it showed up not as a bright spot for America, not as a plus for the ailing US economy, but as an import from China.

The trade deficit with China began widening after 2001, when China joined the World Trade Organization. At first the deficit was seen as a by-product of China's rapid emergence as a low-cost manu-facturer and a burgeoning economic power. In short order, however, the deficit became a symbol of US economic decline and was treated as a symptom of dangerous global imbalances. When the financial crisis of 2008–09 roiled international markets, many pointed directly to the trade deficits between the United States and China as a struc-tural cause.[2] Some warned that continued and deepening trade deficits could lead to the eventual collapse of the US economy, as more and more money left American shores, with only cheap and ultimately dis-posable goods to show for it.

The primary reason that trade deficits are perceived as a liability is that, statistically, they are. They lead to weaker GDP numbers. Every dollar of declared imports is subtracted from the gross domestic prod-uct of the country doing the importing.

And yet, all of the hand-wringing and grim prognostications depend on one simple yet unexamined assumption: that the way we compile these numbers is accurate and reflects something about the relative balance between the country importing a product and the country exporting it. For economists, GDP is a formula: GDP = con-sumption + investments + government spending + trade. If the trade balance is positive, with more exports than imports, then it benefits GDP; if not, it subtracts. That is how the formula was designed in the mid–twentieth century. During a period when the nation-state was more or less a closed economic unit, that may have made some sense. The question is whether it continues to.

Trade deficits have become global symbols of strength and weak-ness, of balance and imbalance. The American public digests negative trade balances with China as proof of decline. European nations are scarcely more sanguine; the Eurozone crisis that plagued those na-tions after 2010 revolved in part around trade and account deficits between southern nations such as Greece and Spain on the one hand and Germany, the manufacturing behemoth, on the other.

But what if the numbers are flawed? What if the assumptions routinely made about the nature of the global economy, of balances between various countries and indeed the balance of the entire system, are wrong for the simple reasons that trade numbers are wrong? If so, we would have to radically rethink many conclusions about the world that are now taken as incontrovertible truths.

Of all the major indicators, trade is perhaps the oldest. Along with collecting grain from harvests, taxing trade was one of the first sources of government income. Ancient empires to modern have tried to gauge the flow of goods in and out of their territory in order to extract revenue. And for just as long, merchants, bankers, and tradespeople have tried to avoid paying those duties. They have smuggled, misreported their cargoes, underreported what they paid for the goods they were selling, and lowballed the amount they planned to sell them for. In seventeenth-century England, King Charles I authorized what may have been the first set of import and export tables. While it's possible to shuffle through thousands of archives around the world and find listings of imports, exports, and customs duties stretching back to the dawn of recorded time, the English effort may have been the first to record exports and imports together. That represented an early recognition that trade is always a matter of flows—flows in and flows out—and that to understand how trade is impacting economic life, the two flows have to be looked at together and not separately.[3]

These English efforts did not lead to a sudden efflorescence of trade statistics. The French followed suit, but the Spanish—even though their colonial empire was at heart a captive trade system that saw Latin America sending silver and gold to Spain—did not. The Americans were precocious. The grievances of the colonists in the mid–eighteenth century focused on trade and duties that the Crown levied, inappropriately and immorally in the eyes of the Americans. So it's not that surprising that one of the earliest demands placed on the US Treasury Department by Congress was to compile detailed trade statistics. It is also not surprising that Alexander Hamilton, the first Treasury Secretary, was one of the champions of that endeavor, given his deep belief in merchants, cities, and industry as the future of America, as opposed to the bucolic agrarian vision of Thomas Jefferson.

Hamilton's *Report on Manufactures* in 1791 made a forceful case that the federal government, formed only recently after the ratification of the Constitution in 1789, should make the promotion of industry one of its primary missions. That meant curbing the competition from abroad—and from England especially—and to do that, the United States would have to place high tariffs on imported manufactured goods. Oddly enough, Hamilton's policies found their fullest expression not in the 1790s, when Hamilton had the most influence (and before his ill-fated and fatal Weehawken duel with Aaron Burr in 1804), but under Thomas Jefferson. Once in office as president, Jefferson defended and implemented numerous policies that he had ideologically opposed in the past, including a near-complete embargo on all imported goods.

Of course, Jefferson's motives weren't to spur domestic manufacturing but instead to harm Great Britain to the advantage of Napoléon's France. Nonetheless, the effect of Jefferson's tariffs after 1807 was to make real much of what Hamilton had desired, and to set the United States on a multidecade course of restrictive taxes on imported manufactured goods. In order to enforce those tariffs, however, someone needed to keep track of imports and exports. After haphazard record keeping in the early days of the nineteenth century, the US government started keeping more rigorous and regular records in the 1820s, and eventually the Census Bureau became responsible for all trade data.[4]

With imports subject to bruising tariffs, which at times in the nineteenth century surpassed 50 percent, the federal government had a strong interest in measuring and calculating trade. The same was true of European countries with far-flung empires. The British and French governments in the nineteenth century were at the center of a lattice of colonies. Even with the free-trade movement gaining momentum in Great Britain, trade with those colonies was designed to benefit the imperial capitals of London and Paris. Tariffs or other forms of economic incentives ensured that the colonies provided raw materials and in return became robust markets for manufactured goods from the imperial power. India, for instance, sent raw cotton to England, whereupon that cotton was transformed on the looms of Manchester into cloth and clothing that then was exported back to India and throughout the empire.

Well into the twentieth century, there was little ambiguity about who made what where. If cotton was planted and reaped in India or Egypt and then sent to the United States or England, it was pretty straightforward to categorize that as an "export to" or an "import from" those countries. It was also relatively uncomplicated to assess what the cotton cost and then write it down. Of course, people tried to fudge and falsify these numbers all the time, to avoid paying higher dues. They often resorted to smuggling to avoid paying any dues. Even so, the process of assigning something to a particular country wasn't that challenging. That was true for finished goods as well. If shoes were made at a plant in Lynn, Massachusetts and then sold abroad, it was simple enough to determine how much they cost and then record them as an "export."

Developments after World War II, and especially after the 1990s, shattered that simplicity. As a result, the neat formula of GDP that assumes a basic accounting of exports minus imports and then a plus or minus for the "economy" began to fray. Categories became more fluid, even as there was no change at all in the basic formula we use to calculate GDP and in the way in which we draw conclusions from these numbers.

Government agencies have also struggled to keep up with the

increased volume of trade. Between 1969 and 1989, the value of US trade increased 1,000 percent, from around $75 billion to nearly $900 billion. Over the next twenty years, between 1989 and 2011, it more than quadrupled to nearly $4 trillion. And with that expansion in dollar amount also came far more goods than ever before.[5] The US Customs Service is the primary source of information about real-time trade flows, which the Census Bureau augments with its own surveys and direct information from Canadian customs officials. By the end of the twentieth century, the Customs Service was providing the Census Bureau with 750,000 documents per month on export and import data, and that was only for shipments above $2,500. The vast amount of small trade in individual goods doesn't even make the cut and is not included in official trade numbers.

Yet the Census Bureau figures tell only one part of the story. To add to the complexity, after 1986 the government began to tabulate not just the trade of goods but also the more amorphous but increasingly important trade of services. That task fell to the Bureau of Economic Analysis. Here, too, there were precursors. Just after World War I, Herbert Hoover's Commerce Department experimented with international accounts that included services. But compared with the trade of goods, services were a small component and hard to measure. By the 1980s, however, services had become an ever-larger part of global trade, especially financial services.

But just what constitutes the trade of services? Say that a branch of an American bank operates in London. Let's call it Goldman Sachs—because everyone likes to use Goldman Sachs as exhibit A for globalized finance, for better and for worse. Goldman's London office arranges a loan to a Swiss business that wants to build a factory in West Africa. That chain of transactions represents "cross-border finance." In the past decades, cross-border finance has become a considerable portion of global economic activity. However, in traditional trade statistics, it is unmeasured and hence statistically speaking, nonexistent.

Recognizing that increasing amounts of global economic activity consist of services rather than things, governments and institutions around the world took steps to measure that activity. In the United States, the Bureau of Economic Analysis started a new series in 1986 that includes not just financial services but also education, travel, data processing, consulting, and insurance, to name a few. In the mid-twentieth century, if Citibank funded a deal in Latin America (as it often did), that wouldn't have shown up as an export in any official statistics—though it might have been noted on one of the many BEA reports on international transactions. Today if Goldman Sachs in New York finances a deal for a Singaporean company to build a Malaysian factory, that will—or at least might—show up as part of the $74 billion in financial services that the United States exported in 2011 alone.

Travel is an even larger "service export." Every time a Londoner buys a ticket on Delta Air Lines to fly to Atlanta, that is an export of travel services, because it's an American company providing a service to a nonresident. Every time a Chinese tour group charters a bus to see the sights in San Francisco or books a block of hotel rooms in Midtown Manhattan, that is counted as a US "export" of services to China. On the flip side, each time an American tour group sees the sites of Angkor Wat or Machu Picchu, that service is counted as an import. Education is another major service export for the United States. Each time a Saudi student enrolls at an American college or a Chinese graduate student completes a PhD at Caltech, those count as an education export. Intellectual property is also a service that can be imported or exported, and so when China Mobile licenses cell phone technology from San Diego–based telecommunications giant Qualcomm, it has—statistically—imported that service from the United States.

The official American trade deficit with China, however, includes only goods, not services. The figures are issued monthly by the Census Bureau, which tracks only goods, and do not integrate the trade in services tracked by the Bureau of Economic Analysis. That matters because while the United States has a substantial goods deficit with China and with the world as a whole, it has run healthy service surpluses. In 2011 the United States "exported" $200 billion more in services than it "imported."

Even with the considerable work done, however, these numbers are hard to obtain, and anyone involved in the compilation recognizes that large swaths of international activity escape measurement.[6] If you read how the BEA measures, say, travel services, the issue becomes even fuzzier. There are no reliable data, in fact, for how much a specific Chinese tour group spends in San Francisco. Instead, to get at that number "the BEA estimates foreign travelers' expenditures in the United States by multiplying the number of foreign travelers by their average travel expenditures."[7] Average expenditures come from airport surveys of travelers and tour groups. This is not rocket science.

But it is increasingly difficult to determine where something is made and how much of its value can be assigned to any one country. The entire statistical edifice of modern trade numbers is built on a simple foundation: each country is a unit. That unit is at heart a closed system. Some foreign ingredients come in (imports), and some domestic ones go out (exports), but we still treat a national economy as a closed-loop unit that is then impacted by trade.

How true is that today? Yes, most people are born, live, and die in one country. In fact, even with the recent expansion of travel and trade, most people still live their days near where they were born. But while people are by and large rooted physically, their economic activity, not so much.

It's not just that our economic lives are becoming more and more defined by services: by travel, education, lives lived online. It's that even our goods can no longer be so easily assigned to one geography. Our trade statistics say that they can, and we then draw profound conclusions with obvious implications for policy and identity. But more than almost any other metric, our trade statistics haven't been able to keep pace with global change. As a result, we are faced with a stark conclusion: we are making decisions based on a world that does not, in fact, exist.

The most glaring example is the trade balance between the United States and China. If the number is more or less correct, then indeed, there is an imbalance. But the number is not correct. In fact, it is possible that if trade numbers measured more accurately how products are made, there would be no trade deficit with China. Think about that: a statistic so core to current global thinking about who is up and who is down, where there is strength and weakness, that statistic is, for the most part, wrong.

It is wrong for the simple reason that the way we determine the origin of goods and the way we measure the amorphous world of services has not evolved quickly enough. That is due not to the limitations of the people who compile these numbers or to the agencies responsible. In fact, everyone responsible for compiling the numbers recognizes these issues. But these agencies are government bureaucracies with mandates and budgetary constraints. They can move only so fast and so far. The evolution of the global economy knows no such constraints.

Contemporary trade figures act as if each product had *one* country of origin, and that the declared value of that product goes to that country. Clearly, even if that was the case in the mid–twentieth century (and before), it no longer is. Continuing to measure trade the same way does has one clear advantage: it allows us to compare trade patterns over the past decades. The value of that should not be ignored. But we shouldn't treat these numbers as the final word on trade, and yet for the most part, we do.

The postwar General Agreement on Tariffs and Trade (GATT) attempted to create uniform standards around the world for how trade was measured and conducted. The precursor to the World

Trade Organization, GATT was to international trade what the United Nations is to international diplomacy or the World Health Organization is to disease and nutrition. It was an idealistic endeavor meant to counter the beggar-thy-neighbor tendencies of countries and the age-old attempts of nations to use trade as both a weapon and an asset in the never-ending struggle for supremacy relative to other nations.

In the spirit of voluntary cooperation, GATT did not demand any one set of standards but rather left each country to determine how it would count exports and imports. Naturally, that led to problems, as some governments were more willing than others to measure in good faith. After all, if imports were counted against national economic output, and if GDP in the second half of the twentieth century became a symbol of national strength, some countries might well want to undercount imports and overcount exports in order to boost their reported GDP figures.

By the 1980s, it was clear that allowing each country to measure trade as it wished wasn't working. A more clearly defined set of rules and standards was needed. As the World Trade Organization came into being in the late 1980s, "rules of origin" were developed that standardized how countries determined where things are made, how to declare goods on customs forms, and then how to integrate that information into national indicators.

So far so good, except that just as these standardized rules came into being, the global supply chain shifted dramatically. One of the hallmarks of the "globalization" of the 1990s was the degree to which the production of manufactured goods began to spread out geographically as companies picked the lowest-cost goods from the lowest-cost countries. Until the advent of accurate software that could track supply chains and transportation networks and ports around the world, that was more complicated and often costly. So auto plants in the Detroit area relied on parts suppliers in Michigan, Pennsylvania, Ohio, and Indiana but rarely parts suppliers in other countries. In the 1990s, that changed.

But rules of origin didn't change as much and still have not. Instead, a product is assigned to the country where that product has undergone its final and "substantial transformation." Under those rules, if a car is assembled in the United States with plastic from Malaysia and parts from China, it counts nonetheless as "Made in America" because that is where that Ford Explorer acquired its final form.

The flip side, however, is the iPhone. It acquires its "substantial transformation" in China and, hence, shows up as a US import from China. In fact, every iPhone that was sold in the United States in 2010 added $229 to the US-China trade deficit, and each iPad added $275, at least according to the calculations of three economists who looked at the issue.[8] That means that by 2013, Apple's sales of the iPhone in the United States had added as much as $6 billion to the trade deficit with China *every year*, and that number is getting larger each year. The iPhone, by itself—and it is just one of thousands of products that American companies have made in China.

The same story could be told, of course, for other countries and their supply chains. Samsung, the Korean conglomerate that makes so many of today's flat-screen television monitors and smart phones, also sources its manufacturing to China, and because of the ubiquitous and standardized rules of origin, its production shows up as imports from China. So does equipment sourced by Japanese companies to China, and by German companies, and so on. No matter how strong a domestic manufacturing base a country has—whether Germany and its touted industrial companies, or Japan, or the United States—everyone sources everywhere, and global production is the norm.

The iPhone 4 sold for an average retail price of $549 in the United States in 2010. However, anyone who has bought a smart phone recently knows that if you buy the phone with a new carrier contract, that carrier gives you a hefty rebate. Sign up with Verizon for two years, and the $549 iPhone becomes a $199 phone to the customer. But for trade purposes, none of that exists. What does exist is the declared imported value (which is, of course, not the same as the price you pay when you walk into an Apple store). And that imported value, registered on a customs form and then processed by the Census Bureau, takes no account of just where and how the various elements of the phone came to be.

It's not as if anyone in the Census Bureau is fooled by that declaration. To the contrary. Everyone involved in the assembly and compilation of these numbers that I spoke with understands the limitations of official trade figures and country-of-origin rules. Dave Dickerson, a twenty-nine-year veteran of the Census Bureau and now deputy chief of the Foreign Trade Division, knows full well the various issues about how the components and intellectual properties embedded in a product might give a rather different picture of "country of origin." But the statistics have been kept for decades. To preserve the usefulness of a long-term set of data that can be compared over time, the Census Bureau, Dickerson explained to me, "uses the agreed-on international standard definition for country of origin as the last country where any significant transformation has taken place. Even with the methodologies and changes in globalization, we felt that it was still valuable to maintain the reporting standards that we had been using."

Over at the Bureau of Economic Analysis, its longtime director, Steve Landefeld, has been concerned about these questions for years. He has chaired working groups to examine the problem and candidly admits that one of the greatest challenges in his world today is "trying to track the value-add of every component of each good." The problem, however, is that a customs declaration is pretty straightforward. Breaking down the components of every single manufactured good is not. As Landefeld explained, "That would require all firms to track each of their products and do so in a consistent classification system across every industry and then report that data in a consistent fashion across industries."

Yet for the iPhone, iPad, and iPod alone, it took groups of skilled economists many hours of careful work to break down who made what where and how much money is attached to each component. Even then, the various groups that have done that analysis do not agree about how to break down one of these devices and assign value to different points along the supply chain. That is because this entire question of value-add—of how to identify which company and then which country received what portion of the final price—is much like a Russian doll. Each time you think you've found the last one, you can go just a bit deeper, and out pops another.

The parts of an iPhone come from multiple different suppliers. Apple, like many high-touch technology companies, goes to considerable lengths to avoid publicizing which companies provide components for its devices. It does so because it wants to control information, prevent competitors from knowing how much it pays for which components, and also keep its own suppliers in the dark so that they have a more challenging time bidding up prices. Some of that secrecy is a direct result of the mercurial nature of Steve Jobs, who was both paranoid and brilliant, a magical showman and a nasty partner. But Apple is not much different than its competitors in this regard, and ascribing too much to the personality of Jobs would be a mistake.

More than a dozen companies supply parts and components for an iPhone or iPad, and intrepid researchers and analysts have identified at least five countries where those parts originate. There is Germany, home to Infineon Technologies, which makes the camera module; Japan's Toshiba, manufacturer of the touch screen; and in the United States, Broadcom, which produces the Bluetooth chips that make it possible to use wireless headsets and hands-free communication in cars.

Where analysts differ is in figuring just how much of the final price tag goes to which country. What no one disputes is that the largest slice does *not* go to China. Instead, the largest slice goes to America. That's because the creation of the intellectual property—the design and the marketing of these devices—takes place at Apple's headquarters in Cupertino, California. Those are services, but more intangible in their way than those services tracked each month by the BEA. The BEA's 2013 official revision of GDP to include the costs of developing intellectual property as part of national income was momentous, but it did not change how trade statistics are currently compiled.

The value of an iPhone, along with thousands of high-tech products, lies not in the materials for the hardware or the bodies that physically assemble the devices. The value is the invention. The innovative mind and master marketing of Steve Jobs, or of his lieutenants Jonathan Ives and his successor as CEO, Tim Cook, led teams that conceived these devices, designed them, patented them, created the packaging, and infused the brand. That intellectual property is the key ingredient, along with the marketing, and that is the largest share of the value-add of each and every iPhone.

That leaves China, the supposed country of origin, with a paltry piece of the pie. It's estimated that as little as $10 of every iPhone or iPad actually ends up in the domestic Chinese economy in the form of wages to those hundreds of thousands of workers at those Foxconn plants—the plants that received such intense and negative scrutiny after a wave of worker suicides in 2010 and 2011. Add to the mix the fact that Foxconn itself isn't even a Chinese company—or at least not a mainland Chinese company. No, it is a contract manufacturer incorporated in Taiwan.

And following the Russian doll metaphor, even the value ascribed to those other countries may not be quite right. When the German company Infineon "makes" the camera module, it has already developed the intellectual property and done the marketing and some of the design, but the actual physical modules may then be produced in factories outside of Germany—perhaps in China, perhaps not. The American company Broadcom doesn't make those Bluetooth chipsets, it designs them. Some other company, likely not in the United States, makes them. So to truly capture the value-add of the Apple ecosystem, analysts would need to go one step further still and slice up the components. And even that might not be enough. Those plastic cases that so many millions buy to house their phones—where did the plastic come from? Malaysia or Indonesia? And what factory made those, and according to which design? Is anything really made anywhere?

These issues are no secret to those immersed in the world of trade and statistics. The Asian Development Bank estimated in 2010 that if the official figures could incorporate a more accurate measure of value-add, the balance of trade for the iPhone alone would add up to a paltry $73 million for China instead of the billions that showed up. More recently, several prominent international groups, including the World Trade Organization, the Organization for Economic Cooperation and Development, and various branches of the Federal Reserve, have tackled the larger question of what the trade balance would be if every product were broken down to each component and each component was then assigned to a specific country.

The World Trade Organization and the OECD have been particularly outspoken about how needed this new approach is and how dramatically it would shift our understanding of global trade. As a recent joint study put it succinctly and bluntly: "With the globalization of production, there is a growing awareness that conventional trade statistics may give a misleading perspective of the importance of trade to economic growth and income, and that what you see is not what you get." There is, however, a vast difference between identifying this problem and doing something about it. The two organizations working in concert have been at the forefront and have started to develop a database to measure "trade in value-added." This would do for tens of thousands of products what has already been partly done for the iPhone.

Preliminary results from this project were unveiled in mid-2012. Assessing trade between the United States and China, the new database showed that the deficit between the two countries would be 26 percent smaller. But while these efforts do a better job of capturing the supply chain and including services as part of the mix, they are still guesstimates for the simple reason that no one has the resources, people, or systems in place to measure every component of every single manufactured product in the world and then add in services in a manner that can be accurately attached to one country or the other. In that sense, this is an issue that everyone may recognize but for which no one has a viable solution.[9]

Shifting to a new set of indicators that capture the value-add of multiple countries is no small task. It would require thousands of extra people tasked with examining global supply chains and individual products. It would require government officials at customs bureaus worldwide to design new surveys and new declaration forms that would, in turn, mandate that exporters and importers declare not the value of goods according to the standards set by the World Trade Organization in the late twentieth century but according to twenty-first-century formulas that have yet to be determined.

It is complicated enough to get nearly two hundred countries to agree on how they will value exports and imports and how that is reported on customs forms. That itself took decades, and it was a necessary step in creating the World Trade Organization and liberalizing global trade. Unless there are uniform standards for how goods are valued and counted, there can't be uniform standards for the tariffs and duties that are the foundation for free-trade pacts and today's globalized supply chains. Love that reality or hate it, it defines the loose global system that characterizes our world today. And yet, as we now know, the numbers that give shape to that world are not clear or even accurate.

In order to make them more accurate, however, these initial

efforts at measuring value-add will have to be intensified exponentially. Companies will have to change the way they report what they have made. Think of nutrition labels that break down a bag of potato chips or a quart of milk, with calories, fat content, protein, and carbohydrates. That is equivalent to what we'd need for each manufactured good, except with categories that included geography and percentage of costs incurred in each different country in the supply chain. We have only partially done that for the much-studied Apple ecosystem. We are nowhere near doing that for the rest of the supply chain.

The result is that there is a wide gap between the world we *think* we are living in and the world in which we live. A not-inconsiderable portion of American identity over the past decade has revolved around the notion that China's rise as a low-cost manufacturing power has undermined the US economy, lowered wages, and contributed to the struggles of the American working class. There's little question that US workers, especially in manufacturing, have seen lower wages and rising unemployment. But if the trade numbers overstate—perhaps dramatically—the balance between China and the United States, then the reasons for that change have been wrongly identified. And that means that the belief that if China would simply revalue its currency or if the United States took a harder stance against Chinese imports and against China's filching of intellectual property, then the domestic US economy would improve could also be wrong. If China isn't the primary cause of these problems, then addressing these issues with punitive China policies won't solve them.

The same argument could be applied to myriad other examples around the world. Japan, for instance, may be benefiting from China's emergence much more than the numbers show. On the flip side, China may be benefiting much less from its vaunted export sector, a fact that the Chinese government has already recognized. That is why Beijing is determined to build a viable domestic consumer economy.

In addition, since 2010, there has been a gradual revival of US manufacturing, but without a sizable increase in manufacturing employment or wages. That has exposed what the trade statistics have obscured: technology, robotics, and the global supply chain have done more to erode wages for workers and eliminate positions than anything else.

Yet our understanding of the world is still framed by our leading indicators. Those indicators define the economy, and what they say becomes the answer to the simple question "Are we doing well?" Trade figures are hardly the only issue. Each one of the leading indicators is fraught with similar tensions.

Without question, we need to have a consistent set of numbers over the course of time. It was the very absence of those numbers that made the Great Depression so challenging. The inability of the Hoover administration and Congress to know what was going on, to be able to compare their present to the past, and to assess whether any of their policies were working was a critical liability. It was a liability for central bankers worldwide, and for the governments. In 1930s Great Britain, the Labor government of Ramsay MacDonald and the Conservative government of Stanley Baldwin flew equally blind; hence, the intensive efforts of Keynes to construct a system of national accounts and metrics.

The statistical framework created in those years and after the war provided for the first time consistent and reliable insight into the workings of the economy. That then made it possible to look at how different policies and different inputs affected these systems over time. Of course, it was over a very short period of time, even taking into account the efforts of statisticians to use these new methods to assemble data from years before. GDP accounts, for instance, were retroactively created for the years before the 1940s, and similar efforts were made to produce inflation and employment statistics for decades well before those indicators even existed.

In recent years, all statistical agencies have expended considerable effort revising how they collect and analyze data. Internationally, there have been repeated updates of the standards of national accounts. In the United States, the Bureau of Economic Analysis has been particularly active in searching for new metrics. Steve Landefeld has headed the agency since 1995, and he is nothing if not acutely aware of both the strengths and weaknesses of our data and indicators. And he has been vocal, in congressional testimony, interviews, conferences, and papers, about the need for our numbers to evolve as the world evolves. For instance, he has urged that more time be spent trying to determine the ultimate domicile of a company, which has implications for whose GDP is benefiting and to what extent. IBM is one of the largest companies in the world, and its corporate headquarters are in Armonk, New York. But it now has more people working for it in India (approximately 110,000) than it does in the United States (around 100,000).

Landefeld has also been adamant about the need for better tracking of value-add. The 2013 revisions to GDP that now include intellectual property will go a ways to providing a better read on an economy that is driven increasingly by ideas and not the sheer making of physical goods. But as right as he is, the BEA is a tiny government agency, with a budget of barely more than $100 million. For the past few years, Landefeld has submitted a proposed budget to Congress of about $10 million in additional funding to develop new data series that would begin to address the many challenges of a changing world. But in a Washington that can spend twice the annual budget of the BEA on one fighter jet but has not passed an actual budget in years, you can guess the odds of getting any money, even if it would provide a clearer sense of the world we are actually living in and how to spend the trillions that are allocated based in part on what those numbers say.

Landefeld has a long list of pressing and compelling questions: How should we account for the expanding and ever more complicated world of services? More of our economic lives are spent online, but how do we measure the economic impact? And how should we assess income distribution more accurately? We know from tax receipts and a plethora of anecdotal information that there is widening income and asset inequality, but we don't really measure all income—from tax rebates, to health care subsidies, to food stamps—nor do we really measure all costs. And what about the vast and significant regional variations that get blended into one smooth number when we compile GDP? Does one simple number obscure too much when a state such as Oklahoma is booming because of oil and natural gas and services, while a state such as Florida is bottoming out because of too much dependence on tourism and real estate?

Over at the Bureau of Labor Statistics, Deputy Commissioner John Galvin has a similar wish list and a similar recognition of what the numbers can and cannot tell us. Galvin abides by an admirable code of public service, seeing the role of the BLS in both pragmatic and moral terms. As he told me, "As long-ago commissioner Carroll Wright said, our job is to be the fearless purveyors of the truth about the economy and about working conditions." The statistical programs of the BLS, Wright concluded, are "instruments of democratic accountability." After all, without numbers that all agree are not susceptible to political manipulation, anyone in public or private life can say just about anything and make just about any statement without the trouble of facts.

Indeed, in 2007 the Argentine government removed the staff of the statistical agency responsible for reporting inflation because the administration didn't like the numbers it was reporting. While nothing comparable has happened in the United States, it's routine for people to believe that the official numbers are "cooked" for political purposes, and these voices are not just a paranoid fringe. In October 2012 Jack Welch, the cantankerous former CEO of General Electric, reacted to news that US employment was stronger than anticipated by claiming that the numbers were a political sham engineered by the Obama administration to improve its prospects on Election Day.

Such an accusation must have shocked Galvin, especially given the measures the bureau takes to avoid any politicization or leakage of any information. Leaks are not high on his list of issues. He is much more concerned about keeping up with a fluid workforce and finding better ways to count discouraged workers and self-employed people, and better ways to gauge costs of goods. In each of these areas, he and the agency staff have identified gaps in how we count and what we count. But the public debate centers almost entirely on the simple, headline numbers and not the wealth of information that comes with them. "Most people," says Galvin, "don't have the time to read through and digest an entire unemployment report," so they seize on the headline number.

The simplicity and regularity of the number are catnip to the media and to politicians. It is easy to report, easy to understand, and easy to digest. That doesn't mean that it is meant to bear the weight that it does. The number is an average that obscures substantial variations between the unemployment rate of college-educated white women (which has stayed consistently below 4 percent even in the worst of the 2008–09 recession) and African-American males with a high school degree or less (which has remained stuck in the double digits and has approached 20 percent in the past years). The "unemployment rate" also obscures the variations from region to region, which can be immense. In 2010, for instance, the unemployment rate in Nevada soared to 14 percent, yet in Nebraska, it barely touched 5 percent. In Florida, the rate peaked at 11.4 percent; in Iowa, it was barely 6 percent.

One round number doesn't tell you any of this. It doesn't tell you that there is, in essence, no national employment rate that can be applied in cookie-cutter fashion to each part of the country or to every person. Levels of education matter greatly, as does where you live. The fiction of a meaningful national number distorts both the public search for answers and people's sense of what is happening. Based on what the numbers actually said, it would have been irrational for a college-educated woman living in Omaha to have any reasonable concern about losing her job in 2010, yet the national discussion of an employment crisis—one which in Las Vegas and swaths of central California was considerably worse than the headline numbers of 8 percent to 9 percent—would have caused substantial and unnecessary anxiety. And the need to tell ourselves one story, in turn, distorts the political debate and the economic policies proposed, because we have not cultivated the tools to break down these numbers and address those regional, educational, and, yes, racial implications.

We have, therefore, multiple challenges. The indicators—through no particular fault of anyone in particular—have not kept up with the changing world. As these numbers have become more deeply embedded in our culture as guides to how we are doing, we rely on a few big averages that can never be accurate pictures of complicated systems for the very reason that they are too simple and that they are averages. And we have neither the will nor the resources to invent or refine our current indicators enough to integrate all of these changes.

Finally, there is the critical lack of international data. The story of the iPhone and statistics shows just how lacking we are in information that is not generated by national governments or organizations. Other than the intermittent efforts of academics and organizations such as the OECD that occasionally dedicate time and energy to new frameworks, we are left with national numbers that are then used clumsily to give a picture of global realities.

So what do we do? That is the question we all must face. Thankfully, some are facing it, in universities, in businesses, in international agencies, and, to the degree that time and budgets allow, in government. These efforts have yielded, as all human endeavors do, mixed results so far, and none more mixed—or more compelling—than the attempts of an obscure country in the middle of the mountains to jettison GDP in favor of something else. That would have been intriguing enough, but it became even more so when that small experiment became a cause célèbre for Nobel Prize economists, for the president of France, and for an amorphous group of advocates worldwide—all of whom decided that the future lay not with better methods for current indicators but instead with an entirely new framework invented by the most unlikely of economic innovators: the king of Bhutan.

9

GROSS NATIONAL HAPPINESS

In 1972, at the young age of sixteen, Jigme Singye Wangchuck became the fourth king of the mountain country of Bhutan. Nestled in the high Himalayas, Bhutan is a landlocked country about the size of Switzerland (or a bit larger than Maryland). It sits north of India, south of China, and on the way to nowhere. The British left India in 1947, but two centuries of their rule still marked the region, and the once and future king had been sent away to English schools in Darjeeling, India, and then in London. He came back to Bhutan as a teen to learn about his future kingdom, which at the time had fewer than a half million people. Most lived in remote fertile valleys in the south. In the vertiginous and steep mountains of the north, the few inhabitants tended herds of sheep and yak. Isolated geographically and culturally—television was banned until 1999—Bhutan was an unlikely venue for a bold experiment.

The new monarch had seen just enough of the world to know that success globally was increasingly being defined by gross national product. And yet, the teenage king had a bold idea: instead of gauging the health of a country by how much stuff it produced, measure it by something else. Instead of emphasizing production and output, emphasize quality of life. And in the world of 1972, that was radical.

We've seen what most countries did: The United Nations had created a framework of national accounts that all countries were expected to use. The United States and the Soviet Union were engaged in a global contest to see whose system could gain the most adherents, and the two primary metrics were how many warheads and allies each had and how much and at what rate its economy was expanding. The royal family of Bhutan was not immune to these pressures. How your country ranked in the global pecking order became a primary pursuit of governments everywhere. The ubiquity of statistics created its own logic: governments looked for legitimacy domestically and internationally by pointing to their material achievements: more food grown, more houses built, more finished goods produced, more wealth created.

Instead of jumping on that bandwagon, King Jigme Singye Wanchuck, the inheritor of the Dragon Throne of Bhutan, jumped off. There is no evidence that the young king was aware of Robert Kennedy's searing 1968 critique of gross national product. He would have been barely twelve years old when Kennedy delivered that speech in Kansas. But somehow, one of the first decisions made by this new king of Bhutan was to replace GNP with something else: happiness. From then on, the goal for Bhutan was not material prosperity but collective well-being. Bhutan, the king believed, would be a successful society only if most of its people deemed themselves happy.

As the Bhutanese started to formulate ways to measure national happiness, material needs weren't ignored. But they were understood to be only one part of a multifaceted mix, along with spiritual contentment, family life, culture, and traditions.

Bhutan was the only country in the world to explicitly reject the national account framework adopted almost everywhere else. Even the Soviets and Communist China measured output according to these international standards, though the Soviets also kept track of what they called "gross social product" (which was the total stated—emphasis on *stated*—output of all their industrial activity). Bhutan, however, said no. In elevating happiness as the primary metric, it was both carving a new path and honoring its own traditions. The first recorded legal code of Bhutan dates from the eighteenth century. Formulated by a ruler who was also a Buddhist *Rinpoche*, or high-ranking monk, the code stated, "If the government cannot create happiness for its people, there is no purpose for the government to exist."[1] In Bhutanese lore, the current dynasty of kings descends directly from the monks who established the kingdom centuries ago, and there is a belief that each new king is, in fact, an embodiment of the spirit of the previous one. In that sense, the sixteen-year-old who ascended the throne in 1972 was far older than his earthly years. Or so many Bhutanese believed.

It was one thing for the king to pronounce that Bhutan would use a different measuring stick; it was another thing to create the measures. That process is still not complete, but over the subsequent decades, Bhutan did design an actual index and built a staff to conduct surveys, collect data, analyze it, and produce an official statistic. They drew on the expertise not just of statistical agencies and the United Nations but also on academics who had concluded that the way national economies were being reduced to gross national (or domestic) product distorts the way we answer vital questions.

Stemming from centuries of Buddhist teachings and an isolated culture steeped in that legacy, the methodology of the gross national happiness index bears more resemblance to New Age teachings than it does to the statistical mantras of the Bureau of Economic Analysis. Given the degree to which New Age teachings have been shaped by Buddhism, that shouldn't come as a surprise. Many of the Bhutanese charged with developing the framework for the index trained as Buddhist monks, including Karma Ura, who combined an Oxford University education and Buddhist discipline to head the Centre for Bhutan Studies. The index defines happiness as "the creation of enabling conditions where people are able to pursue well-being in sustainable ways." Happiness for the Bhutanese is as much a collective phenomenon as an individual one, and true happiness is said to encompass "spiritual, material, physical, and social needs."

It's hard to overemphasize how far this framework departs from the economic metrics developed in Great Britain and the United States in the middle of the twentieth century. For most of the individuals who invented and championed the leading indicators, it was inconceivable that softer, subjective factors such as happiness and well-being would be part of the mix. Yes, there were glimmerings of dissent, from Simon Kuznets advocating that unpaid housework ought to be included in national income to George Katona arguing for a strong link between subjective confidence and consumer behavior. But even those efforts were in the context of a belief that "the economy" was grounded in the material world and bounded by the decisions of rational actors. In that world, spiritual and social needs were at best invisible and at worst irrelevant.

In rejecting the then-accepted framework, tiny Bhutan started a movement that has since become global. While every country in the world except for Bhutan now uses GDP as the primary proxy for economic success, most countries in the world have begun to reconsider whether using GDP as *the* primary indicator is such a good thing. Even before Bhutan, of course, we had Robert Kennedy's critique, and that, in turn, was only one eloquent expression of a larger cultural questioning. The 1960s and 1970s in the Western world witnessed a wholesale reexamination of core tenets and values, including the intense emphasis on economies as engines meant to maximize material output. Most of that questioning, however, was a cultural phenomenon that barely changed established institutions. At the same time that Arthur Burns was battling inflation and Washington policy makers were trying unsuccessfully to find the right mix of economic policies, popular culture was turning on, tuning in, and dropping out. There may have been a link between training and inflation, but if so, no one could see it.

And yet, in academia, some economists started to reconsider the major indicators and wonder if something vital wasn't being left out of a framework that said the more GDP, the better, the less inflation, the better. Some began to ask whether established economic systems were creating more happiness or less, and whether the pressures of modern society to maximize output were, in fact, satisfying the needs and wants of citizens.

Even here, there were powerful precedents. In the nineteenth century, Western philosophers such as Jeremy Bentham and John Stuart Mill, tapping into similar memes as their Buddhist doppelgängers, championed happiness of the greatest number of people as a key goal of society. By the twentieth century, as the mania for measurement took hold, so did the desire to quantify the softer sides of life, from family satisfaction, to sex, to subjective well-being. In the 1960s, the Gallup Organization started polling people about health and general life satisfaction. But until the 1970s, these efforts were ad hoc. The primary focus internationally remained on including all countries in the same statistical regime and standardizing indicators around the world.[2]

By making happiness the national priority, Bhutan broke with that trend. As small as it is, it is nonetheless a nation, represented in the United Nations and accorded the respect of a sovereign entity. In that sense, its embrace of happiness as opposed to output was more significant than millions of people around the world living their lives geared toward personal fulfillment or a few private institutions arguing that GDP was not the way to measure societal success. Bhutan was the first—and, to date, the only—sovereign nation that has rejected the core metric of modern economies. Though no government has yet joined Bhutan in this exclusive club, in the years since 1972, more and more questions have been raised about what we are measuring and how we measure it.

Bhutan itself has spent the past decades refining what it means to measure gross national happiness. In one key respect, the Bhutanese have come to a different understanding of happiness than many in the West. As Ura explains, "Gross national happiness in Bhutan is distinct from the Western literature on happiness . . . it is not focused on subjective well-being to the exclusion of other dimensions." Or as Bhutan's prime minister explained in 2008, "We distinguish between the happiness in GNH from the fleeting, pleasurable feel-good moods so often associated with that term. We know that true happiness cannot exist while others suffer, and comes only from serving others, living in harmony with nature, and realizing our innate wisdom and the true and brilliant nature of our own minds."[3]

It is almost impossible to imagine a public figure in the Western world using this language. And yet, in the past few years, the underlying ideas have crept into the once-unassailable halls of Western culture and pushed themselves to the center. It's as if there are two parallel tracks: one continues and deepens the work of Ethelbert Stewart and the twentieth-century children of Keynes and Kuznets, and seeks precise calculations of the components of an iPhone or the definition of *employment*; the other looks at society as a holistic mix of the spiritual, material, collective, and personal. The chairman of the Federal Reserve and government economists might never speak in such terms explicitly, and would likely react with a mixture of perplexity and derision if asked to revise current metrics along Bhutanese lines. Yet that is precisely what Nicolas Sarkozy did as president of France between 2007 and 2012.

Sarkozy struck no one as a man of contemplation. If anything, he was described by friends and adversaries alike as a whirlwind of id determined to haul the French economy into the twenty-first century by making it more ruthless and competitive. Fair enough. Yet in his few years as president, he convened a high-level commission with the explicit mandate to rethink GDP as the measure of all measures and replace it with something akin to what that sixteen-year-old Bhutanese king had set in motion in 1972.[4]

"I hold a firm belief," Sarkozy explained, "[that] we will not change our behavior unless we change the ways we measure our economic performance . . . Our statistics and accounts reflect our aspirations, the values that we assign things. They are inseparable from our vision of the world and the economy . . . Treating these as objective data, as if they are external to us, beyond question or dispute, is undoubtedly reassuring and comfortable, but it's dangerous . . . That is how we begin to create a gulf of incomprehension between the expert certain in his knowledge and the citizen whose experience of life is completely out of synch with the story told by the data." And in that spirit and with that conviction, in 2008 Sarkozy asked Nobel Prize–winning economists Joseph Stiglitz and Amartya Sen, along with French-born economist Jean-Paul Fitoussi, to chair a commission to revamp and potentially replace GDP.

It's hard to know for sure what motivated Sarkozy. If any country in the Western world might be expected to question the unequivocally material basis of the leading indicators, it would have been France. There has long been a French strain of skepticism, if not outright hostility, to the overweening emphasis on money and growth that characterizes American society and much of modern capitalism. Those metrics are notoriously bad at capturing much of what French culture has held dear: a carefully prepared family meal adds much less to national income than a Peugeot made in a factory by a robot, yet few French would admit to valuing the latter more than the former. And while the French are no more comfortable with the Buddhist language of Bhutan than any other European country or any developed

Anglo-Saxon nation, they are perhaps more likely to focus on values such as beauty and a life well lived as key components of society's well-being.

Culture is fuzzy, easy to caricature, amenable to oversimplifications, and often used as a catchall when all other explanations fail. But even with those caveats, culture does matter, and it shapes our metrics. The leading indicators are the products of a particular phase of Western history. Even more, they are largely the result of what American and English economists and policy makers believed to be important in the middle of the twentieth century. They saw economies as industrial systems that obeyed scientific laws. They invented statistics to measure material output. And if economies became unstable and unbalanced, it was because the wrong tools were being used or because the data and the statistics were faulty.

As the United States became more powerful at midcentury, it essentially exported that way of viewing an economy to every part of the world. Yes, the Soviet bloc and Communist countries championed an alternate vision that rested on collective wealth rather than individual affluence. But even the Soviets attempted to prove that their system was superior based on material output. Much of the Cold War consisted of each side saying that it produced more stuff and better stuff, from better weapons to better cars.

A few countries and voices objected. In India, Prime Minister Jawaharlal Nehru spoke for a different set of principles and metrics that could guide national success. He also rejected the good versus evil mantra of the Cold War and articulated a vision of peaceful coexistence that stemmed from ancient Buddhist and Hindu precepts. But these efforts, whether noble, self-interested, or both, couldn't stem the global rush to choose sides in the Cold War and use the economic statistics promulgated by the United States and the United Nations.

The choice of those statistics created a particular pathway that emphasized industrialization and "modernization." In the process, other societal values got pushed to the side or relegated to private life rather than public policy. Many would say that the relentless emphasis on output, employment, prices, commerce, trade, industrialization, and consumption created untold affluence worldwide by the early twenty-first century, and they would be right. Economic indicators allowed societies to steer a course toward greater productivity and more material goods for more people as surely as earlier scientific innovations had ameliorated disease and alleviated hunger.

The fact that the Western societies succeeded so spectacularly does not, however, mean that they satisfied all human needs. Their very success, in fact, generated a new wave of self-examination and allowed people to say, Hold on! What are these numbers not measuring? What key aspects of human life get short shrift, and is ever-greater output actually generating more contentment? Do modern economies, in fact, produce the greatest good for the greatest number? And are the way that economies are measured and structured likely to maintain the same level of prosperity in the future as they have in the past?

Those questions led the Bhutanese to opt out, and they also spurred Sarkozy's challenges. But whereas Bhutan at first could draw only on a cultural legacy, by the late 2000s, Sarkozy could tap decades of academic research on happiness and subjective well-being.

Many societies, the United States included, describe happiness as a core social value. The American Declaration of Independence famously defended the right of citizens to "life, liberty, and the pursuit of happiness." Then as now, however, defining happiness is devilishly difficult. We all know that our subjective experience of life frames how we view reality. Economic statistics take little account of those subjective factors. In part, that's because the economy isn't a person. It doesn't have feelings or expectations. It is a statistical construct. At the same time, we all know that human emotions, beliefs, fears, hopes, and expectations shape individual behavior and have profound implications for commercial activity. How, then, to translate that into usable numbers? That question led to a series of efforts to create an objective measurement for subjective experiences.

You might ask why even bother. If happiness, contentment, and well-being are all subjective states, then coming up with a number to represent them would seem a fool's errand. If you create a 1 to 10 scale and ask people to state their happiness number, one person's 6 could be another person's 9. Traditional economists take as a given that people can lie to themselves and others about what they feel. But they cannot hide their economic actions, and actions don't lie. That means you can measure actions and their real-world consequences with some degree of certainty, but not well-being.

At some point in the past thirty years, however, scholars interested in human behavior and economics began to craft ways to measure and quantify subjective experiences. Very much in the spirit of George Katona, Daniel Kahneman (who would earn a Nobel Prize for his work in 2002), Edward Diener, Alan Krueger (who later became President Obama's chairman of the Council of Economic Advisers), and William Nordhaus all began to investigate how best to come up with standardized measures of well-being. Given their training as economists and social scientists, they sought to match behavior and observations with numbers and formulas. They sought, in short, to create metrics for happiness that were equivalent to the statistics for inflation, employment, and GDP.

They did so because they believed that GDP was both mismeasuring society and creating incentives that might not lead to a better world. Even a government uninterested in increasing the well-being of citizens would be troubled by the thought that economic indicators were hampering efforts to become stronger and more competitive in a competitive world. As Stiglitz, Sen, and Fitoussi explained in unveiling the results of the work commissioned by Sarkozy, "In an increasingly performance-oriented society, metrics matter. What we measure affects what we do. If we have the wrong metrics, we will strive for the wrong things. In the quest to increase GDP, we may end with a society in which the citizens are worse off."

The most obvious example of the way that GDP can distort and even be at odds with well-being is a factory that produces a lot of products but also pollutes the local environment. Its production shows up as a positive. Then, if the local community doesn't like the rivers running green and people getting sick, the expenses incurred to fix those problems also show up as a positive for GDP. Even higher health care costs show up as a positive for national output. But the costs of the factory's activities for the surrounding inhabitants, in terms of disabled workers, a ravaged environment, and broken communities—those never show up as negatives in our indicators.

Of course, many factories do no harm to their local environment and indeed create community, jobs, schools, stores, and homes. GDP, however, is neutral about those effects. It makes no distinction between constructive and destructive outputs and no judgment about which enhance and which don't. And it takes no position and says nothing about whether people are more or less content and secure as a result of that output.

The limitations of GDP along with the incentives it creates for countries to maximize output led to happiness research and the quest for new metrics. Those moves were supported by voices starting in the 1970s that questioned the materialism of the Western world and asked whether the undeniable ability of modern industrial societies to produce ample amounts of goods was actually leading to the happiness that had been promised. Or to put it another way, having striven for centuries to generate the affluence that the United States and Europe produced from the mid–twentieth century on, people assumed that securing not just the bare necessities but also a good deal of luxury would lead to widespread contentment that, if short of utopia, was pretty close indeed. Yet that was not what people felt in the 1970s.

Instead, they agonized over inflation, wondered what it all meant, and questioned whether Western societies had gone off the proverbial rails.[5]

Into that maelstrom, happiness researchers moved to the fore. By the end of the twentieth century, they were able to draw on an ever-larger body of surveys and studies. It wasn't just Gallup that had been asking questions about happiness. Multiple countries had undertaken their own assessments of happiness and well-being. Starting in the 1990s, the World Values Survey brought together European and American scholars to conduct surveys in more than a hundred countries about people's experience, beliefs, and happiness. The Pew Foundation funded its own set of global surveys. Surveys are the raw material for indicators, and by the late 1990s, there was enough data to begin to answer the question of how much happiness modern economies were generating.

This booming field of happiness research, however, did not simply expand the principles articulated by Bhutan. In fact, Bhutan's definition of happiness is different from the definition of happiness seized on by Western scholars. Given the Western belief in the sanctity of the individual, happiness is often understood as a personal value. For Bhutan, happiness is equally a collective phenomenon and not just an answer to the question "Am I happy?" The goal of Bhutan's happiness index isn't for each individual to say "I'm happy." It's for the collective to conclude that it has a workable formula for a sustainable and equitable present and future. In that sense, Bhutan is not nearly as subjective but instead defines what every individual should have—enough land, shelter, food, and community—and whether or not society makes that possible.

In fact, though Bhutan is now routinely described as one of the happiest nations in the world, its version of happiness would likely fall flat in the United States and much of Europe. The country is still quite threadbare, with minimal modern luxuries and very low income.

Yet basic needs are met and spiritual ones valued. Says Karma Ura, "The true forms of wealth are a ravishing environment, vibrant health, strong communal relationships and meaning in life and freedom to have free time."[6] It sounds wonderful, but it comes at the cost of renouncing growth and output, which are at the core of the modern economic systems of the rest of the world. Renouncing that is acceptable in Bhutan, but much less so in countries that have defined their economies as perpetual growth machines.

The happiness research outside of Bhutan essentially replaces "output" with "happiness." If the goal of modern economies is to produce more stuff for the greater good, the goal for Western happiness indicators is to produce more happiness for more individuals. It is, in short, happiness maximization.

Nowhere is that more evident than in the far-ranging work of what are called "national time accounts." Two of the leading figures here are Alan Krueger, a Princeton University economics professor who briefly served as chairman of Obama's Council of Economic Advisers, and Daniel Kahneman, whose lifelong interest in how behavior shapes economics segued nicely with developing these accounts. National time accounts are based on a large ongoing survey of people who fill out a meticulous diary of how they spend their time and whether their activities are pleasant or unpleasant. With this data in hand, Krueger and his colleagues created a "U-index," shorthand for "unpleasantness index." The U-index is a numerical representation of how much time people spend doing things they find unpleasant, such as commuting to work in heavy traffic, doing the laundry, shopping for food, or taking care of young children. (People may say in retrospect that parenting young kids was the most rewarding and meaningful part of their lives, but asked at the time, many are, well, miserable about it.)

Part of the rationale for a U-index might come as a surprise. Happiness surveys across cultures have shown in the past few decades that most people think they're happy. Percentages vary by society. In some cultures such as the United States, people think that they should be happy and so tend to say they are. In other cultures, such as Armenia, happiness isn't seen as a primary social good, and so people are somewhat less likely to emphasize it. Why a greater percentage of people in Latin America tell Gallup that they are happy, and why Colombia and Honduras are among the happiest of them all, is a cultural mystery. Nonetheless, happiness surveys have shown worldwide that people tend to look on the bright side of life. As Krueger et al put it, "[T]he predominant emotional state for the majority of people during most of the time is positive, so any episode when a negative feeling is the most intense emotion is a significant occurrence."[7]

The problem with time studies, which its innovators recognize but have no easy remedy for, is that things that people find unpleasant may also be things that they must do in order to have a good life. Household chores are a drag. Who likes to scrub the bathroom or vacuum? (Though apparently some people do claim to enjoy doing the laundry and perfecting the art of folding.) Not doing household chores, however, is a much greater drag. Taken to an extreme, you get the life of one of those hoarders whose horror stories make for lurid reality shows but whose actual lives are not models to emulate. Commuting may be unpleasant, but not having a job that provides an income to offset that unpleasantness is substantially worse. Time accounts provide lots of microinformation, but they can miss the bigger picture. They rectify some of the deficiencies of GDP, but they have their own blind spots.

As new indicators such the U-index evolve, it becomes clear that while they don't suffer from the same limitations as the old indicators, they have their own nonetheless. The proliferation of happiness metrics shows that each new methodology comes with its own issues. Happiness is so difficult to define that each of the major happiness indicators and surveys—from Gallup, to Pew, to the World Value

Survey, to the rather extensive and impressive work now being done by the Legatum Institute in London—comes up with a different ranking of nations. Colombians score high on individual happiness but not on happiness as defined by Legatum, which adds in collective wealth, opportunities for entrepreneurship, education, personal freedom, and health. Different methods, different numbers. Different numbers, different conclusions.

The Sarkozy commission seemed to understand the conundrum that all metrics will be in some way flawed. It called for a "dashboard" approach that takes as a given that "well-being is multidimensional." The commission also integrated another key challenge: the tendency of people and societies to define happiness in relative terms, or what might be called the "keeping up with the Joneses" paradox. Behavioral psychologists such as Kahneman and Amos Twersky have demonstrated time and again that a fair number of people will feel better having less as long as they believe they have more than neighbors and colleagues. They establish a "reference point," which then becomes a baseline. To wit, many would rather earn $50,000 a year knowing that everyone else around them earns $40,000 than earn $75,000 knowing that most others are earning $100,000. Keynes noted this phenomenon as well, and most of us have encountered it in our own lives without the benefit of having economists point it out.[8]

Stiglitz in particular, after a long career at the World Bank and in academia, has been especially concerned about the ways in which inequality isn't part of the national equation of success insofar as GDP is indifferent to it. So is the often-used statistic "per capita income," which simply divides GDP by the population of a country. In the United States, Warren Buffett has the same per capita income as his secretary (the one he famously mentioned as paying a higher tax rate than he), but that only creates an illusion of income equality that we know doesn't exist. There are established global measures of income inequality within societies; the wonkiest and most frequently used (but not without its own issues) is called the Gini coefficient. But Stiglitz urged that any new set of national measures should include a statistical consideration of income inequality, and, indeed, one of the pilot programs of the Bureau of Economic Analysis is to find a way to do just that.

All of these efforts dance around the core challenge of what to do with a set of entrenched indicators that frame the way almost every country in the world—Bhutan notwithstanding—assesses its economic success and the viability of its national economic policies. You can't just say that because GDP fails to measure private goods and much else that it should therefore be discarded in favor of other statistics that might rectify those issues but then create others. The dashboard approach, which could also be called a smorgasbord approach, addresses the shortcomings but at the cost of throwing in variable after variable. A statistic that says everything matters isn't appreciably more helpful than one that says only certain things matter.

Recognizing the limitations of current indicators is a start. We do an increasingly good job of measuring commercial transactions, from home sales to retail purchases, from sales online, to sales at big box stores, to sales at independent outlets; from prices paid by companies for their goods, to prices paid by families in Minneapolis for theirs. And the same can be said of many other countries. The Germans have ample data about income in Bavaria and output in Hamburg, and the Chinese—though many question the integrity of official data—keep better track of energy consumption, pollution levels, and life expectancy than was ever the case under Mao or the emperors that preceded him.

We do not yet, however, do a good job of incorporating happiness and satisfaction, and as we saw with trade numbers and employment figures, our established indicators have significant limitations—at least in how they are used if not in how they are compiled. For instance, there is nothing wrong per se with the unemployment figure, provided you know that the definition of employment is a construct, not a counting exercise. As we discussed earlier, to be unemployed, according to the Bureau of Labor Statistics, you have to be in the workforce. To be in the workforce, you have to have a job or be looking for a job. To be looking for a job, you have to answer when surveyed that you have *actively* sought employment at some point in the past four weeks. If you haven't, you aren't actually unemployed. You are a *discouraged* worker, are *marginally attached to the workforce*, and are not counted as part of said workforce. And if you haven't been looking for a year, you're not, statistically speaking, even discouraged. You simply, statistically speaking, don't exist. You do, of course, actually exist (though that is a whole other topic), but not in the statistical universe of employment data.

The result of such methods is that it is possible, and not just theoretically, for the unemployment rate to drop not because more jobs were created or more people were hired but simply because more people gave up looking for work and dropped out of the workforce. That is, in fact, what happened in the United States and swaths of Europe after 2009, though in America, there were also real job gains in 2010 and after. Nonetheless, the unemployment rate, which receives so much public scrutiny, went down in part not because the economic system was creating so many new jobs but because it was failing to do just that. To be fair, the BLS keeps multiple unemployment statistics and different unemployment rates, including ones that include underemployed, marginally attached, and part-time workers, but there is only one headline number. That is what the BLS points to in its monthly release; that is what the media pick up; and the other numbers are at best footnotes.

Jobs are particularly important because there is ample evidence— from surveys, at least—that increasing employment adds more to social contentment and stability than increasing income and output. That is true even for lower-paying jobs, though an economy that creates mostly low-paid and unskilled jobs is not a good foundation for a competitive system in the twenty-first century. That is a challenge for the United States today. Still, while GDP going from 2 percent to 2.5 percent might increase the happiness of a political party promising growth, unemployment dropping .5 percent, especially if that reflects jobs created rather than discouraged workers departing the workforce, adds to collective well-being.[9] On that basis, economic policies that maximize employment serve collective happiness more than ones that maximize output. More cynically, policies that showed widespread employment would serve politicians seeking reelection more than good GDP growth. True, some jobs pay so little that they create stress without meeting material needs. That too needs to be addressed statistically, and it is not by current unemployment figures that do not distinguish between well-paid jobs and poorly paid ones.

Happiness research has added a vital dimension to economics and led to a new set of statistics. Those have in no way supplanted the established indicators; happiness indices are still second-class citizens in statistics land. But the investigation into what makes individuals happy and what adds to collective well-being has done more than expose the failings of traditional numbers and traditional economic policies. It has also highlighted how the world has changed in the past fifty years and how much the present marks a departure from most of the past.

When the indicators were invented, the vast arc of human history had been scarcity. People had clawed and scraped for enough food, enough shelter, enough health. Economic theory assumes scarcity, hence there was no concept of unemployment until the late nineteenth century. You couldn't truly be unemployed if you needed to eat, unless you were willing to starve. Until the twentieth century, it was possible to have too few workers to meet society's demand for manufactured goods; in almost every part of the world, land was abundant, and labor was scarce. With the population explosion of the twentieth century and technologies that allowed land to produce far more food with far fewer farmers, that equation shifted to scarce land and abundant labor.

It also shifted from a constant state of want and all the attendant insecurities to a state of abundance. That reality was perfectly captured for midcentury America by Harvard social scientist, sometime *Fortune* writer, advisor to John F. Kennedy, and occasional public servant John Kenneth Galbraith. In 1958 Galbraith wrote a book with the provocative title *The Affluent Society*. It was a huge seller and touched a cultural nerve, and it remains startlingly relevant.

Galbraith's central point was that the classical economics that had been framed by a world of scarcity no longer made sense in postwar America. Instead, that world was (and is) characterized by abundance, not want; by a surfeit of things, not a dearth. The modern American system was geared not just to meet basic needs but to generate new ones. The economic indicators only reinforced that tendency. Instead of celebrating an affluence that would have been the envy of almost any person alive before 1900, twentieth-century Americans were trapped in a loop of never-ending consumption, never satisfied, endlessly fueled by marketing and capitalism, to the point where private needs and wants trumped the common good.

Subsequent scholars called this the "hedonic treadmill." Americans and increasingly Europeans and then citizens of successive countries throughout the world have been caught in an endless cycle of never having enough. Those feelings were fueled by a system that demanded more consumption in order to produce growth, as determined by GDP and by other numbers (home sales, car sales, advertising spending) and in the end by how much each person could satisfy his or her wants.

Galbraith warned that this process would in the end impoverish the common good, endanger the supply of natural resources, and lead to a law of diminishing returns. Soon enough, that process acquired a name, the Easterlin paradox, named after USC professor Richard Easterlin. In 1974 Easterlin argued *pace* Galbraith that at some point, the acquisition of more goods ceases to increase happiness. As more surveys were conducted and analyzed, it appeared that richer people and richer nations were not necessarily happier than poorer ones and that the increased acquisition of material goods or even greater social stability does not make people happier.

But while Easterlin identified a variant of "Money can't buy you love," his observation was only partly true. To begin with, subsequent research has indicated that money does lead to happiness when you start from a very low base. It's just that at some point, it buys less and less of it. In addition, much like reference points, people develop happiness set points. One day you have a 1,500-square-foot home and a quarter of an acre, and you feel, hey, this is pretty good. Then you get a better job, or a raise, have a few kids, and buy a 2,500-square-foot home and think, hey, this is pretty good. But then you plateau, or worse, lose that job and eventually sell that house—if you can—and downsize to a 2,000-square-foot home in a less compelling neighborhood. Your set point in that equation was the high point, not where you began. And given that no society generates endlessly increasing set points for everyone, eventually more income produces smaller increases in happiness and larger amounts of disappointment.[10]

Or so many studies suggest. The evidence is far from clear-cut, and decades of surveys have only muddied the picture. There's been considerable debate over the link between material well-being and happiness. Not surprisingly, these debates tend to break on ideological lines. Those who champion the free market as an unalloyed good reject the Easterlin paradox, and they can point to ample survey evidence to support that view. Those who decry the hedonic treadmill and the relentless consumerism of contemporary capitalism point to the Easterlin paradox as proof that something is awry in our current system. Environmental degradation and climate change have added additional weight to those arguments. Not only does the hedonic treadmill cease to generate happiness once basic needs are taken care of, but it begins to undermine the sustainability of these systems for future generations.[11]

Or so the argument goes. These issues are a matter of belief and values, not clear evidence. What is clear is that our static sets of indicators fail to address these fundamental questions. Nor were they designed to in the first place. As we saw, men like Irving Fisher, Arthur Burns, and Richard Stone, not to mention the orthodoxy of mid-twentieth century economics, purposely excluded multiple categories of activity and experience in the belief that those were just too fuzzy and subjective to measure and too amorphous to address with specific economic policies. In that sense, the leading indicators are not wrong at all. They measure precisely what they were designed to measure.

Yet the pressure after the 1970s to address other crucial aspects of economic and material life has continued to grow. Bhutan provided one example, and happiness research and subjective well-being studies followed suit. None of those, however, represented a systematic formula that could substitute for GDP and the other indicators. Yes, Bhutan by the late 1990s had developed a coherent happiness index, but so much of what Bhutan valued was steeped in its own culture of agriculture, farming, mountains, and Buddhism that its index wasn't one that others were likely to adopt.

Then there is the United Nations. The critique of the UN is that it is an ineffective assemblage of nations, with every voice heard ad infinitum. The result is that little gets done, everything is by committee, and final products are years behind and have all edges smoothed. "We stand for world peace"—yes, and who does not? But those very qualities made the UN an ideal place to develop a new index to measure societal success, and while its recent endeavors haven't supplanted the leading indicators, they have provided a compelling alternative.

The Human Development index debuted in 1990, under the aegis of the United Nations Development Program. It was a child with many fathers, but Amartya Sen was clearly one of the driving forces.

Born in West Bengal in 1933, Sen was shaped by elite education, a cosmopolitan family, decades at Cambridge and the University of London, and rough-and-tumble exposure to some of the worst violence and famine of the India partition in 1947. No one can fully say what turns someone into who they are, but the net effect for Sen was a lifelong dedication to understanding the causes of poverty, inequality, development, and the mysterious interplay between individual behavior and the larger society.

His academic career took him to the leading universities of the world, with professorships at Trinity College, Cambridge, at MIT, and at Harvard. In 1998 he was awarded the Nobel Prize, in no small measure for his work on the Human Development index. "Human beings," he wrote, "are the real end of all activities, and development must be centered in enhancing their achievements, freedoms, and capabilities. It is the lives they lead that are of intrinsic importance, not the commodities or income that they happen to possess. Income and wealth do have . . . importance but they do not constitute a direct measure of the living standard itself."[12]

The goal of the Human Development Index is to craft a more comprehensive metric than GDP. Sen argued that such an index would also be more useful, especially for developing nations seeking the right policy mix to end poverty, staunch disease, and educate the illiterate. In short, Sen contended that measuring GDP didn't do developing nations much good, except to highlight the gap between what they produced and what the developed world produced. The new index would give countries throughout the world better tools. Emerging countries in the second half of the twentieth century had dutifully set up statistical offices to measure the same variables that were measured in the United States, because that was what they were expected to do. But GDP and unemployment numbers didn't make much sense for Bangladesh in the 1970s, or for Peru, Senegal, and dozens of other states. The Human Development Index was tailored to the needs and makeups of developing nations. It also attempted to grapple with one of the glaring weaknesses of GDP, income inequality, and the huge disparities in quality of life within developed nations as well as developing ones.

Reflecting these concerns, the Human Development Index quantifies life expectancy, infant mortality, literacy, education levels, health, diet, differences between genders, between urban and rural, and between rich and poor, to name just a few of the questions it addresses. Each category is scored and assigned a number on a scale, and those scores are blended into one final number. The result in an international ranking according to "human development" rather than GDP, although such rankings often harmonize with GDP. Wealthier nations tend to score higher, with the United States, Germany, Japan, and Scandinavian countries routinely in the top ten and sub-Saharan African nations routinely at the bottom. The goal of the index was not, however, the ranking but rather what the many sub-indices said about development, about what was working and what was not, and which countries were dealing more effectively or less so with crucial problems.

From its debut in 1990, the index has been refined and revised. It has also been used as the basis for the *Human Development Report*, which every two or three years summarizes the latest data and introduces a new theme. In 1999 the topic was globalization; in 2002 it was democracy; in 2011 the focus was on development and sustainability, particularly the impact of emerging nations on climate and the environment. The 2013 report addressed the "Rise of the South." In addition to the omnibus global reports, there have been hundreds of regional and country-specific reports using the index as a starting point for a larger discussion of challenges faced, met and still unresolved.

These efforts have their own limitations. As Eva Jespersen, the deputy director of the Human Development Report Office, explicitly cautioned when I spoke with her, because the index is compiled by the UN, it relies entirely on information supplied by member nations.

If a country wants to misrepresent its levels of literacy, there is no way for the Human Development Index or the staff responsible for it to correct for that. Of course, this isn't a problem particular to this index or these reports. Countries can lie about GDP and employment whenever they want; certainly the Soviet Union boosted statistics during the Cold War to make it appear that it was economically stronger. More recently, many have voiced suspicions of China's official data, convinced that because the central government establishes economic targets in its five-year plans and then rewards local authorities who meet those targets, there are huge incentives for said officials to report that they have met or exceeded those targets whether or not they have.

The difference with China is that Beijing seems to understand that false numbers may look good, but they do the country no good. That doesn't mean that data emerging from official China is without fault, but the central government takes seriously the risks inherent in wrong or politicized statistics. If you are responsible for a plane reaching its destination safely and on time, it does no good and immense harm if the pilot says that there's enough fuel and good weather to make it on time when neither is true. In 2011 the Beijing government suspended its national reporting of housing prices after a prolonged period during which the housing index chronically failed to reflect how sharply prices had been going up. The reason? Each time the central government mandated a slowdown in real estate speculation, regional officials duly reported that prices had decreased. Critics claimed that Beijing ended the data set because it could no longer hide the fact that prices were surging, and officials wanted to stop drawing attention to their futile efforts to conceal it. That was one way to interpret the moves. Taken in conjunction with an overall effort to gauge its own economy correctly and manage growth, however, it seems more the case that the decision reflected a government that wants to know what is going on, not one that is more interested in optics and Potemkin villages.

Because the Human Development Index relies on the integrity of national reporting, it is vulnerable to governments that care more about how statistics make them look than in accurately depicting their societies. That doesn't make the HDI invalid; it simply indicates that it has its own problems, as all major indexes do. In the decades since the first report, not only have development measures proliferated but so have other indices and indicators, ranging from climate and sustainability (the Global Reporting Initiative), to energy consumption, to studies from the World Bank and the IMF. In 1960 the World Bank began to create its own "World Development Indicators," and these alone now cover more than two hundred countries in more than three hundred categories.

With happiness research, subjective well-being indexes, the United Nations Human Development Index, and enhancements to established numbers such as inflation, trade, and employment, the early twenty-first century has witnessed indicator proliferation. While a forest of indicators doesn't create the same risks as too many weapons, as far as our ability to gauge the world around us, more is less. We are left globally with a set of leading indicators that were crystallized in the mid–twentieth century and exported to every country in the world. New metrics, many of which were created by trade groups such as purchasing managers associations (who provide one of the leading measures of industrial activity) or Realtors (who generate some of the best statistics on the housing market) have entered the canon. Other metrics are the products of international and multinational institutions that recognized the weaknesses of the statistical framework and have tried to reform it, add to it, and broaden it.

There's another group, however, that has charted an entirely new course. The Human Development Index may look at different variables than national income accounts, but it is still a product of national measures that take the states as the starting point and the end point and rely on data gathered by governments. The happiness studies look at individuals rather than industries or economic variables, but they do so primarily with the aim of determining how well a nation is meeting the needs of citizens.

Yet there is another type of innovation occurring, care of individuals who are measuring "the economy" in novel and eclectic ways. They build on the efforts of the past, but they aren't beholden to them. They understand the importance of states, but they don't necessarily see them as the most important unit. And they recognize above all that the world seen through the lens of current indicators is not *the world*. It is a world: a construct built on numbers derived from surveys and statistical formulas.

The immensely popular 1999 movie *The Matrix* began with a simple premise. The world we think of as real and substantial is just a program designed by others to keep us from recognizing reality as it actually is. The appeal—in addition to vertiginous special effects, cool leather costumes, and a New Agey lingo of spiritual empowerment backed up by kick-ass martial arts training—was that many people feel that the world they experience daily departs in small and large ways from the truth society accepts and defines. They feel that the world around them has the qualities of shadows on a cave wall, reflecting moments of reality but missing the mark and hiding some deeper truth.

Our suite of leading indicators is also a construct, a statistical matrix. They create a virtual world defined by a set of numbers that may reflect aspects of reality but also obscure and distort. Hence, the example of how trade statistics fail to account for the way an iPhone or iPad is actually made. The degree to which unemployment is a statistical construct rather than a state of being (you're not statistically unemployed if you are out of work yet have given up looking because there are no jobs for you) isn't far behind.

No, our leading indicators do not construct an entirely fictional world, and only the lunatic fringe and the paranoid fringe are convinced that government maintains indicators as mechanisms of control. Our indicators are good-faith efforts to understand and respond to complicated issues of how we manage our economies. However, they are limited in their ability to guide us, and that is getting worse, not better.

The hero of *The Matrix*, Neo, was the one who saw through the construct and could then grapple with the multiple other realities that existed simultaneously. In a less dramatic fashion, many people have recognized that "the economy" delineated by our economic indicators is only one of many stories. It paints only one of several possible pictures of what is unfolding domestically and internationally. The economic innovators of today are striving to reframe how we understand the world to allow us to see things that our current indicators do not reveal. These efforts, and these Neos, are where we turn last.

10

THE AVATARS

In 1749 the king of Sweden authorized the compilation and publication of the *Tabellverket*, which was essentially a census of his realm—a realm that had only a century before fielded the most powerful army in northern Europe but which was then in a slow decline. The king hoped that with a better understanding of the trends in his kingdom, he might find a way to reverse the slow, not altogether traumatic but still undesired march into the twilight of continental influence.

The Swedes never did regain their imperial glory, but they managed to craft a highly effective society that serves the needs of its eight million people about as well as anywhere on earth. Because of the *Tabellverket*, Sweden claims to be the first country to collect official government statistics on births, deaths, marriages, and the like. Two hundred fifty years after the king commissioned the census, a quirky epidemiologist named Hans Rosling, then teaching his rather provincial yet alert and passionate students at Uppsala University, began to rethink the way statistics are used. He recognized that the eyes of his students grew heavy with boredom when statistics appeared; they had long become desensitized to numbers presented blandly and inertly as static markers intended to mean something.

Rosling was also struck, as many professors are, by what his students did not know and by what they assumed they did. He was particularly surprised by the widely held assumption that there is a huge divide between the developed world and the developing world, between the industrialized and affluent nations of Europe (and especially Sweden) and the industrializing and still relatively poor countries of Africa, Asia, and Latin America. That assumption pervades almost all discussions about the state of the world, and as Rosling knew from his statistical work, it is fundamentally wrong. How then to communicate that knowledge to his students using numbers without their attention waning and the lesson being lost?

First, there was the fact that the dramatic divide between the developed and developing worlds no longer exists. "There is no such thing as 'we' and 'they' with a gap in between," Dr. Rosling is fond of saying. "The majority of people are living in the middle."[1] But simply saying that and then pointing to income, life expectancy, health, education, and output statistics isn't quite enough. Most people do not relate to or retain columns of numbers, however much those numbers reflect something that they care about deeply. Statistics can be cold and dull. Rosling knew that if numbers were to make an impact on students who were not inclined to see the world statistically, he had to present the data differently.

The result was a rather simple yet stunning invention: a new software system that allowed Rosling (and, indeed, anyone else) to present statistics not as inert numbers, in tables or graphs, but as fluid and dynamic. Few people may think statistically, but most can relate to things visually. It's hard to describe in words the visceral effect of Rosling's technique, which is the point. He developed a visual system that put those numbers in motion along a graph, using shapes that morph and move. On a computer or tablet running Rosling's program, circles representing health statistics of multiple countries, or wealth, or employment rates, or indeed any set of variables, start pulsing and migrating, like proverbial Mexican jumping beans. The effect is quirky, funny, captivating, and unlike any presentation of data anyone has ever seen. You have to see it to appreciate it fully, and that's the point. His dynamic program makes the numbers kinetic. It transforms them into shapes, and those shapes move in ways that make intuitive sense.[2]

A lifelong statistics aficionado, Rosling had found an exciting way to communicate the importance of numbers viscerally. That matters greatly, he believes, because "statistics tell us whether the things we think and believe are actually true." The way they are traditionally communicated, however, prevents most of us from using statistics as the powerful tool that they are. Hence, he developed his program to show the data in ways that people enjoy and understand. His students were thrilled, but when he presented the software in a scintillating talk at a TED (Technology, Entertainment, and Design) conference in 2006, he became something of an international celebrity—the modest Swedish academician who managed to make statistics "come alive" and managed to make them cool.

Since then, Rosling has been an apostle of visual statistics and free data. Though Google invested in his software for its Motion Chart app, everything Rosling does he offers for free on his Gapminder website. He draws on an eclectic mix of data from agencies and government worldwide in order to create a composite picture of how the world has evolved over the past few centuries. For him, the leading indicators are only one of many different inputs. For a more complete picture of the world, he draws on health statistics, education data, energy figures, demographics, and multiple others data points. Scanning the globe, Rosling assembles a statistical smorgasbord, translates it into compelling, fluid graphics, and helps people understand the world they inhabit.

Inevitably, Rosling has become aware of the limitations of our current data maps. One major issue is that the minute you change how you collect information or how you analyze it, you potentially sacrifice the greatest benefit of today's indicators: they may not have been around for very long, but there is now just enough history to provide useful comparisons and to allow people to gauge how things have evolved either for the better or the worse. As he told me, "The problem of changing statistics is that you lose the ability to compare across time. The longer the time series, the harder it is to change it, but you want to be able to compare. How do you replace GDP? And if you do, you lose the past sixty years of relevance. This has been a problem for centuries—take the Spanish silver trade. Anything you measure will become increasingly irrelevant over time."

Even if we accept the limitations of our current suite of statistics, even if we invent new ones and significantly refine old ones, we are left with the age-old challenge of how to implement those without inadvertently creating a new set of problems. If we were to engage in a radical revision of the way we kept GDP, for instance, how would governments, the United Nations, the World Bank, tens of thousands of nongovernmental organizations, the global media, and billions of people be able to assess what those numbers meant without being able to compare them to points in the past? Statistics are meaningless unless they exist in some context. One reason why the indicators have become more central and potent over time is that the longer they have been kept, the easier it is to find useful patterns and points of reference. GDP growth of 4 percent could be good, bad, or mediocre until you know that the average over the past twenty years is 3 percent.

As Rosling recognizes, "No country has a debate on statistics. It is never a political issue; too boring." And yet in the past few years, the nature of statistics and how they frame our lives has started to receive more attention. Rosling's simple yet radical insight was to recognize how ready and willing most of us are to use statistics to understand the world but are brought up short by the arcane methods and presentation. Those methods may be vital for statisticians, but for statistics to be used more constructively to shape policies and inform debates, they need to be expressed and presented accessibly.

The desire for just that may explain the small cottage industry of books on statistics that has developed of late. One of the unexpected darlings of the 2012 election cycle in the United States was the former baseball statistician turned political poll analyst Nate Silver, whose *FiveThirtyEight* blog on the *New York Times* website drew almost a quarter of the online traffic to the paper's website in the second half of the year. That worked out to as many as six million page views each day turning to Silver for his analysis of the myriad polls shaping the 2012 election.

Poring over polling data is in itself hardly evidence of some mania for statistics, but what set Silver apart was the perception that he had turned the fuzzy art of political prognostication into something more akin to a science. His dispassionate use of polls and subjecting them in toto to statistical analysis proved remarkably accurate, which in turn seemed to justify those methods as tools that can be widely applied to answer critical societal questions.

Silver himself is modest about when statistics can help predict outcomes and when they cannot. The media demand for black-and-white clarity—which itself reflects a very human and widely shared demand for such clarity—is at odds with what we can actually know about the future. And as Silver has been at pains to demonstrate, it is at odds with what statistics can in fact tell us. Economic forecasts based on our leading indicators are even trickier. Unlike polling data, which is a fairly narrow universe, the inputs into any economic system are numerous and getting more so. Even more important, the numbers are constantly revised and rerevised.[3]

As we've seen, the first Friday of each month, the BLS releases unemployment figures. The unemployment rate and the number of new jobs get attention, but each month the previous months' numbers are also revised, and those revisions get less attention even though they can fluctuate by hundreds of thousands of jobs. The same happens with GDP figures, which go through three initial estimates and then are subject to further revisions years later as the various data get integrated into the national accounts and then assessed by the Bureau of Economic Analysis.

But economic forecasters tend to focus on the initial data, not the multiple revisions, and the needs of the media, the financial industry, and many companies dictate a level of certainty from these initial releases that the numbers simply cannot support. If you are the chief economist for the company Caterpillar, for instance, there is considerable pressure to make a conclusive statement about GDP, construction spending, and the housing market, not just in the United States but also in China, Latin America, and throughout the world. These conclusions then help determine how much inventory to stock and how much to spend on raw materials for expected production. Governments do much the same and try to match future GDP assumptions with tax revenues to come up with budget projections.

As Silver highlights, however, the best we can hope for is a spectrum of probabilities, not a clear and shiny path forward. As our debates about the economy have become ever more central, so too has the misuse of statistics. All too often, indicators are treated as absolutes rather than as provisional and limited. That is the tendency for the senior policy makers who framed the 2009 stimulus bill, and it's true for journalists and pundits who pronounce with certainty future outcomes based on what the indicators say. Far better would be a degree of modesty and an air of humility about the inherent complexity of these systems and the degree to which future outcomes cannot be determined based on a limited set of data points in the past. The indicators suggest various probable outcomes, but that is all.

Rosling's work highlights how indicators can best be used: as ways to understand what has happened and what is emerging; as descriptions, not prescriptions. Rosling calls on data to illuminate the past and highlight trends in the present, not to predict the unpredictable. The problems of our leading indicators are less what they say and don't and more how we use and misuse them. GDP was created to measure national output, not collective well-being, not whether a particular nation is succeeding or failing in meeting collective needs, wants, and hopes. Unemployment was invented as a snapshot of labor conditions in a time of duress, to give workers and unions more leverage in negotiations with management and to give policy makers in government more clarity about the effects of various measures to bolster employment. It was not meant as an indicator of the quality of life; that is one reason why there is no effort in the unemployment numbers to distinguish between a job that pays less than a living wage and one that allows for a comfortable retirement.

And, yes, there are other problems with the indicators as they currently exist, as we saw with the way the trade statistics have not kept pace with the globalization of supply chains. The primus inter pares of our indicators is GDP. As we've seen, it is now enshrined as an all-encompassing indicator of national success, even though it came into prominence in the United States only in 1991, when the Bureau of Economic Analysis made it, rather than gross national product, the primary gauge. Yet, neither GNP nor GDP have kept pace with technological change. Through no fault of statisticians, the economic systems that GDP and national accounts measure have evolved more rapidly than the methods used to measure them.

One of the most perceptive critics of contemporary GDP is a Massachusetts Institute of Technology professor named Erik Brynjolfsson. A self-described "econ nerd," Brynjolfsson has been part of a group at MIT asking hard questions about many of our core assumptions about macroeconomics.

For instance, Brynjolfsson and his colleague Andrew McAfee have looked intensively into the reasons for the breakdown in the traditional correlation between economic growth (as measured by GDP) and job creation. As we saw with the 2009 stimulus bill, the concept of an output gap and a natural relation between GDP and employment framed the size of the bill and the expectations behind it. Using a combination of intensive quantitative work and careful analysis, Brynjolfsson and McAfee explained why the traditional model has collapsed, and they did so with a level of simplicity that even Occam would admire.

The leaps in technology since the 1990s, ranging from robotics to software, have led to significant gains in measured productivity but not significant gains in either wages or employment. That trend is, in their view, in its infancy, simply because technological change and the relentless corporate hunger for technology-enhanced efficiencies are driving a wedge between the assumed connections between economic growth, employment, and average income. Had Obama's economic team in 2009 taken this analysis into greater account, they might have been that much more careful about making the assumptions they did.

The role of technology in enhancing profits and growth while undermining traditional forms of employment is only one way that GDP is missing tectonic shifts. Brynjolfsson, along with his postdoctoral colleague Joo Hee Oh, has also been investigating the way in which GDP hasn't quite kept pace with technology. This is not for lack of awareness or attention at the Bureau of Economic Analysis. The BEA has a budget and staff determined by Congress and has always relied on primary data assembled elsewhere. It can do only so much only so quickly unless public and political priorities were to change dramatically. The last time Congress took an urgent interest in crafting official statistics to meet the demands of the present was during the Great Depression; there's no indication such urgency is building again or will anytime soon.

In the meantime, researchers and academics such as Brynjolfsson perform a vital role in drawing attention to the gaps in our understanding. Starting in the 1990s, economies everywhere have been transformed by the revolution in information technologies. While the utopian ardor of the 1990s faded quickly, the degree to which these technologies have become ever more central to most aspects of social, political, and corporate life is hard to overstate. Yet these changes have only been captured by traditional measures of economic activity with a lag if at all. In the 1990s, as we saw earlier, the only impact that the personal computer was having on measured output of the economy was whatever hardware a company such as Dell computers produced domestically. The use of the Internet, the ease of data analysis and processing, the speed of communications—while still minimal compared with the 2010s—did not meaningfully register in productivity statistics and GDP.

That attracted the interest of researchers such as Brynjolfsson, but more important at the time, it attracted the notice of Alan Greenspan. Brynjolfsson's work is in many respects the next generation of a process Greenspan started when he urged those Fed economists to consider how information technology was enhancing productivity. The 2000s have seen an efflorescence of the next wave of these technologies, ranging from Web-based tools to games to social networking applications that have been adopted by hundreds of millions of people in a short amount of time. It's no surprise that official statistics, which are the product of years of testing and calibrating, have yet to integrate the effects of these new tools, but the fact that they have not may be creating an untenable divide between the economy as measured and economic life as lived.

In much the way that the economy of the 1990s received a boost from the proliferation of personal computers and then the Internet, the economy today receives a boost from a host of "free goods" available online. Google, Wikipedia, Facebook, Yelp, online and mobile banking, YouTube, Expedia, and thousands of other applications allow individuals and institutions to perform tasks that used to consume considerably more time and money. However, none of these tools exists statistically, and why would they? These goods are not only new, they are free. The consumer price index will eventually register a new product as long as it is bought and sold, because the basket of goods changes over time to reflect purchasing behavior. But free goods will never show up, because they are free and so not technically part of the market exchanges that constitute "the economy." Just as domestic work and the black market and volunteer work are invisible statistically, so are these free goods on the Internet.

Brynjolfsson, however, argues that because they are almost invisible statistically, we are undercounting our overall output. That is easier to hypothesize than prove. In order to measure just what those free Internet goods are adding, he developed a methodology that uses something called *consumer surplus* as a way of determining what consumers consider to be the cost of these free goods. The goods may not have a price, but they do require time. In a capitalist society, time is money, and, thus, you can create a formula that translates time spent into money spent. Sounds simple, but it took Brynjolfsson and Joo Hee Oh many months of hard work to craft the formulas, refine time-survey data of consumer behavior, and come up with a credible, peer-tested calculus of how much these free goods are adding to our overall output.

Their preliminary findings are that Internet tools added as much as $34 billion a year to consumer surplus between 2002 and 2011, a figure that undoubtedly has only increased annually in the years since. Remember that *consumer surplus* is a term of art, a statistical construct in itself. And that number does not capture what these goods contribute to overall economic activity. It simply attempts to put a number on how much value via their time consumers are assigning to these tools.[4]

In fact, the enhancements to overall activity are probably a multiple of the figure calculated by Brynjolfsson and his colleagues. The next generation of information technologies is a mixed bag when it comes to enhancing productivity. Much of Facebook is pure entertainment. It also allows people to nurture social connections. The fact that it is in addition a powerful marketing tool for Nike to Disney to a small business in Dubuque is part of the mix but hardly the most prominent. The decision in the 1930s to omit nonmarket activities from national accounts was challenged at the time by Simon Kuznets, and with the efflorescence of social media tools in the 2000s, that decision has ever more consequences.

How much does social connectivity facilitate commerce or enable business to be better organized internally? No one really knows. Human resource professionals at larger companies will tell you that tools such as LinkedIn are changing the way they find new recruits and making it far more efficient and less time consuming to fill needed roles with qualified personnel. Marketers swear by the power of Facebook, Twitter, Yelp, Foursquare, and a dizzying array of new applications that aren't yet ubiquitous but soon will be. Advertisers have embraced the algorithms offered by Google that offer the hope of solving—if not yet, then soon—that age-old conundrum of department store magnate John Wanamaker that half of advertising dollars are wasted, but you don't know which half.

The effect of software and digital storage is dramatic as well. Software systems have enabled companies to globalize supply chains, whether that's a corporate behemoth such as Apple or a small company making a specialized product. You can assemble parts made worldwide only if there are advanced software and inventory control management systems. For all of its initial challenges, the Boeing 787 Dreamliner was among the purest examples of supply chains gone global, with hundreds of parts sourced worldwide and then shipped on massive container ships to be assembled at Boeing factories in the Pacific Northwest. The fact that there were glitches should be less surprising than the fact that they could build a plane that way at all. And then there's digital storage, which has had a profound effect on the explosion of information worldwide. The cost to store a byte of data has plummeted, and so hardware has become less necessary because of the worldwide data cloud of massive servers humming along while people take their smart phones and tablets and slip the contents of their lives seamlessly into their purses and pockets.

Yet GDP, because it is a measure of current market value of goods (as well as government spending and investment, of course), does not "value" these efficiencies unless they lead to more market value of goods. As Brynjolfsson and others have noted, if the cost of something falls precipitously, that may reflect positively in lower inflation numbers and may make lots of people better able to afford it and hence potentially add to their lives, but it will not boost GDP. Plummeting market values may hurt companies as well. Hundreds of millions of people have had access to more music more cheaply since the widespread digitization of music in the 1990s. That, however, decimated the traditional music industry and statistically led to the declining value of music sold. The plunging price of personal computers had a similar boon for widespread connectivity, as has the surge in tablets recently. But the effect on GDP has been more muted because of plunging sticker prices.

The net result of all of these new technologies, says Brynjolfsson, could be as much as "trillions of dollars of benefits that are not measured in the Bureau of Economic Analysis's official GDP statistics." That's an astonishing figure, but not one that the BEA and its director, Steve Landefeld, would necessarily dispute. We began the book citing how in mid-2013, the BEA released a revised set of GDP tables going back to 1929 that showed that "intangible assets" had not been adequately measured in national accounts and that, as a result, the US economy in 2012 was about 3 percent larger than previously thought. These "intangible assets" are things such as brand equity (the value of the name "Pepsi," for instance) and research and development investment, which had previously been treated as expenses.

The BEA is well aware of the limitations of its methods and works intensively to keep pace. It's not a stretch to assume that at some point in the coming years, GDP will indeed reflect more accurately the benefits of the information economy. But the BEA has neither the budget nor the mandate to reframe the raw data that it relies on from multiple sources, and that is where academics such as Brynjolfsson and economists at the various Federal Reserve banks are vital. As the BEA's Landefeld explained dryly, "The Federal Reserve has higher salaries," and its banks can more easily attract top talent than the salary-constrained federal bureaucracy. The result is that the Fed and academia have been the leading sources of innovation in rethinking our indicators and how they might evolve.

Of course, if the effect of information and other technologies was fully reflected in GDP and national accounts, the result might be more overall wealth but not necessarily more individual affluence. Yes, when GDP is revised upward, we all magically become wealthier on a per capita basis, because per capita income is just GDP divided by population. But if I told you that statistically your income was actually 3 percent more over the past decade than you thought, you wouldn't have 3 percent more income to spend than you did. Not only that, but the effects of these still uncalculated aspects of economic life are not evenly distributed. In fact, the people who benefit more from the free goods on the Internet are the same people who are currently benefiting the most from the structural changes affecting the developed economies: the people who have access to education, who have access to technology, who know how to use social media tools for their enjoyment and benefit, and who are connected to the most dynamic areas of economic life today. They are not people with no more than a high school diploma, not men over fifty who had careers in manufacturing, and not those who have seen global competition for their jobs and skills and downward pressure on wages.

The divide between those doing well in a shifting economy and those faring badly is not well captured by GDP statistics. Yes, incomes are traced by the government and broken down into various tranches, and that information is available both from the Bureau of Labor Statistics and from the BEA. But as Steve Landefeld will attest, there is much work to be done providing a better picture of various income brackets and who is reaping the current benefits of GDP growth. Part of the challenge is that so much of our data comes from people voluntarily responding to surveys. That would be fine if everyone told the truth, and if everyone responded in the same proportion regardless of income, geography, and race. But they don't. Says Landefeld, "There is different data from lots of sources on inequality and distribution. But most of it is from the middle. Low- and high-income households don't tend to respond to household surveys." These limitations make it even more difficult for official data to reflect the import of Brynjolfsson's work. If he is correct, then a fair number of people are doing much better than our current statistics suggest. On the flip side, however, a large number of people are faring much worse, because of the digital divide and the educational divide.

These issues about how we calculate GDP, of course, also underscore the limitations of unemployment statistics. We have come a long way from Ethelbert Stewart in our ability to survey multiple occupations, to have businesses feed data electronically into a centralized system at the BLS, and to conduct tens of thousands of household surveys every month. Across Europe and much of the world, statistical agencies are busy doing the same in their respective countries. Not every country has exactly the same methodology. In the United Kingdom, for instance, one of the primary sources of unemployment data is the number of people receiving unemployment benefits. In the United States, that metric is kept as well but not used to determine the unemployment rate. In addition, the very definition of employment in a world of increased self-employment is certainly fuzzier than it was for much of the twentieth century.

Yet the greatest challenge with unemployment statistics is not the categories so much as the fiction of one round number meant to reflect a national condition. In truth, there are vastly different employment rates depending on education, gender, race, and location. Those with higher education and skills to navigate an information economy (where even factories demand skilled workers able to manage computer-calibrated machines) are in high demand. There is no unemployment crisis for those workers, not in the United States and not in much of Europe. But those without those skills and degrees have an unemployment challenge much greater than even the worst headline unemployment number would suggest—much worse than the 8 percent number in the United States in 2008 or the 11 percent number in the United Kingdom and France. You can find those other figures in the pages and pages of supplemental material published each month by the BLS, but because they are buried in reams of text and tables, they remain obscure and less examined.

The limitations of national indicators are far greater in countries with even less of a tradition of keeping them. Not only are there questions about the reliability of the data, there are often problems of political pressure on those who assemble the statistics. Those issues are of a different order than the ones identified by American academics and economists. They may criticize methodologies, but they have full faith that the agencies responsible for the indicators are operating honorably. In some other countries, however, indicators are subject to political challenges. Imagine the scandal in the United States if a group that believed the real inflation rate was being woefully underreported by the BLS persuaded the president to sack the head of the division responsible and put someone else in charge who was more "sensitive" to the problem. Yet that is precisely what happened in Argentina, and it led one intrepid researcher to consider ways to calculate inflation that would bypass government agencies altogether.

In early 2013 Argentina earned a dubious distinction: it became the first country ever threatened with expulsion from the International Monetary Fund because of its failure to maintain the integrity of its official economic data. The executive board of the fund called on Argentina to align "these indicators with the international statistical understandings and guidelines that ensure accurate measurement," or else face sanctions culminating in suspension from the fund. The reason? In 2007, INDEC, the National Institute of Statistics and Census of Argentina, reported that inflation for the month of January was 1.5 percent, suggesting an annual rate close to 20 percent. President Néstor Kirchner wasn't pleased. High inflation would undermine his claim that the Argentine economy had turned a corner. In response, he fired the head of INDEC, Graciela Bevacqua, on the grounds that her methods were inaccurate and replaced her with someone who, unsurprisingly, reported several months later that inflation was, as Kirchner had supposed, rather less than had initially been announced.[5]

The firing caused an international uproar. The political intervention was seen, rightly, as a threat not just to Argentina's ability to gauge its economic life independent of political pressures but as a dangerous precedent for other leaders around the world who might take the cue that when the indicators aren't favorable, the best course of action is to fire those responsible for calculating them and find someone else to present you with figures more to your liking. The Argentine government's meddling didn't stop with pressuring the official statistics agency. In the following years, a number of independent, private groups began to assemble their own reports of inflation in an effort to provide more accurate data. When one of these, a nonprofit group that surveyed grocery store prices, reported an inflation level three times what INDEC announced in 2012, it was informed by the economy ministry that its nonprofit status was being revoked. After years of such shenanigans and increased questions about the reliability of its official data, Argentina found itself on the verge of ostracism from one of the world's most significant financial institutions.

Aside from a cautionary tale and a reminder of how vital independent indicators are to not just our understanding of the world but to the smooth functioning of international diplomatic and economic affairs, the Argentine story served as a spur for academics thousands of miles away, at MIT. There, two professors, Roberto Rigobon and Alberto Cavallo, saw what was happening with the politicization of data in Argentina and had an idea. Cavallo, himself born and raised in Argentina, was particularly interested in what could be done to create indicators that the government couldn't interfere with. A government can fire official statisticians; it can harass domestic private institutions that provide independent analysis; and, presumably, it can also make foreign funding of such domestic institutions difficult or impossible. But what it cannot prevent so easily is a computer program from scanning through all prices online.

The result was the Billion Prices Project. Working with programmers, Rigobon and Cavallo developed a real-time index of consumer prices. Increasingly in the United States and throughout the world, the primary point of sale for consumer goods is online. Yes, online sales are still small compared with brick-and-mortar transactions, constituting less than 10 percent of all purchases in the United States and lower in most other countries. But websites of brick-and-mortar stores offer prices for much of their inventory, which means that a well-designed program can find and record all of those prices, every day. Plugged into the same formulas used by the BLS and other national statistical agencies, those prices can be used in precisely the same way as prices obtained through the laborious process of sending out surveys and then inputting the responses. And where the BLS and most national agencies spend thousands of man-hours obtaining the information, adjusting the basket of goods, and then producing monthly indices, a computer program designed to scour the Web acts far faster.

The Billion Prices Project collects vast amounts of data. While it is still a work in progress, in 2013 it already encompassed more than seventy countries. In the United States and the United Kingdom, it digests more than five hundred thousand different prices from more than one thousand different retailers.[6] Unlike the BLS or the BEA, Rigobon and Cavallo don't "weight" the basket of goods created by these scans. The only adjustment in the composition of the basket is what items appear or disappear from the websites of the retailers that they scan. If a certain flat-screen television or mobile device is replaced by a next-generation model, that change is reflected seamlessly because the older models just stop being sold. There aren't many iPhone 2s being offered these days.

You might think that an index that electronically assembles hundreds of thousands of prices and just adds them up and averages them would diverge from "inflation" as calculated by official agencies that use a more sophisticated methodology of weights. But no. The Billion Prices index tracks to a remarkable degree the official inflation numbers in every country—with the notable exception of, yes, Argentina.

The work of Rigobon and Cavallo is vital in several ways. First, it makes it much harder for inflation conspiracy theorists to argue that government statisticians are purposely and deviously understating actual inflation. The electronic bots that scour the Internet for retail prices have no political agenda. They move at inhuman speed, dispassionately assembling information. Of course, a good conspiracy never lets facts get in the way. One could credibly argue (in the absence of any information to the contrary) that the professors at MIT have a secret agenda and are receiving hidden financing from powers-that-be who wish to perpetuate the optic of low inflation in order to rob the masses of their hard-earned income and undermine the value (what little there is) of the ever-dwindling social safety net. But barring such beliefs, the work of the Billion Prices Project has the virtue of confirming official statistics using a different methodology and technology.

It also has the advantage of creating a key indicator in real time at far less cost. The budgets of statistical agencies may be pennies compared with other programs such as defense and health care, but such budgets still amounts to billions in the United States and substantial sums in other countries. Calculating the CPI alone costs Americans more than $200 million each year, and even then, it is released with a time lag and subject to revisions and statistical massaging to compensate for erratic but nonrecurring factors such as extreme weather. Both chained CPI (which adjusts the basket of goods based on consumer spending patterns) and traditional CPI generate intense debate and political controversy, as the proposal in 2013 to shift Social Security payments to chained CPI (thus lowering the increase of future payments) demonstrates. The Billion Prices Project avoids those problems because it is almost entirely electronic, does not involve much human mediation, makes no distinction between different products, and attempts no value judgments about what people buy and in what quantities. And it is much less expensive.

Cost, of course, is only one consideration. Indicators are economic equivalents of sentries: we spend money to collect and refine them because of a collective imperative, and it is thus money well spent. As we've seen, however, a major limitation of our current statistics is the degree to which services, technologies, and changed global dynamics have rendered some of the assumptions anachronistic. Intensive human collection of price information is a legacy from a time when that was the only way to obtain the data. With today's information technologies, there are now other ways, and those happen to be speedier and cheaper. Without question, the agencies that collect and disseminate these statistics have avidly integrated information technologies themselves, but not to the extent of the Billion Prices Project.

The idea that we could develop a real-time gauge of inflation is not unique to Professors Rigobon and Cavallo. Google, with its franchise of information and its uses, has devoted a small portion of its considerable firepower to assessing economic activity in real time. Google dominates the online advertising and search market in the United States and globally except for China. Its algorithms capture terabytes of data daily, and its engineers and analysts have a unique window on the daily activity of entire societies. That includes what people are interested in, worried about, and desirous of. That fact has not, of course, been lost on Google itself, which has dedicated some of its energies to analyzing its vast data stream from various angles. With such large and extensive inputs, Google has studied whether it can develop predictive algorithms for crises, for elections, for markets, and for just about any core concern we humans have.

Hal Varian has served as Google's chief economist for years. Most major corporations employ one or more economists as part of their efforts to judge the prevailing economic winds. Fundamental decisions about how much to spend, how much to staff, how much inventory to order and where to invest in future growth (if at all) hinge on what management believes about the future. If a company such as General Electric or Honeywell, which must spend heavily on capital equipment to make sophisticated and expensive machines worldwide, believes that industrial activity tied to China will strengthen and that US manufacturing will weaken, that shapes how aggressively to ramp up production and where. The assessment of interest rates and economic growth will determine whether to borrow money, buy back stock, and how much to tie employee compensation to equity prices or offer larger cash bonuses instead.

Varian's role is a bit different. He has focused on investigating what questions Google could answer but hasn't. For instance, Google has developed a measure of GDP for most countries in the world that is based on transactions and activity it can identify on its servers. It has tried to determine employment trends in actual time and by industry, and it has looked at ways of calculating "knowledge worker productivity," which isn't just the productivity of its own employees but anyone involved in the burgeoning world of information technologies and social media. And in a similar vein to the Billion Prices Project, Varian hatched the idea of using Google's reach to calculate a "Google Price index" that would supplement and perhaps one day supplant the consumer price index maintained by statistical agencies around the world.

Trained as an economist and for many years a professor of economic theory and business, Varian was always drawn to the implications of new technologies and the exponential growth in the amount of data and information created. That made him a good fit for Google, which is at the epicenter of that trend. Naturally, Varian was struck by how little official statistics have been reframed by technological changes. "If you look at the private sector in the past ten to fifteen years," he told me, "everyone has created some sort of data warehouse, from UPS to WalMart, to Visa and MasterCard, and indeed just about all major companies. They all have these real-time information systems to gauge what they are doing, and those systems are sophisticated and robust. But the public sector data hasn't changed that much, nor does it have the same tools. Note the way we take the census, sending out forms to be filled out in pen or pencil and then mailed back. We have all this real-time price information, but we don't use scanner data for the CPI." Hence, the Google Price index.[7]

Like the Billion Prices Project, the Google index (which has not been widely published and may not be continued) did not depart dramatically from the CPI. Rather, it confirmed the same basic trends, with modest differences. For instance, it showed more deflation in 2010 than the headline CPI did, and that reading proved to be more accurate. Interestingly, both these alternate inflation measures leave out one substantial component of the consumer price index: housing prices. Yet even though housing (via "owner's equivalent rent") is a large percentage of CPI, its absence from the Billion Prices Project and the Google index seems to make little difference. That suggests that housing prices, save for the mid-2000s housing bubble, tend to move in sync with overall prices and income. Home prices, of course, can be volatile, as can food and energy, but an electronic index that looks only at online retail prices ends up tracking quite closely the official inflation indicator that includes housing.

Statisticians watch these innovations closely. In fact, out of the wreckage of the financial crisis of 2008 emerged an entirely new government statistical office, mandated by the Dodd-Frank Act of 2010. The Office of Financial Research was established only in 2011, but it is now a $100-million-a-year agency tasked with finding or creating statistics and models that might identify critical problems before they again threaten to bring down the global financial system. The thinking is that an agency tasked with analyzing the system might have recognized the dangers of too many derivatives well before 2008. While not responsible for improving our current set of leading indicators, the formation of this new agency does reflect the degree to which governments, and not just creative individuals, recognize the need to update how we gauge the behemoth we call "the economy."

Our final avatar, however, has little use for government indicators or for most of the private indicators disseminated by businesses and academics. He does employ teams of analysts who study those indicators, whether issued by government agencies, or the National Association of Realtors, or the Institute of Supply Management, or the National Association of Business Economists, or any of the hundreds of other sources nationally and globally. But he treats none of these indicators as anything more or less than data points—variables in a sea of variables, subject to interpretation and always, always open to question. He runs one of the largest, most successful, and more lucrative hedge funds in the world, with assets well north of $100 billion. He himself is a billionaire and then some, but outside the insular and privileged world of high finance and economic policy, he is anonymous. His name is Ray Dalio.

In 1975 Dalio founded his firm, called Bridgewater Associates, which now occupies a campus hidden in the woods of Westport, Connecticut. Though hardly a remote area, the firm's headquarters is all but invisible unless you know it's there. That somehow matches the insularity of the firm, which has in recent years opened up a bit more to outside questions but still retains an aura of mystery. During the worst years of the financial crisis after 2008, Bridgewater managed to generate double-digit returns for its clients, who are predominantly large institutions such as endowments and pension plans. While not every year has been stellar, the average for the past twenty years is nearly 14 percent annually, even with massive contractions in global markets in 2002 and again in 2008–09.

One reason for the mystery surrounding the success of Bridgewater is the personality of its founder. Dalio is not entirely media shy, but he has not shown much interest in public appearances. That began to change around the time of the financial crisis, but only marginally. Like many successful hedge fund managers, Dalio tends toward the private and secretive, as if there is a proprietary magic formula that he has discovered that must be closely guarded. That his fund has managed to generate substantial returns during times when the preponderance of other market participants have stumbled lends that perspective some credence. What does he know that others don't? What secret insight into the working of economies and markets does he possess that the rest of us have missed?

The competition in the asset management industry also plays a part in cultivating mystery. If you are competing for a mandate from a state's pension fund—a chunk that can easily exceed $500 million— you need to make the case why your approach to investing will yield better returns than someone else's approach. Why else should you be paid millions to manage that money actively when the trustees of the pension plan could just invest in index funds and Treasury notes and pay much less for potentially similar (or even better) results? Making the pitch that you have a unique insight into how the world works and what is likely to unfold in the near future, and that your insights have generated superior results for your clients over time, is imperative in winning that business.

Yet Bridgewater and Dalio take the argument one step further. Dalio contends that he has discovered a unique set of principles, and that these principles allow his firm to analyze the world more accurately and make better investing decisions. After years of refining his philosophy, Dalio published his approach in a small book that each new employee of Bridgewater receives and is told to study. It begins with an exhortation more familiar to self-help and New Age books. Called simply *Principles*, Dalio's guidebook has one primary goal: "Above all else, I want you to think for yourself—to decide (1) what you want, (2) what is true and (3) what to do about it. I want you to do that in a clear-headed thoughtful way, so that you get what you want. I wrote this book to help you do that. I am going to ask only two things of you—(1) that you be open-minded and (2) that you honestly answer some questions about what you want, what is true, and what you want to do about it."[8]

The book is part autobiography, part how-to-live manual. A self-described ordinary kid who grew up on Long Island, Dalio developed several guiding mantras: opinions are often wrong and the only way to be less wrong is to test opinions relentlessly; "success is achieved by people who deeply understand reality and know how to use it to get what they want;" "Pain + Reflection = Progress;" and, above all, individuals and systems, including economies, are at heart "machines" that can be understood with intense effort by skilled people.

Dalio's gestalt is easily ridiculed, and has been. When copies of *Principles* trickled out after they were published in 2011, there was some inevitable chortling among the cynical financial set and in the media as well. *New York* magazine caviled that Dalio's little book of aphorisms read "as if Ayn Rand and Deepak Chopra had collaborated on a line of fortune cookies."[9] Others labeled Bridgewater "a cult," nothing more, nothing less, complete with a dear leader and a lexicon that the firm's employee-acolytes were told to embrace. The fact that many of the professionals at the firm were hired straight out of college or business school with little other work experience reinforced the view that Dalio is as much in the business of shaping minds and crafting a culture as he is about making money.

If Bridgewater were any less successful, it would be easy to dismiss Dalio and his methods completely, and easy to ridicule them if ridicule is your thing. Yet another peculiarity of the company is that most meetings are taped. That way, any dispute about what is said, any questions of interpretation, can be answered by referring back to the tape, and those records can also be used for self-criticisms and group criticisms. But the anomaly of the firm's returns year after year suggest that either Dalio has indeed found a way to both analyze the world and act on the analysis or that he has been extraordinarily lucky. You could make an argument for luck, especially since the firm reportedly stumbled for much of 2013. But what marked Bridgewater for many years wasn't a fully developed governing philosophy replete with rules and jargon; it was a maverick approach to reality and to the way that the investing community and economists understood that reality via the suite of statistics and indicators that have been the subject of these pages.

Dalio has a healthy skepticism of all opinions, including opinions of experts. That skepticism extends to the way that the world is depicted through statistics. Dalio has his team analyze hundreds of indicators worldwide, and rather than take them at face value, he tries to find patterns and relationships over time that others may not see. That means he rejects the economic laws and rules that others tend to hold dear. He believes that the world is a machine that can be understood but also recognizes that almost no one actually understands it. Bridgewater treats established statistics and indicators as part of an array of available inputs that are assembled by fallible human beings and, hence, cannot be taken as absolute or sacrosanct.

Instead, Dalio and his team start from the assumptions that everyone and every data point is limited and may be wrong. Interest rates, GDP, inflation, the price of gold, consumer sentiment—they are the raw material for understanding reality and making decisions. Because Dalio is never convinced that anyone can be right about anything, his funds make many, many different bets on outcomes. Because he has a large team of analysts skilled in both quantitative and qualitative analysis, he has been able to develop proprietary models that integrate statistics and daily information such as who is buying what, which institutions are taking large bets on what stocks, who is buying Japanese bonds or US Treasuries, which central banks are purchasing gold or undertaking quantitative easing, and who is doing what, when, and for how long. These indicators are then put into computer models programmed to find linkages between these variables that suggest one trade or another.

In short, Dalio built an institution that digests global indicators, adds a suite of new, proprietary indicators, and then creates a picture of the world that suggests certain types of trades. It is a system of bespoke indicators, built on a philosophy and fueled by what has certainly been many millions of dollars of annual research over the course of years, executed by extremely smart, very dedicated individuals who are part of an offbeat, even bizarre culture. Bridgewater doesn't trade based on an analysis of leading indicators, or based on the world that a limited set of limited statistics tell us exists. It makes decisions based on its own set of indicators.

In time, Bridgewater may have a major stumble. Neither 2012 nor 2013 were stellar years for the firm, which suggests that its systems (or Dalio himself) misjudged how the global economy would evolve, or misjudged how different financial assets would perform in response. The multiyear performance of the firm stills stands out, but investing is humbling insofar as you can get the big picture right and still lose money, and you can get the big picture wrong and make it. Good companies do not always equal good stocks, and identifying risks and problems does not always mean that those will unfold in a familiar fashion. Dalio may have a unique set of principles attached to a firm that has had the success and resources to create its own statistical map of the world. Even then, at one point or another, it will fail to capture a three-dimensional reality that is constantly in flux.

If governments had the resources of a Bridgewater (or in the case of the United States, the willingness to allocate resources), they might just be able to more effectively refine and update the leading indicators. They would still make mistakes from ignorance or misjudgment. But they might be able to integrate the work of Brynjolfsson and dozens of other whip-smart economists and theorists, not gradually over the course of the next decade, but now. They might be able to think about what inflation means now that prices are increasingly determined not just locally and nationally but globally, with everything from the price of vital commodities such as oil and iron ore to wages for labor determined in a global marketplace. They might be able to rethink what employment means and why we count a job that earns barely more than the poverty level as a plus, but we treat a college graduate who takes eighteen months to find her first full-time position that pays substantially more as an unemployment problem. Those issues were insignificant in the 1930s, when these numbers were created. But they are vital now. And we might be able to reframe our trade data to reflect where value is flowing; we might be able to think more intensively about what GDP does not measure but needs measuring, and what nothing will ever measure but needs attending to.

The avatars in this chapter are only a smattering of the voices saying that the world we live in departs in radical ways from the world that our indicators say that we are living in. These avatars do not, for the most part, say that these indicators are wrong. In fact, they recognize, as they should, that most of our indicators are vital tools that have been overseen by diligent and thoughtful stewards (Argentina notwithstanding). But as we have seen, the problem is not just that our economic numbers have the DNA that they have and were designed to measure mid-twentieth-century industrial nation-states rather than early-twentieth-century information economies that increasingly transcend the nation-state. The even greater problem is that we place so much collective weight on our indicators. We treat them as absolute markers rather than as the limited guideposts that they are. We ask them to determine how we spend what we spend, when all they can do is speak to certain aspects of our material and economic life.

The final question, then, is what do we do about it? We can't all build multibillion-dollar hedge funds, and, frankly, most of us don't want to. Better hedge funds will not ameliorate the larger social need unless the industry is suddenly transformed by a social mission. We can't all be "economics geeks" like Erik Brynjolfsson, and most of us wouldn't want to create the Billion Prices Project in our spare time. Most companies won't and can't take the risk to reject the correlations of the past; Caterpillar's executives won't just decide to build more plants and make more earth movers because they had a strong feeling that the growth of the emerging economies will continue. They need data and indicators to support their decisions, and they rely on the indicators we have. What, then, is to be done other than to do our best with the tools we have and think critically?

There is, in fact, something to be done. It's not a golden bullet. And it's not a shiny new set of indicators per se. To find the answer, we first need to go back, not quite to the beginning, but before we lived in a world so intimately defined by these indicators. Not go back to the same world, but look back, if only for a moment, for insight about how to move forward.

CONCLUSION: MADE TO MEASURE

When Simon Kuznets began to develop tools to quantify the national income of a country, he was answering a simple question: How do you measure an economy? In doing so, he was also defining "the economy" as the commercial activities measured at prices set by the market. As we've seen, that framework left out, purposely, swaths of human existence, from domestic work to volunteer work to commercial transactions that aren't recorded anywhere, that exist in cash or are conducted privately or illegally. Nonetheless, it was a start.

When Ethelbert Stewart and his heirs at the Bureau of Labor Statistics began to develop ways to measure unemployment, they were also answering a simple question: What does it mean to be unemployed, and how many people meet that definition at any given moment? Unemployment as a statistic was and is related to unemployment as a state of being, but it isn't the same thing. Being unemployed statistically isn't the same as not having a job. To be unemployed meant that you wanted a job and were actually looking for one, because in the late nineteenth century and the early decades of the twentieth century—when there was no social safety net, no unemployment insurance, no pension plans, no retirement age—there was no such thing as voluntary unemployment or "ceasing to look for work." You had a job, or a farm, or an inheritance, or you risked starvation. The creation of a statistic called unemployment gave advocates of workers' rights a tool, especially in times of duress, which the Great Depression certainly was. It allowed defenders of labor to insist on some support for workers displaced and without jobs, and to puncture Herbert Hoover's illusion that government was doing enough and should do no more.

When George Katona championed a set of surveys to measure how people felt about economic conditions, he was looking for quantitative evidence that how people feel shapes both future prices (inflation) and how they behave. That was vital during World War II because any severe disruption in domestic economic activity could imperil the ability of the United States to meet its war production needs. Kuznets as well was brought into that process, along with so many others, to gauge just how much America could devote to war production without jeopardizing the essential needs of daily life at home.

When Irving Fisher tackled the thorny question of how to measure the cost of living, he was motivated by an intellectual passion to create the most accurate index. As he and all those who came after grappled with the definition of inflation and how best to quantify prices, they focused on "the economy" as a closed, statistical system, not on whether or not that system met the needs, desires, and aspirations of millions of individuals. Over time the consumer price index became an emotional gauge as much as an economic one. As a tool for bankers and policy makers to assess the stability of the system, it has largely been a success. As a marker used by millions to grade the economy and the government, it has been a source of angst and controversy, and it continues to be.

Not one of our leading indicators was designed to carry the weight they now do. They were not invented to be absolute markers of whether we are doing well or poorly, whether our nations are succeeding or failing, and whether our governments are visionary or destructive. They were not created so that a college graduate looking for a job in Chicago can assess her opportunities, or to help someone interested in starting a small business figure out whether now is a good time. And they were not worked on by generations of economists and statisticians in government and academia in order to determine whether Congress should take on more debt or spend more, whether General Electric should build a factory in Mississippi or China, and whether our economic priorities are correct.

This wasn't always the case. The indicators were created to provide clarity where there had been none. In the early 1930s, governments and businesses flew blind when it came to whether what they were doing was having the desired effect. By the 1950s, the new indicators provided a state-of-the-art statistical dashboard. It gave those who used them and studied them a new confidence in their ability to monitor and steer this new thing called "the economy." And by dint of the Cold War and the phenomenal success of the United States as a nation of affluence in the mid–twentieth century, the indicators became woven into daily life and began to assume a place of prominence that no one had intended and few had anticipated.

The transformation of these numbers from statistics used by bureaucrats and managers into markers of societal success happened so quickly yet subtly over the course of a few decades that no one quite noticed what was happening. Debates over the validity of the consumer price index had been heated during negotiations between union leaders, the Department of Labor, and companies in the 1940s and 1950s, but only in the 1970s did inflation migrate to the center of public life in the United States. Yes, inflation had left a searing memory in Germany because of the 1920s and 1930s, but for most countries, the statistic of inflation, determined by CPI, assumed its pride of place at the center of public consciousness only in the 1970s. That was when the United States flirted with runaway inflation, and when Latin American countries were severely roiled by spiraling prices and plunging currencies.

Many of the progenitors of our economic indicators might have smiled with pride at the thought that their work had become so pivotal to national identity, but most would have blanched at the way their statistics are now used. Take the example mentioned at the very beginning of the book: During the 2012 US presidential election, it was said routinely that "no president has been reelected with an unemployment rate above 7.2 percent." Sometimes the number changed in the reporting, but the central claim was the same. As we know, the 2012 election did not play out according to that truism. Barack Obama returned to the Oval Office with an unemployment rate of 7.9 percent.

But the real problem with these statements, as Ethelbert Stewart might have recognized, and which his heirs at the Bureau of Labor Statistics surely did, was that they made unequivocal conclusions based on an extremely limited set of data points. As we know, there was no published unemployment rate until the late 1940s, and not until the late 1950s did the monthly average attract much in the way of publicity. The only way that the unemployment rate can have a dramatic effect on an election is if that rate is part of the public discussion. Yes, a widespread sense that millions are suffering and the economic system is failing has always challenged political incumbents. But that's not the same as believing that there is a direct causal relationship between a statistic and voter behavior. And even if there was, no statistician would be comfortable making definitive statements when the entire available data set consists of at most sixteen distinct examples. That's the number of presidential elections from 1948 through 2012. And in that period, there were only five presidents reelected (Eisenhower,

Nixon, Reagan, Clinton, and George W. Bush) and two defeated in their attempts to be reelected (Carter and George H. W. Bush).[1]

The statement that "no president has ever been reelected with an unemployment rate above 7.2 percent" is exhibit A for how we place too much weight on our indicators to dictate something meaningful and predictive about the world. A thousand years from now, if we are still keeping these numbers (doubtful), we would have more than enough data and patterns to make definitive (albeit still provisional) statements about probabilities, correlations, and possible causations. With a bit more than fifty years of data, however, we are nowhere near that. Yet we now routinely discuss these numbers as if there is a sufficient amount of information over a long enough period of time to make such conclusions.

Even the notion that there is one static number that can encapsulate employment is a problem in a rapidly morphing economic system. Many have noted that in the United States especially, monthly job reports are constantly subject to revision, and these revisions can be quite large both up and down. For instance, in the May 2013 jobs release from the BLS, numbers for February were revised up from 268,000 to 332,000, while numbers for March increased even more dramatically from 88,000 new jobs to 138,000. Yet it is only the initial release that receives attention in the media, which is the primary way that most people digest these numbers. The statisticians at the BLS would never suggest that the initial monthly number be used as gospel, yet the relentless demands of the twenty-four-hour news cycle dictate just that. Some nuance occasionally creeps in, but there's yet to be a headline saying, "Jobs Picture Quite Different Than What We Said Last Month Because of Revisions."

You could argue that directionally, these numbers are correct. That is, they rarely point up when the actual trajectory is down. But even here, the easy simplicity of an "unemployment rate" clouds our understanding of what's going on. Given the scrutiny that unemployment statistics come under in every developed country, this is a serious problem. The illusion of the unemployment rate is that it is a national number that represents national realities, whether that nation is Spain or the United Kingdom or the United States. Yet as we've discussed, the unemployment rate masks just how unevenly distributed unemployment is, by age, race, gender, geography, and, above all, by education level.

The myth of national numbers that reflect national realities distorts how we attempt to solve these problems collectively and inhibits how we meet our challenges individually. In the United States, the federal government spends billions on national unemployment insurance. European countries spend even more. Those tens of billions of dollars are supplemented by programs sponsored by the Department of Labor and other agencies for job training and placement. And that does not even add in the almost trillion dollars of emergency spending at the heart of the 2008–09 crisis designed, as we saw, to save and create jobs.

These budgets are large, but they are also extremely blunt instruments. They rely on macroeconomic theories that have grown more rigid since the nimble Keynes. Input in, output out. Yet unemployment is not a scythe that cuts through society indiscriminately. It is high in Spain, and not in Germany; high in some American states and hardly a blip in others; at crisis levels for young Hispanic or African-American men without a college degree, and barely a factor for college-educated women. And then there is that crucial issue of jobs that pay so little that they barely leave the person working two of them with enough money to meet his or her needs. He is fully employed statistically, as an orderly in a health care facility, or in "business services"—that ubiquitous BLS category that can include building custodians, mailroom clerks, and minimum-wage retail sales associates. These are jobs, yes, honorable ones and difficult, but not often jobs that form the foundation of a more vibrant economy. Rather than spending indiscriminately on a problem that we treat as simple and national, we would be far better off tailoring our public policies to the specific nature of the problem.

These numbers were invented to give policy makers needed tools to derive the best policies to remedy the most egregious economic problems. In the 1930s, policies were creative and innovative by default: there was little legacy of governments attempting to ameliorate systemic economic issues using data and statistics. These indicators were invented to help those policy makers navigate the many and varied policy experiments. Today the leading indicators are not used that way. Instead, our national statistics often act as barriers to innovative approaches rather than facilitating them. The congressional straight-jacket that forces the CBO to project growth rates is a high barrier to investing for the future. Companies that tether capital spending to inflation numbers may find themselves underinvesting for the future.

What, then, is to be done? It would be satisfying to unveil a new framework and to outline a new set of statistics that would better serve our present needs. That would have the virtue of simplicity, and it would be easy to digest. Instead of GDP, let's have a version of gross national *contentment*. Instead of the unemployment rate, let's have the employment-education ratio. Problems with our current numbers? Well, then, let's invent new ones.

Yet we *are* inventing new ones and updating old ones. We touched on only a few new indicators in these pages but enough to demonstrate that the world is not without extremely adept individuals tackling the limitations of our economic numbers, refining them and deriving alternatives. Within the BEA, there are already multiple variants of income and price deflators; within the BLS, there are a half dozen established alternate unemployment measures that take into account underemployment, hours worked, and other factors, just as there are multiple measures of prices.

All indicators, however, are simple numbers. That is the problem.

The reason GDP falls short of measuring our economic lives is because no one number can measure our lives. Any *one* number will have shortcomings, even if those shortcomings are different for different numbers. GDP does not account for happiness, contentment, or domestic work. It also does not—and cannot—account for nonmarket activities such as hanging out with friends and family. It cannot encompass activities that exist beyond the reach of the state, such as the so-called invisible economy of cash transactions, cash remittances sent home by wire or by mail from migrant workers, and trade of services, all of which certainly add up to many trillions of dollars globally. But if we replaced GDP with another number, it too would leave out something.

Say we created a number that included all variables we think are vital to a stable, prosperous economy. How would those be weighted? What percentage should be happiness versus output? What part should be the "invisible economy" and what part should be the value-add of goods and services? There would have to be some methodology, some way to weight these new variables. Creating that formula would, in turn, involve value judgments no more or less valid than the ones that Kuznets and Richard Stone and then Amartya Sen and the UN Human Development Project used to derive their indices and those indicators.

No one number will suffice. That is the key limitation of GDP: not its methodology, not what it includes or excludes, but the very fact that it attempts to distill into one figure complicated, ever-changing economic systems. The same can be said of each of the indicators invented in the twentieth century and so prevalent today. They were and still are more than adequate to answer a specific set of needs. They are far better than nothing, and they still serve a purpose for policy makers, for business, and for individuals as markers that offer some provisional guidance about what to do and when to do it.

That is a far cry from how these numbers are used. Rather than tools to augment decisions and provide guidance, they are more often than not taken at face value and treated uncritically as absolute mirrors of reality. Instead, they should be used as limited guideposts that describe one reality known as "the economy" but not all reality known as "the world we live in."

So, again, what should be done? What do we need to know and how will we find the information we require? That answer varies, depending on who you are and what you need. Governments, institutions, businesses, and individuals have different imperatives and different questions. There is no "one size fits all" answer that suits all of these needs.

First, all of these indicators are built on a foundation of immense amounts of data. Statistics are what humans do with the data they assemble; they are constructs meant to make sense of information. But the raw material is itself equally valuable, and rarely do we make sufficient use of it. Each unemployment report comes with a wealth of data about which sectors are doing well and which are not, how employment varies by age, education, occupation. Every inflation reading comes with vast tables of information about the movements of televisions versus bread, gasoline versus legal services, smart phones versus power drills. Each housing report shows the vagaries of geography, and each trade report allows insight into dozens of industries and sectors. And, of course, every GDP report has literally hundreds of charts and tables that trace national income by sector.

Our needs going forward will be best served by how we make use of not just this data but all data. We live in an era of Big Data. The world has seen an explosion of information in the past decades, so much so that people and institutions now struggle to keep pace. In fact, one of the reasons for the attachment to the simplicity of our indicators may be an inverse reaction to the sheer and bewildering volume of information most of us are bombarded by on a daily basis. Cognitive studies have shown that faced with a large number of choices, people tend to be less able to choose; faced with a limited number of choices, they find selecting easier. The lesson for a world of Big Data is that in an environment with excessive information, people may gravitate toward answers that simplify reality rather than embrace the sheer complexity of it.

Yet embracing it is the only way forward. The reality of Big Data is that never before have so many people had so much power to measure their lives. Never before have so many people had the power to craft their own solutions to their problems and challenges. What we need is not an alternate set of equally limited indicators but indicators tailored to our own particular needs and our own particular questions. With the immense ease of computing tools, with the capacity to scan the web for information, and with the plethora of information floating through our ether daily, we can do that, and we must. We don't need new indicators that replace old simple numbers with new simple numbers. We need instead bespoke indicators, tailored to the specific needs and specific questions of governments, businesses, communities, and individuals.

HOW TO USE BESPOKE INDICATORS

Bespoke is a word rarely used today. It comes from a time when people of means would go to a tailor and have clothes made to fit them and them alone. After all, every body is different, and if you truly want what you wear to work perfectly for your body, having clothes made to measure is the way to go. Granted, the cost is prohibitive, and few have ever been able to afford that route.

But the cost of bespoke indicators is minimal. Anyone with a computer can be their own tailor and create bespoke data maps to answer their own questions. And in a world that is increasingly less served by one-size-fits-all economic statistics, crafting bespoke indicators isn't a luxury; it's a necessity.

Different aspects of society have different questions and different demands. There is no one methodology or one set of indicators that can serve governments, multinational institutions, large corporations, small businesses, and individuals. Yet today, all of them rely on the same suite of metrics. That is a mistake.

Governments and multinational institutions are the ones that benefit most from the current leading indicators, and given how those indicators evolved to meet the needs of policy makers, that's to be expected. Even so, we've seen the limitations. The gravest is the lack of global indicators that has been alluded to several times. All international data is essentially national data aggregated. There is no systematic global measure of prices and inflation that assesses costs and currency valuations worldwide. If you had unlimited funds, one priority would be to set up a new organization—not beholden to national governments as the UN is—to begin the laborious process of producing data on global economic systems such as finance and trade. Then we could develop some basic statistics, though with the strong caveat that these would have to be used modestly and not become fetishized as "the truth" the way current indicators have been. While there are efforts here and there, from groups such as the World Health Organization and the World Bank, for the most part, we are left with numbers compiled at a national level, and that looks as if it will be the case for a very long time.

For governments, the most important thing is to be less slavishly dependent on what the numbers say and much more modest about making predictions. Governments everywhere must broaden the array of numbers and make smarter the plethora of data collected and analyzed. As we saw, the commission convened by former French president Nicolas Sarkozy has already suggested a dashboard approach to national economic indicators. That, in effect, means expanding the array of statistics that are utilized in determining policy. To be fair, some policy makers already do that. The US Federal Reserve Board does not rely on a few select macroeconomic numbers to determine policy but instead canvasses a wide range of data and numbers, and has hundreds of economists on staff to add their own layer of analysis. That is precisely the right direction, but it needs to be embraced at all levels of governments, especially legislative bodies. Granted, that is a high bar for legislatures and congressional representatives who often have only a minimal economic awareness. Still, high bar or not, this is what is needed, and it will arm policy makers with a wider array of tools to address the myriad challenges of our world today and tomorrow.

But simply broadening the array isn't sufficient. Governments must also become more nimble in how they use data and what data they use. Local governments have been leading the way, with cities such as Chicago, Denver, New York, Sydney, Paris, Singapore, and Rio de Janeiro collecting information on everything from traffic to tourism to create data maps and statistics that allow them to allocate resources more efficiently and target municipal challenges more effectively. The data that a municipality collects on energy consumption can be used along with "smart meters" to reduce usage and save money. That information, which can then be compared with other cities' and juxtaposed to local economic indicators, matters more to the health of that community than national GDP or unemployment statistics do.

National governments almost always lag in their ability to shift gears and be innovative. A more nimble use of Big Data for the federal government in Washington would mean analyzing the reams of information collected by federal agencies with the understanding that most problems are not truly national; at least, not in a large country. In Singapore, perhaps; in Norway, maybe; in the United States, no. Most issues are best addressed not by using one synthetic number but by looking more closely at the underlying data. If you want to know why repeated policies emanating from Washington have not succeeded in bringing down the unemployment rate substantially, it's in part because of the convenient fiction that there is a national unemployment challenge. Policy makers could make more productive use of the underlying data to meet the challenges of unemployment. They could focus on states and even counties where unemployment is especially high because of a collapsed housing industry, or because of inadequate education levels. The data are there, but the current indicators don't reveal them. That once made sense. In the 1930s, no one crafting the New Deal could chart in real time wages in Tennessee as compared with those in New Hampshire, or employment patterns in West Virginia compared with those in Texas. Policy approaches were blunt because that was the only option.

Now policies are still blunt, but there are other options. Some federal programs take that approach, but on the whole, the fiction that problems are national clouds the responses, and the failure to craft new bespoke statistics hobbles the ability of government to design effective policies. Of course, governments in general face multiple issues, of which indicators and statistics are admittedly low on the totem pole. But changing how governments use statistics and encouraging policy makers to rely not on a static set of indicators but instead adopt a fluid approach that uses the wealth of data at our fingertips—well, it is at least worth suggesting.

For businesses, the bespoke need is clear. For a company such as Caterpillar, it should matter less whether GDP in the United States grows at 2 percent or 4 percent and whether it is up 6 percent or 10 percent in China. It should matter whether the specific need for its earthmovers and mining equipment and excavators is expanding or contracting. Traditionally, demand for such products was closely correlated with GDP growth. But in a world with subeconomies, with GDP itself not capturing swaths of activity, and with a global system without any global data per se that allows us to measure it, Caterpillar is less tied to national leading indicators than it was. And this is for a company with a core business that is inherently linked to several variables measured by GDP, including construction and industrial activity.

For hundreds of other companies, that link is even more tenuous. Amazon.com and eBay have some connection to consumer incomes and employment, but much less than you'd think. Their need to gauge future spending based on the traditional indicators is marginal and becoming more so with every passing day. The questions they have are best answered by their own expanding database of information that flows to them from their customers, and not on whether inflation is up or down and whether the GDP of any particular country or market is expanding.

Or say you are global company X. The inclination in past years would be to gather as many indicators as possible to come up with a best guess as to what the future held. If the economists and financial officers and assorted members of the management team gleaned from the leading indicators that unemployment was on the rise, GDP contracting, inflation heading up, stock prices weakening, and the housing market slumping, they might rationally decide to trim their employment rolls, halt plans for a new plant or a new product line, and cancel the annual Christmas party.

Doing the same today would be a mistake. One of the most recent statistical conundrums in the United States is that high levels of unemployment are going hand in hand with multiple companies unable to fill open positions. The reason? There is a skills mismatch between jobs that need to be filled and applicants able to fill them. This is nowhere more acute than with factory jobs. These used to be line jobs: repetitive tasks that most able-bodied men could fill or at least learn. Now many factory jobs require facility with software and robotics, the capacity to learn complicated "just in time" production techniques, and flexible factory floors that frequently are adjusted for different lines. Many of these jobs require either some level of college or, at a minimum, some degree of certification.

One consequence is that companies should not use national economic indicators to steer corporate strategy. Or, rather, those indicators can't be relied on to work according to past patterns. It isn't just unemployment. It's numbers such as inflation. That is where the absence of global indicators is acute. Price indices may be collected by national governments, but many prices of goods and materials are now determined by global supply chains. A retail clothing company must use global prices to determine how much material to buy and at what price, and then do the same to price its finished goods.

Many well-run companies, of course, no longer rely on traditional indicators for operational decisions. Yet if you listen to CEOs discuss the landscape of their industries, it's remarkable how much they fall back on the twentieth-century indicators. The way they run their businesses may have de facto changed, but the mind-set has yet to shift.

Finally, for individuals and small businesses, relying on the leading indicators is a bad idea. Yes, it's good to be aware of what the indicators are saying at any given moment, but using them to make most meaningful decisions is a mistake. As we saw with inflation, these statistics were not invented and aren't designed to give individuals clarity about their economic lives. They were constructed as tools to augment government macroeconomic policy. The newer indicators—the private ones developed by various industry groups in particular—are tailored to the needs of companies and industry. Housing data isn't meant to help an individual decide whether now is a good time to purchase a home.

Just as companies are better off developing their own proprietary indicators, so too are individuals and small businesses. Let's say you are contemplating starting a small business. Unless the national economy is in complete free-fall, GDP figures will not make much difference. Let's say "the economy" is growing by 2 percent annually. Does that mean that it's a good time to open a nail salon? Or if GDP is contracting by 2 percent, does that mean you should wait? For the vast majority of small businesses, GDP is irrelevant.

You wouldn't know that listening to the plethora of commentary and analysis. Given that we all swim in a sea of commentary and statistics, it is almost impossible to filter out that noise completely. Enough headlines trumpeting economic weakness are bound to have an effect on how we view the future, and a climate of anxiety and fear is never conducive to starting a business. Financial markets are particularly sensitive to the buzz of data. When the economy is contracting, it is often harder to convince banks to make loans, which in turn makes it harder to open that nail salon, or expand a current franchise, or even raise the money from friends and family that you might need to create a Web-based business or design a robust app for mobile use.

Yet myriad activities can and do thrive regardless of whether GDP is contracting or inflation is rising (or falling). On the flip side, many new businesses fail even when the overall economy is growing. GDP is simply not a useful number, and it shouldn't guide how banks lend nor whether businesses form. Some businesses may thrive even when the national and local economies are sagging. "Affordable luxuries" such as Starbucks seem to weather ups and downs for the simple reason that in times of stress, people need those luxuries, just as in flush times they may just desire them. Nor should the unemployment rate or inflation or wholesale prices control your actions, unless, of course, you are starting a business that revolves around an activity that a specific indicator captures.

For instance, a local staffing agency will see more or less business based on employment trends, but only based on local employment trends, not the national employment picture. The headline unemployment rate or underemployment rate as calculated by the BLS has little impact on the fate of a staffing agency in Omaha. What LinkedIn (a rapidly growing online jobs and networking site) does will have far greater impact than the leading indicators. And if you are opening a restaurant, the CPI isn't what matters. No, you need to know the prices of local goods, and how much you have to pay people in your area, not the level of income nationwide.

In short, almost all small businesses demand bespoke indicators rather than national ones. National housing data will tell a contractor little about his own community, except in rare circumstances such as 2008–09 when there was such panic and contraction overall that it affected just about everyone everywhere.

Finally, what do we do individually? It may, of course, be impossible to ignore the leading indicators. They form a reference point for too many debates, and they offer a peg for thinking about how "the economy" is doing. But unless you are arguing about the economy over dinner, they do not help you navigate your own life. The amount of time we spend digesting these national numbers, whether consciously or simply because they seep into our awareness via multiple outlets, is disproportionate relative to how much the indicators actually shape either our daily existence or the outcome of our decisions.

Take unemployment. The focus on the unemployment rate generates substantial anxiety. Every time the national rate ticks up, people become legitimately anxious about their job security. How many stories have been written about the "crisis of youth unemployment" decrying the difficulties of even recent college graduates? And yet, no one has a personal unemployment rate of 7.2 percent.

None of our individual needs are adequately served by a national number. National housing being flush or tight doesn't matter to the calculus of whether you should buy a home now. All that matters is whether you have a job; whether it is in an industry or business that is stable; whether you have skills that are in demand locally or nationally; and whether you can get a mortgage to buy said home. Average mortgage rates nationally also don't matter. What rate you can get does. Average home costs don't matter. Home prices in your community matter. The fact that there is too much inventory in Miami or Las Vegas has little bearing on a decision unless you are buying there. Average prices don't matter unless you are living on a fixed income such as disability payments or Social Security, and even then, those payments are adjusted regularly in sync with such prices.

In short, individuals need bespoke maps. Thankfully, designing those maps costs very little and requires only an Internet connection and some facility using Google and math. All of us need to be clear about what questions we have. That, then, will allow us to tailor our bespoke indicators to answer many of the central material questions we have: should we buy a home and where; what skills should we learn and for what; what are the costs of having a family; do we have enough income to meet our needs? And of course, it goes without saying that none of the indicators—unless you live in Bhutan—give much guidance about whether you are happy. Those questions are best answered in other ways and by other means.

Never before have we collectively relied on our economic numbers so much, and never before have we needed to less. The search for the right numbers a century ago involved statisticians, economists, and policy makers trying to sketch a credible and useful map of our economic system. Today the search for the right numbers should begin with one question: What do you need to know in order to do whatever you need or want to do?

The rise of Big Data means that all of us now have the ability to assemble our own data maps. That ability will only increase in years to come as technology evolves. As of now, we can answer any relevant question and find the information we need with incredible ease. By relevant, I mean those questions that frame a particular government policy or objective, that determine corporate strategy, or that shape a person's life. Existential questions, philosophical questions—those are of a different order. How to act collectively to solve certain problems, how to run an effective business, how to buy a home, afford college, whether to go to college, when to retire—all of those can be answered not by our indicators but by ourselves.

The free tools that the Internet provides make much of this possible. Of course, to make best use of those tools, you need to learn how to use them. Schools should teach that, and often do; they should teach the skills to empower anyone to find the information he or she needs and analyze it. Our reliance on twentieth-century leading indicators to craft a common narrative of "the economy" is an obstacle. We can all obtain the data we need to address the problems we have, and we can do that quickly and easily. The only thing that inhibits us is the myth that there is something called "the economy" that affects all of us equally.

The indicators invented in the twentieth century were one of the most important innovations of their time. Far less flashy than the innovations of science and technology, they nonetheless enabled us to craft economies whose fluctuations may still be violent but which are—for now—far more benign than was the case for most of human history. The fact we came to rely too heavily on these indicators is not an indictment of the good they have done and the needs they continue to fill.

But in a world where anyone with a smart phone can access more data than a team of statisticians could in 1950, we have the power to craft bespoke indicators. We have come a long way since the *Domesday Book*. Our questions need to be specific, and answers must be bounded by a sense of how to parse information, but the result should be a welcome liberation from "the economy" defined by our leading indicators. That may not be easy, but it will be real. It's a new paradigm we can embrace, nodding in thanks that we developed our statistical edifice in the first place, and then turning to our futures armed with the numbers we need and graced with the tools to discover them.

Acknowledgments

When I studied to be an historian, my ever-astute professors emphasized that everything has a story and a point of origin. Those origins are too often forgotten, but they shape everything. Individuals have their biographies; nations have their histories; and it turns out that our numbers have a story as well.

The idea for this book germinated over many years while I was working at Fred Alger Management as both a portfolio manager and senior executive. Alger has a unique culture of questioning and probing, and it was often the case that investing according to what the leading indicators said would lead to exactly the wrong decision. I continued to wonder about all of this when I ran my own investment fund and started writing more about economic affairs. I listened and watched (and still do of course) as predictions of what was in store for "the economy" proved to be incorrect. So many of those assessments seemed to depend on what leading indicators said, which in turn led to the central questions of how these numbers came to be and what they were originally designed to measure.

In doing the research for the book, I was more than ably assisted by several researchers who found vital material for me. Caroline Esser, Annie Zhou, Lea Bogner, Nicole Tosh, and, above all, Charles Bonello provided invaluable help. I also interviewed and discussed these questions with a range of people at the Bureau of Labor Statistics, the Bureau of Economic Analysis, the United Nations, and in academia, think tanks, and companies—some quoted in the book, some not. So many thanks to James Poterba, James Galvin, John Glasser, Eva Jespersen, Hal Varian, Erik Brynjolfsson, Andrew McAfee, Steve Landefeld, Hans Rosling, Alan Greenspan, Steve Haugen, Lew Daly, John Greenlees, Dave Dickerson, Ed Diener, and Alberto Cavallo.

Clear eyes and sharp minds are always needed as a reality check, and once again I called on those near and dear to read my drafts and call me out. Timothy Naftali, Eric Olson, Nicole Alger, David Karabell, and Phil Powers did yeoman work on less-than-polished early drafts and pushed me to hone and refine.

At Simon & Schuster, I benefitted from the incisive observations and gentle (and at times not so gentle) prodding of my editor and doyenne of the realm, Alice Mayhew. Jonathan Cox was a regular and refreshing source of insight, on everything from titles to narrative arc. Jonathan Karp, Simon & Schuster's ageless publisher, understood this book from Day One, and it's hard to imagine it being published without him. The book was wonderfully produced and designed by Beth Maglione, Joel Breuklander, Jason Heuer, and Ruth Lee-Mui. Elisa Rivlin made sure that no legal boundaries were unnecessarily overstepped, and Maureen Cole and Stephen Bedford undertook the arduous task of creatively marketing the book hither and yon.

This project began with Scott Moyers once again representing me, and when he decamped back to publishing, Andrew Wylie shepherded the book to completion. I could not have asked for more professional, engaging, and thoughtful agents, and to James Pullen, for disseminating this abroad, thank you as well.

Finally, to those who patiently (and otherwise) gave me space and time to hash out these pages: my wife Nicole, whose eye and ear have always been essential and whose touch and words I cherish, and my two boys, Griffin and Jasper, who still can't fathom why I would write this book or others, but who genially support their father's passion.

Notes

Introduction

1. "Preview of the 2013 Comprehensive Revision of the National Income and Product Accounts: Changes in Definitions and Presentations," www .bea.gov/scb/pdf/2013/03%20March/0313_nipa_comprehensive_ revision_preview.pdf.

Chapter 1: The Ripples of Domesday

1. Quotations from Victoria King, "The Domesday Book," *History Magazine*, October–November 2001.
2. Keith Devlin, *The Unfinished Game: Pascal, Fermat, and the Seventeenth-Century Letter That Made the World Modern* (New York: Basic Books, 2008).
3. Stephen M. Stigler, *The History of Statistics: The Measurement of Uncertainty Before 1900* (Cambridge, MA: Belknap Press of Harvard University Press, 1986), 100–135.
4. Frederick Bohne, *Two Hundred Years of Census Taking* (Washington, 1989), report prepared by the Bureau of the Census, www.census .gov/history.
5. The history of the census and these debates is covered extensively in Margo J. Anderson, *The American Census: A Social History* (New

Haven, CT: Yale University Press, 1990). Also, A. Ross Eckler, *The Bureau of the Census* (New York: Praeger, 1972).

6. Quoted in *The Story of U.S. Agricultural Estimates* (US Government Printing Office, 1969), 37.

Chapter 2: Unemployment

1. Chester McArthur Destler, "A Coffin Worker and the Labor Problem: Ethelbert Stewart and Henry Demarest Lloyd," *Labor History* 72, no. 3 (1971); Richard Barry, "Human Cussedness Causes Labor Disputes," *New York Times* (August 6, 1916); Joseph P. Goldberg and William T. Moye, *The First Hundred Years of the Bureau of Labor Statistics* (Washington, DC: US Government Printing Office, 1985), chapter 5; Ethelbert Stewart, "Irregularity of Employment," *Annals of the American Academy of Political and Social Science* 154, no. 1 (March 1931): 7–11.

2. David Card, "Origins of the Unemployment Rate: The Lasting Legacy of Measurement Without Theory," February 2011. Paper prepared for the 2011 meetings of the American Economic Association. http://davidcard.berkeley.edu/papers/origins-of-unemployment.pdf.

3. Udo Sautter, *Three Cheers for the Unemployed: Government and Unemployment Before the New Deal* (Cambridge, UK: Cambridge University Press, 1991).

4. See, for instance, "Address of Carroll D. Wright, President of the American Statistical Association, at its Annual Meeting in Boston, Jan. 17, 1908," *Journal of the American Statistical Association* 11, no. 81 (March 1908): 1–16. Also, see Carroll Wright: "Setting the Course," chap. 2 in Goldberg and Moye.

5. Joseph W. Duncan and William C. Shelton, *Revolution in United States Government Statistics, 1926–1976* (Washington, DC: US Government Printing Office, 1978), 168; Janet L. Norwood and John F. Early, "A Century of Methodological Progress at the U.S. Bureau of Labor Statistics," *Journal of the American Statistical Association* 79, no. 388 (December 1984): 748–761.

6. Meeker quotation from Goldberg and Moye, 84. Also, see Royal

Meeker, "The Dependability and Meaning of Unemployment and Employment Statistics in the United States," *Harvard Business Review* (July 1930).

7. William E. Leuchtenberg, *Herbert Hoover* (New York: Times Books, 2009); Herbert Hoover, *The Memoirs of Herbert Hoover—The Great Depression, 1929–1941* (1953); Robert H. Zeigler, "Herbert Hoover, the Wage-Earner, and the 'New Economic System,'" *Business History Review* 51, no. 2 (Summer 1977); Ellis Hawley, "Herbert Hoover, the Commerce Secretariat and the Vision of an 'Associative State,' 1921–1928," *Journal of American History* 61, no. 1 (June 1974).

8. Hoover quoted in Vincent Gaddis, *Herbert Hoover, Unemployment, and the Public Sphere: A Conceptual History, 1919–1933* (Lanham, MD: University Press of America, 2005), 19. Also, see Ellis W. Hawley, ed., *Herbert Hoover as Secretary of Commerce 1921–1928: Studies in New Era Thought and Practice* (Iowa City: University of Iowa Press, 1982).

9. The quotation is from Joel Best, *Lies, Damned Lies and Statistics: Untangling Numbers from the Media, Politicians, and Activists* (Berkeley: University of California Press, 2001). Also see, David Salsburg, *The Lady Tasting Tea: How Statistics Revolutionized Science in the Twentieth Century* (New York: Henry Holt, 2001); Michael Blastland and Andrew Dilnot, *The Numbers Game: The Commonsense Guide to Understanding Numbers in the News, in Politics, and in Life* (New York: Gotham Books, 2009).

10. Quoted in Adam Cohen, *Nothing to Fear: FDR's Inner Circle and the Hundred Days That Created Modern America* (New York: Penguin Press, 2009), 60.

11. Michael Hiltzik, *The New Deal: A Modern History* (New York: Free Press, 2011); Anthony J. Badger, *The New Deal: The Depression Years 1933–1940* (New York: Hill and Wang, 1989). For a more supportive view of Hoover, see Amity Shlaes, *The Forgotten Man: A New History of the Great Depression* (New York: HarperCollins, 2007).

12. Kirstin Downey, *The Woman Behind the New Deal: The Life and Legacy of Frances Perkins—Social Security, Unemployment, Insurance, and the Minimum Wage* (New York: Anchor Books, 2010).

13. Goldberg and Moye, "Isador Lubin: Meeting Emergency Demands" chap. 6 in *First Hundred Years*.

14. For some of the challenges and how they were faced, see Duncan and Shelton, *Revolution*, ibid.; George B. L. Arner, "The Census of Unemployment," *Journal of the American Statistical Association* 28, no. 781 (March 1933): 48–53; Mary van Kleeck, "The Federal Unemployment Census of 1930," *Journal of the American Statistical Association* 26, no. 173 (March 1931): 189–200; Philip Hauser, "The Labor Force and Gainful Workers—Concept, Measurement, and Comparability," *American Journal of Sociology* 54, no. 4 (January 1949): 338–355; John N. Webb, "Concepts Used in Unemployment Surveys," *Journal of the American Statistical Association* 34, no. 205 (March 1939): 49–59.

15. Duncan and Shelton, *Revolution*, 40.

Chapter 3: National Income and the Man from Pinsk

1. Quoted in Joel Popkin, "Data Watch: The U.S. National Income and Product Accounts," *Journal of Economic Perspectives* 14, no. 2 (Spring 2000): 215–24.

2. There are not as many studies of the history of GDP as one might think, given the importance of the subject. See Paul Studenski, *The Income of Nations* (New York: New York University Press, 1961); Angus Maddison, *Monitoring the World Economy, 1820–1992* (Paris: OECD Development Centre, 1995), www.ggdc.net/Maddison/Monitoring.shtml. For a comprehensive yet searing account of the evolution of GDP, see Lorenzo Fioramonti, *Gross Domestic Problem: The Politics Behind the World's Most Powerful Number* (London: Zed Books, 2013). Also, Marc Fleurbaey and Didier Blanchet, *Beyond GDP: Measuring Welfare and Assessing Sustainability* (New York: Oxford University Press, 2013).

3. Jonathan Schlefer, *The Assumptions Economists Make* (Cambridge, MA: Belknap Press of Harvard University Press, 2012).

4. The discussion of Simon Kuznets and the early history of national accounts are taken from Kuznets's own writing as well as the following: Carol Carson, "The History of the United States National

Income and Product Accounts: The Development of an Analytical Tool," *Review of Income and Wealth* 21, no. 2 (June 1975): 153–81; Robert Fogel, "Simon S. Kuznets, April 30, 1901–July 9, 1985" (working paper 7787, National Bureau of Economic Research, Cambridge, MA (July 2000), www.nber.org/papers/w7787.pdf.; Eli Lederhendler, "Orphans and Prodigies: Rediscovering Young Jewish Immigrant 'Marginals,'" *American Jewish History* 95, no. 2 (June 2009): 135–55; Erik Lundberg, "Simon Kuznets' Contribution to Economics," *Swedish Journal of Economics* 73, no. 4 (December 1971): 444–59; Yoram Ben-Porath, "Simon Kuznets in Person and Writing," *Economic Development and Cultural Change* 36, no. 3 (April 1988): 435–47; Vibha Kapuria-Foreman and Mark Perlman, "An Economic Historian's Economist: Remembering Simon Kuznets," *Economic Journal* 105, no. 433 (November 1995): 1524–47; Moses Abramovitz, "Nobel Prize for Economics: Kuznets and Economic Growth," *Science* 174, no. 4008 (October 29, 1971): 481–48B.

5. Thomas McGraw, *Prophet of Innovation: Joseph Schumpeter and Creative Destruction* (Cambridge, MA: Belknap Press of Harvard University Press, 2010). Also, Joseph Schumpeter, *The Theory of Economic Development*, first published in 1911.

6. Patrick J. Maney, *Young Bob La Follette: A Biography of Robert M. La Follette, Jr., 1895–1953* (Columbia: University of Missouri Press, 1978); David A. Moss and Joseph P. Gownder, "Origins of National Income Accounting," Harvard Business School Case 799–080 (December 1998).

7. For these early attempts, see Studenski, *Income of Nations*, ibid.

8. Richard Stone, "The Accounts of Society," Nobel Memorial Lecture (December 8, 1984). Also, Simon Kuznets, "On the Valuation of Social Income—Reflections on Professor Hicks' Article," *Economica* 15, no. 57 (February 1948): 1–16. Kuznets, *Toward a Theory of Economic Growth*: With "Reflections on the Economic Growth of Modern Nations" (New York: W. W. Norton, 1968); Kuznets, *National Income and Capital Formation, 1919–1935* (Cambridge, MA: National Bureau of Economic Research, 1937).

9. In addition to Skidelsky's three-volume opus, see Robert Skidelsky, *John Maynard Keynes, 1883–1946: Economist, Philosopher, Statesman* (New York: Penguin Books, 2005); Skidelsky, *Keynes: The Return of the Master* (Philadelphia: Public Affairs, 2010); Benn Steil, *The Battle of Bretton Woods: John Maynard Keynes, Harry Dexter White, and the Making of a New World Order* (Princeton, NJ: Princeton University Press, 2013). Also, John Maynard Keynes, *The General Theory of Employment, Interest, and Money* (Palgrave Macmillan, 1936).

10. John Kenneth Galbraith, "The National Accounts: Arrival and Impact," in *Reflections of America: Commemorating the Statistical Abstract Centennial*, ed. Norman Cousins (Washington, DC: Bureau of the Census, 1980); Rosemary D. Marcuss and Richard E. Kane, "U.S. National Income and Product Statistics: Born of the Great Depression and World War II," *Survey of Current Business* 87, no. 2 (February 2007): 32–46, https://www.bea.gov/scb/pdf/2007/02%20 February/0207_history_article.pdf.

11. Milton Gilbert, "Measuring National Income as Affected by the War," *Journal of the American Statistical Association* 37, no. 218 (June 1942): 186–98; Simon Kuznets, "National Income: A New Version," *Review of Economics and Statistics* 30, no. 3 (August 1948): 151–79; Marcuss and Kane, *"U.S. National Income,"* ibid.

12. "GDP: One of the Great Inventions of the 20th Century," *Survey of Current Business* 80, no. 1 (January 2000): 6, www.bea.gov/scb/pdf/ BEAWIDE/2000/0100ed.pdf.

Chapter 4: The Invention of the Economy

1. Quoted in Andrew L. Yarrow, *Measuring America: How Economic Growth Came to Define American Greatness in the Late Twentieth Century* (Amherst: University of Massachusetts Press, 2010), 118.

2. Alan Brinkley, *The Publisher: Henry Luce and His American Century* (Knopf, 2010).

3. Quoted in Yarrow, *Measuring America*, 115. Also, Michael Augsburger, *An Economy of Abundant Beauty: Fortune Magazine and Depression America* (Ithaca, NY: Cornell University Press); Kevin S. Reilly,

"Dilettantes at the Gate: *Fortune* Magazine and the Cultural Politics of Business Journalism in the 1930s," *Business and Economic History* 28, no. 2 (Winter 1999), www.thebhc.org/publications/BEHprint/v028n2/p0213=p0222.pdf.

4. The term "the affluent society" was coined by economist John Kenneth Galbraith, who was also a sometime contributor to *Time* and *Fortune*. See Galbraith, *The Affluent Society and Other Writings, 1952–1967* (New York: Library of America, 2010).

5. Schlefer, *Assumptions Economists Make*, ibid.; Justin Fox, *The Myth of the Rational Market: A History of Risk, Reward, and Delusion on Wall Street* (New York: HarperBusiness, 2011); Duncan K. Foley, *Adam's Fallacy: A Guide to Economic Theology* (Cambridge, MA: Belknap Press of Harvard University Press, 2006).

6. Stanley Meisler, *United Nations: A History* (New York: Grove Press, 2011).

7. Brian Urquhart, *Ralph Bunche: An American Life* (W. W. Norton, 1993).

8. Michael Ward, *Quantifying the World: UN Ideas and Statistics* (Bloomington: Indiana University Press, 2004); United Nations Statistical Commission, *Sixty Years of Leadership and Professionalism in Building the Global Statistical System, 1947–2007* (New York: United Nations, 2007), http://unstats.un.org/unsd/statcom/doc07/UN_Stat_Commission_1947–2007_bookmarks.pdf.

9. "Sir Richard Stone and the Development of National Economic Accounts," *Survey of Current Business* 72, no. 3 (March 1992): 27; M. Hasem Pesaran, "The ET Interview: Professor Sir Richard Stone," *Economic Theory* 7, no. 1 (March 1991): 85–123.

10. *Measurement of National Income and the Construction of Social Accounts; Report of the Sub-Committee of National Income Statistics of the League of Nations Committee of Statistical Experts* (Geneva: United Nations, 1947); Richard Ruggles, "The United States National Income Accounts, 1947–1977: Their Conceptual Basis and Evolution," chap. 1 in *The U.S. National Income and Product Accounts*, ed. Murray F. Foss (Chicago: University of Chicago Press, 1982), www.nber.org/chapters/c7783.

Chapter 5: The Economic Gestalt

1. Daniel Horowitz, *Anxieties of Affluence: Critiques of American Consumer Culture, 1939–1979* (Amherst: University of Massachusetts Press, 2004), 65–70. Also, David Bird, "George Katona, 79, Leading Economist," *New York Times*, June 19, 1981; Jan Logemann, "George Katona (1901–1981): Behavioral Economist and Consumer Researcher," *Transatlantic Perspectives* October 18, 2011. www .transatlanticperspectives.org. George Katona, "Psychology and Consumer Economics," *Journal of Consumer Research* 1, no. 1 (June 1974): 1–8; Katona, "Analysis of Dissaving," *American Economic Review* 39, no. 3 (June 1949): 673–88.

2. In June 2013 the fact that Thompson Reuters had been providing the consumer sentiment a few seconds before the general release to high-paying clients created quite a controversy.

3. Katona, "Psychology and Consumer Economics."

4. John McNeil, "Federal Programs to Measure Consumer Purchase Expectations, 1946–1973: A Post-Mortem," *Journal of Consumer Research* 1, no. 3 (December 1974): 1–10.

5. James Tobin, "On the Predictive Value of Consumer Intentions and Attitudes," *Review of Economics and Statistics* 41, no. 1 (February 1959): 1–11; James P. Smith and Robert J. Willis, eds., *Work, Wealth and Health: Innovations in Measurement in the Social Sciences* (Ann Arbor: University of Michigan Press, 1999).

6. Jeff Dominitz and Charles F. Manski, "How Should We Measure Consumer Confidence (Sentiment)? Evidence from the Michigan Survey of Consumers" (working paper 9926, National Bureau of Economic Research, Cambridge, MA, August 2003), www.nber.org/ papers/w9926); Christopher D. Carroll, Jeffrey C. Fuhrer, and David W. Wilcox, "Does Consumer Sentiment Forecast Household Spending? If So, Why?," *American Economic Review* 84, no. 5 (December 1994): 1397–1408.

7. Fabian Linden, "The Consumer as Forecaster," *Public Opinion Quarterly* 46, no. 3 (Autumn 1982): 353–60.

8. History of the Institute for Supply Management can be found in

brief on ISM website, www.ism.ws/ismreports/content.cfm?Item Number=10742. Also, Michael R. Leenders and Harold E. Fearon, "Developing Purchasing's Foundation," *Journal of Supply Chain Management* 44, no. 2 (April 2008): 17–27.

9. Geoffrey H. Moore, "Wesley Mitchell in Retrospect," *Journal of Economic Issues* 12, no. 2 (June 1978): 277–86; also, see the intriguing essay on Mitchell by none other than Joseph Schumpeter, "Wesley Clair Mitchell (1874–1948)," *Quarterly Journal of Economics* 64, no. 1 (February 1950): 139–55.

Chapter 6: Inflation: From Leading Indicator to Government Con

1. Aaron Steelman, "The Federal Reserve's 'Dual Mandate': The Evolution of an Idea" (paper published by the Federal Reserve Bank of Richmond, December 2011), www.richmondfed.org/publications/research/economic_brief/2011/pdf/eb_11-12.pdf.

2. Goldberg and Moye, *First Hundred Years*, 150.

3. Andrew E. Kersten, *Labor's Home Front: The American Federation of Labor During World War II* (New York: New York University Press, 2006).

4. Quoted in Goldberg and Moye, *First Hundred Years*, 179.

5. James Tobin, "Irving Fisher (1867–1947)," *American Journal of Economics and Sociology*, 64, no. 1 (January 2005): 19–42; William J. Barber, "Irving Fisher of Yale," *American Journal of Economics and Sociology* 64, no. 1 (January 2005): 43–55. Sylvia Nasar, *Grand Pursuit: The Story of Economic Genius* (New York: Simon & Schuster, 2011), 281ff; Irving Fisher, *Booms and Depressions: Some First Principles* (New York: Adelphi, 1932); Fisher, *The Money Illusion* (New York: Adelphi, 1928).

6. Moore, "Wesley Mitchell." Simon Kuznets, "Wesley Clair Mitchell, (1874–1947): An Appreciation," *Journal of the American Statistical Association* 44, no. 245 (March 1949): 126–31; David Breslau, "Economics Invents the Economy: Mathematics, Statistics, and Models in the Work of Irving Fisher and Wesley Mitchell," *Theory and Society* 32, no. 3 (June 2003): 379–411; Wesley Clair Mitchell, *Business*

Cycles and Their Causes (Berkeley: University of California Press, 1960).

7. H. Spencer Banzhaf, "Quantifying the Qualitative: Quality-Adjusted Price Indexes in the United States, 1915–1961," *History of Political Economy* 33, supp. 1 (2001): 345–70; Banzhaf, "The Form and Function of Price Indexes: A Historical Accounting," *History of Political Economy* 36, no. 4 (Winter 2004): 589–616.

8. Milton Viorst, "The Burns Kind of Liberal Conservatism," *New York Times Magazine*, November 9, 1969; Leonard Silk, "The Man at the Money Throttle," *New York Times Magazine*, August 10, 1975; Arthur Burns, *Reflections of an Economic Policy Maker: Speeches and Congressional Statements*, 1969–1978 (Washington, DC: American Enterprise Institute, 1978). Alan S. Blinder, "The Anatomy of Double-Digit Inflation in the 1970s," chap. 12 in Robert E. Hall, *Inflation: Causes and Effects* (Chicago: University of Chicago Press, 1982), www.nber.org/chapters/c11462.pdf; Edward Nelson, "The Great Inflation of the Seventies: What Really Happened" (working paper 2004-001, Federal Reserve Bank of St. Louis, Saint Louis, MO, January 2004), http://research.stlouisfed.org/wp/2004/2004-001.pdf. Also, for an overview of the 1970s, see David Frum, *How We Got Here: The 70's—The Decade That Brought You Modern Life—For Better or Worse* (New York: Basic Books, 2000).

9. Quoted in Goldberg and Moye, *First Hundred Years*, 232.

10. Quoted in *First Hundred Years*, 231. Also, Jerry Hausman, "Sources of Bias and Solutions to Bias in the Consumer Price Index," *Journal of Economic Perspectives* 17, no. 1 (Winter 2003): 23–44; F. Thomas Juster and Paul Wachtel, "Inflation and the Consumer," *Brookings Papers on Economic Activity* 1 (1972): 71–121.

11. There were two stages: the first was the shift to owner's equivalent rent in the CPI-U Index (CPI for All Urban Consumers) and then for the CPI-W (CPI for Urban Wage Earners and Clerical Workers). "The Effect of Rental Equivalence on the Consumer Price Index, 1967–82," *Monthly Labor Review* 108, no. 2 (February 1985): 53–55; Robert Poole, Frank Ptacek, and Randal Verbrugge,

"Treatment of Owner-Occupied Housing in the CPI," Office of Prices and Living Conditions, Bureau of Labor Statistics (December 9, 2005); Ann Dougherty and Robert Van Order, "Inflation, Housing Costs, and the Consumer Price Index," *American Economic Review* 72, no. 1 (March 1982): 154–64.

12. Brian R. Moulton, "Bias in the Consumer Price Index: What Is the Evidence?," *Journal of Economic Perspectives* 10, no. 4 (Autumn 1996): 159–77.

13. William H. Gross, "Investment Outlook: Haute Con Job" (October 2004), www.pimco.com/EN/Insights/Pages/IO_Oct_2004.aspx; Austan Goolsbee, "The Index of Missing Economic Indicators: The Unemployment Myth," *New York Times*, November 30, 2003.

Chapter 7: Diminishing Returns

1. See the explanation from the US Bureau of Economic Analysis, http://www.bea.gov/faq/index.cfm?faq_id=1003.

2. www.frbsf.org/publications/economics/letter/2009/el2009-19.html.

3. Noam Scheiber, "The Memo That Larry Summers Didn't Want Obama to See," *New Republic*, February 22, 2012; Scheiber, *The Escape Artists: How Obama's Team Fumbled the Recovery* (New York: Simon & Schuster, 2012); Ryan Lizza, "The Obama Memos: The Making of a Post-Post-Partisan Presidency," *New Yorker*, January 30, 2012; text of the Summers memo, www.newyorker.com/online/blogs/newsdesk/2012/01/the-summers-memo.html. Also, see Michael Grunwald, *The New New Deal: The Hidden Story of Change in the Obama Era* (New York: Simon & Schuster, 2012).

4. Alan Greenspan, *The Age of Turbulence: Adventures in a New World* (New York: Penguin Press, 2007).

5. Data from the US Department of Agriculture, http://www.ers.usda.gov/data-products/food-expenditures.aspx#26654.

6. Charles R. Hulten, "Price Hedonics: A Critical Review," *Federal Reserve Board of New York Economic Policy Review* (September 2003:5–15); Zvi Griliches, "Hedonic Price Indexes and the Measurement of Capital and Productivity: Some Historical Reflections," in Ernst

R. Berndt and Jack E. Triplett, eds., *Fifty Years of Economic Measurement: The Jubilee of the Conference on Research in Income and Wealth* (Chicago: University of Chicago Press, 1991); Alan G. White, "Measurement Biases in Consumer Price Indexes," *International Statistical Review* 67, no. 3 (December 1999): 301–25; Jerry Hausman, "Sources of Bias and Solutions to Bias in the Consumer Price Index," *Journal of Economic Perspectives* 17, no. 1 (Winter 2003): 23–44.

7. Milton Friedman, *Capitalism and Freedom* (Chicago: University of Chicago Press, 1962).

8. Quoted in Adam Fletcher and Trenton Hamilton, "Scoring and Revenue Estimation," Briefing Paper no. 5, Harvard Law School Federal Budget Policy Seminar 2008, www.law.harvard.edu/faculty/hjackson/ScoringRevenueEstimation_5(rev).pdf.

9. Dudley Jackson, *The New National Accounts: An Introduction to the System of National Accounts 1993 and the European System of Accounts 1995* (Chettanham, UK: Edward Elgar Publishing, 2000).

10. Eli Saslow, "'Jobs Day': Monthly Release of Employment Data an Economic, Political Obsession," *Washington Post*, March 9, 2012.

11. Simon Kuznets, *National Income 1929–1932: A Report to the U.S. Senate, 73rd Congress, 2nd Session* (Washington, DC: US Government Printing Office, 1934), quoted in Robert Costanza et al., "Beyond GDP: The Need for New Measures of Progress," published by the Pardee Center at Boston University, 2009, www.bu.edu/pardee/files/documents/PP-004-GDP.pdf.

Chapter 8: Where's Waldo?

1. See a Pew survey from September 2012, summarized at http://money.cnn.com/2012/09/19/news/world/china-economic-threat/index.html.

2. See Heleen Mees, "How China's Boom Caused the Financial Crisis," *Foreign Policy*, January 17, 2012. Here is only one of many.

3. Faith M. Williams, "The Origin and Development of Modern Trade Statistics," *Quarterly Publications of the American Statistical Association* 17, no. 134 (June 1921): 732–42.

4. Douglas A. Irwin, "Historical Aspects of U.S. Trade Policy," *NBER Reporter*, Summer 2006, www.nber.org/reporter/summer06/irwin .html.

5. *Trade in Goods with World, Seasonally Adjusted*. Report prepared by the Bureau of the Census, www.census.gov/foreign-trade/balance/c0004 .html.

6. www.oecd.org/finance/financial-markets/1923208.pdf. Also, see Olivier Cadot and Jaime de Melo, "Why OECD Countries Should Reform Rules of Origin," *World Bank Research Observer* 29, no. 1 (Spring 2008), http://www.hec.unil.ch/crea/publications/autrespub/ oecd.pdf.

7. See Bureau of Economic Anaysis website for articles on the methodology used to compile US international transactions accounts, http:// www.bea.gov/international/pdf/bach_concepts_methods/Travel .pdf.

8. Kenneth L. Kraemer, Greg Linden, and Jason Dedrick, "Capturing Value in Global Networks: Apple's iPad and iPhone" (July 2011), http://pcic.merage.uci.edu/papers/2011/Value_iPad_iPhone.pdf.

9. "A Better Way to Track Trade Than 'Made In' Labels," *Bloomberg View Editorial* (January 21, 2013). For the OECD database, see www.oecd.org/industry/ind/measuringtradeinvalue-addedanoecd- wtojointinitiative.htm. For the assessment by the OECD and the WTO, see "Trade in Value-Added: Concepts, Methodologies and Challenges," www.oecd.org/sti/ind/49894138.pdf. Also, Yuqing Xing and Neal Defert, "How the iPhone Widens the United States Trade Deficit with People's Republic of China," Asian Development Bank Institute Working Paper (December 2010).

Chapter 9: Gross National Happiness

1. Karma Ura et al., "An Extensive Analysis of GNH Index" (May 2012), www.grossnationalhappiness.com.

2. Professor Edward Diener of the University of Illinois has been central to the development of subjective well-being studies over the past, and he helpfully provided me with some history of how this field evolved.

3. Quoted in Ura et al., "An Extensive Analysis."

4. Nicolas Sarkozy, foreword to Joseph E. Stiglitz, Amartya Sen, and Jean-Paul Fitoussi, *Mismeasuring Our Lives: Why GDP Doesn't Add Up* (New York: New Press, 2010).

5. Donella Meadows et al., *The Limits to Growth* (New York: Signet, 1972); Herman E. Daly, *Beyond Growth: The Economics of Sustainable Development* (Boston: Beacon Press, 1997).

6. Quoted in Timothy W. Ryback, "The U.N. Happiness Project," *New York Times*, March 28, 2012.

7. Alan B. Krueger, ed., *Measuring the Subjective Well-Being of Nations: National Accounts of Time Use and Well-Being* (Chicago: University of Chicago Press, 2009), 19. Also, Bruno S. Frey, *Happiness: A Revolution in Economics* (Cambridge, MA: MIT Press, 2008).

8. Daniel Kahneman, *Thinking, Fast and Slow* (New York: Farrar, Straus and Giroux, 2011).

9. This point has been made time and again, most recently by Derek Bok, *The Politics of Happiness: What Government Can Learn from the New Research on Well-Being* (Princeton, NJ: Princeton University Press, 2010). Also, Arthur C. Brooks, *Gross National Happiness: Why Happiness Matters for America—and How We Can Get More of It* (New York: Basic Books, 2008).

10. Carol Graham, "Some Insights on Development from the Economics of Happiness," Economic Studies Program, Brookings Institution (April 2005), www.brookings.edu/~/media/research/files/articles/2005/4/globaleconomics%20graham/200504.

11. For a critical examination of the paradox and a superb take on the issue of measurement, see Diane Coyle, *The Economics of Enough: How to Run the Economy as If the Future Matters* (Princeton, NJ: Princeton University Press, 2011). Also, Robert Skidelsky and Edward Skidelsky, *How Much Is Enough? Money and the Good Life* (New York: Other Press, 2012).

12. Sudhir Anand and Amartya K. Sen, "Human Development Index: Methodology and Measurement," in Human Development Report Office Occasional Papers (July 1994). Sen has published

voluminously over the years, and the above is simply the most relevant for HDI.

Chapter 10: The Avatars

1. "Making Data Dance," *Economist*, December 9, 2010. Dr. Rosling also said much the same in an interview with me on February 27, 2012.

2. You can find representative samples at Gapminder, www.gapminder.org.

3. Nate Silver, *The Signal and the Noise: Why So Many Predictions Fail—but Some Don't* (New York: Penguin Press, 2012).

4. Erik Brynjolfsson and Joo Hee Oh, "The Attention Economy: Measuring the Value of Free Goods on the Internet" (preliminary and incomplete draft, July 2012). Also, Erik Brynjolfsson and Adam Saunders, "What the GDP Gets Wrong (Why Managers Should Care)," *MIT Sloan Management Review 51, no. 1* (Fall 2009); Erik Brynjolfsson and Andrew McAfee, *Race Against the Machine: How the Digital Revolution Is Accelerating Innovation, Driving Productivity, and Irreversibly Transforming Employment and the Economy* (Digital Frontier Press, 2011). And author interview with Brynjolfsson, March 2013.

5. Jude Webber, "Argentine Statistics: A Guessing Game with Plenty of Losers," *Financial Times*, July 2, 2010, http://blogs.ft.com/beyond-brics/2010/07/02/argentine-statistics-a-guessing-game-with-plenty-of-losers/#axzz241qDRds2. Also, Ian Mount, "Argentine Inflation: Shoot the Messenger," *Financial Times* (August 28, 2012).

6. Author interview with Professor Alberto Cavallo, January 19, 2012; also, http://bpp.mit.edu/usa. Annie Lowrey, "Do We Need Google to Measure Inflation?" *Slate*, December 20, 2010.

7. Author interview with Hal Varian, February 13, 2012; Robin Harding, "Google to Map Inflation Using Web Data," *Financial Times*, October 11, 2010.

8. For the full text of Ray Dalio's *Principles*, see www.bwater.com/Uploads/FileManager/Principles/Bridgewater-Associates-Ray-Dalio-Principles.pdf.

9. This citation actually comes from a thoughtful profile of Dalio by John Cassidy, "Mastering the Machine: How Ray Dalio Built the World's Richest and Strangest Hedge Fund," *New Yorker*, July 25, 2011. And, full disclosure, I had several discussions with Bridgewater about a possible job in 2008 and had been following its progress for years before, when I worked with Fred Alger Management.

Conclusion

1. Aaron Blake, "The Most Overrated Stat of the 2012 Election," *Washington Post*, September 14, 2012, www.washingtonpost.com/blogs/the-fix/wp/2012/09/14/the-most-overrated-stat-of-the-2012-election.

Index

About the Author

Zachary Karabell is an author, money manager, commentator, and head of global strategy at Envestnet. He is also president of River Twice Research and River Twice Capital. Educated at Columbia, Oxford, and Harvard, where he received his PhD, Karabell has written eleven previous books. He is a regular commentator on CNBC and MSNBC. He writes the weekly "Edgy Optimist" column for *Reuters* and *The Atlantic*, and is a contributor to such publications as *The Washington Post*, *The Daily Beast*, *Time*, *The Wall Street Journal*, *The New Republic*, *The New York Times*, and *Foreign Policy*.